INTRUSIVE PARTNERS

ELUSIVE MATES

INTRUSIVE PARTNERS

ELUSIVE MATES

THE PURSUER-DISTANCER DYNAMIC IN COUPLES

STEPHEN J. BETCHEN

Routledge
Taylor & Francis Group

NEW YORK AND HOVE

Published in 2005 by
Routledge
Taylor & Francis Group
270 Madison Avenue
New York, NY 10016

Published in Great Britain by
Routledge
Taylor & Francis Group
27 Church Road
Hove, East Sussex BN3 2FA

© 2005 by Taylor & Francis Group, LLC
Routledge is an imprint of Taylor & Francis Group
Formerly a Brunner–Routledge title

No claim to original U.S. Government works

Printed in the United States of America on acid-free paper
10 9 8 7 6 5 4 3 2 1

International Standard Book Number-10: 0-415-94801-0 (Hardcover)

Library of Congress Cataloging-in-Publication Data

Betchen, Stephen J., 1954–
    Intrusive partners — elusive mates : the pursuer–distancer dynamic in couples / Stephen J. Betchen.
        p. cm.
    Includes bibliographical references and index.
    ISBN 0-415-94801-0 (hardbound)
    1. Couples—Psychology. 2. Married people—Psychology. 3. Intimacy (Psychology)
    4. Interpersonal conflict. 5. Sexual disorders. 6. Marital psychotherapy. I. Title

HQ801.B495 2005
616.89'1562--dc22   2004027506

Taylor & Francis Group
is the Academic Division of T&F Informa plc.

Visit the Taylor & Francis Web site at
http://www.taylorandfrancis.com

and the Routledge Web site at
http://www.routledgementalhealth.com

Dedication

To Maria,
my wife and best friend in the struggle of life

Contents

Preface

Nearly every therapist who works with couples will eventually cross paths with the pursuer–distancer (p–d) interaction. It is one of the most common relationship dynamics and, when problematic, is one of the most formidable to alleviate. As a consequence, I have heard numerous colleagues and supervisees express frustration about it as it has pertained to several different relational contexts (*e.g.*, affection, sex, money, work). To my surprise, the general public has demonstrated a certain fascination with the interaction, as well. After a speaking engagement, a woman from the audience approached me and confessed that she was a distancer. The talk I had given, however, focused on an entirely different topic — I only mentioned the p–d dynamic in passing. Also, several couples have asked me over the years for reading material on the subject.

My interest in the pursuer–distancer dynamic was not capricious; it evolved slowly. At first, I was only aware of my academic fascination with the concept. This seemed to spur me on to publish a scholarly article on it as it related to sexual difficulty in marriage. My belief at the time was that it was a common dynamic and that it would be somewhat unique to examine it within the context of sexuality. More and more, however, I came to realize just how important a role it played in the scope of relationship difficulty; this and the recent focus on intimacy in the professional psychology literature continued to spark my pursuit.

I do not pretend to have discovered this dynamic nor do I feel that I have mastered it; I'm not sure that the latter is at all possible. I wrote this book for several reasons: (1) I believe that the inability to achieve intimacy underlies most relationship problems, (2) I have a respect for the complexity of the dynamic and of relationships in general, and (3) I recognized a need for couples therapists to have a specific model from which to treat this most challenging dynamic more effectively.

While it may seem paradoxical to mix systems therapy with psychoanalytic conflict theory, as I have here, I am convinced that this is a most powerful and reasonably compatible approach for treating the p–d dynamic. After many years of working with couples, I have come to accept that change for most people is extremely difficult and that, although they may not like their present state, they would rather find a way of remaining the same without the pain. In essence, most partners I have seen have been unconsciously looking for a way to support their internalized conflicts so that they could avoid the arduous process of change; this is the unconscious basis on which they have chosen one another — to balance or support their individual conflicts.

This model does not pretend to shy away from viewing couples from a pathological perspective when deemed appropriate, but it is wholly optimistic in its belief that, with insight and in some cases education, each partner of a couple will be presented with the opportunity to gain control over his or her conflict and any associated symptoms. It is the exposing and resolution of these conflicts that can ultimately lead couples past any chronically deleterious p–d dynamics and into a more consistent state of intimacy. I hope this book will be a guide to that end.

Acknowledgments

Because the process of becoming a psychotherapist depends on the knowledge and skill of many others, I feel compelled to pay homage to certain individuals who have trained, supervised, and influenced me in my work with couples. My thanks go to those at the Marriage Council of Philadelphia (renamed the Council for Relationships) and, in particular, to Ellen Berman, Larry Hof, Harold Lief, Gerald Weeks, and April Westfall. At the Marriage Council, I learned that marital therapy and sex therapy are inextricably linked and that training in one of these areas alone is partial training for one who wishes to work with couples.

I spent seven studious years at the University of Pennsylvania, and I loved nearly every minute. My thanks to the academic and administrative staffs at the university's School of Social Work and the other departments that I utilized to form my specialization in marriage and family therapy. I am especially grateful to my doctoral chairperson, the late Anne-Linda Furstenberg, for her commitment to me as well as her guidance and open-mindedness.

The late Helen Singer Kaplan, former Director of the Human Sexuality Training Program at the New York Hospital–Cornell Medical Center (renamed the New York Weill–Cornell Medical Center), was also instrumental in my theoretical and clinical development. As a clinician, teacher, and supervisor she was unsurpassed. She had the gift of being able to critique you and yet simultaneously communicate that she cared for and supported you unconditionally. I consider my time spent with her invaluable. Elaine Kleinbart's clinical supervision was also influential during my time in the New York program, and my relationships with former Fellows were and still are inspirational to me.

I would also like to pay homage to Gerald Margolis and Bernard Fried-berg, my mentors in the Psychoanalytic Fellowship Program at the Institute of the Philadelphia Association for Psychoanalysis (renamed the Psychoanalytic Center of Philadelphia). Special thanks also go to David Rackow and Walden Holl, Jr., of the Institute. Without Dr. Holl's support, insight, and wisdom, in particular, this book might not have been written. Classical psychoanalysis still lives and has added invaluable depth to my work with couples.

Mindy Schiffman of New York University School of Medicine also deserves my gratitude for her comments and criticisms on earlier portions of this work. In such hectic times, I cannot thank her enough for taking time out of her busy schedule to aid in the shaping of this manuscript. My appreciation also goes to all those at Routledge, particularly George Zimmar, Publishing Director, and Dana Bliss, Associate Editor, for their professional expertise and for giving me the opportunity to present my work in book form, and to Sarah Nicely Fortener of Nicely Creative Services for her accurate and expedient editing on behalf of Routledge.

I would also like to acknowledge those who have helped to develop the pursuer–distancer dynamic over the years, especially Thomas Fogarty. While I have never met him personally, I have seen his work live and remain impressed with his knowledge and skill. The world of marriage and family therapy will be forever grateful to him for his great contribution to the field.

And, finally, I would like to extend heartfelt gratitude to my wife, Maria, and to my daughters, Jennifer and Melanie, as well as my friends and colleagues whom I have no doubt eluded while in the process of writing this book. These special people have amazingly tolerated my distance with grace and patience.

Introduction

Understanding the
Pursuer–Distancer Dynamic

Professional couples therapists consistently witness partners who claim to want intimacy in their relationships but behave in ways that run counter to this objective. In fact, being emotionally, physically, and spiritually close to one's mate is more difficult to achieve than anticipated. Nearly 8 million unmarried people cohabitate, and 95% of all people will eventually marry (Fields & Casper, 2001). Yet, the anxiety that often results when intimacy is pursued can provoke partners to search for ways to provide relief without totally ruining their relationships. For many, it is a big enough feat to "connect at a distance."

A Definition of Intimacy

Levine (1991) referred to intimacy as "an elusive and transient state of grace that initially creates great private excitement and promises happiness. It is the original glue of important relationships" (p. 260). Hallowell (1999) called it the "ultimate of connection" (p. 84). I define an intimate couple as one in which partners can be open and honest with one another about their innermost thoughts and feelings without being coerced, controlled, or made to suffer consequences. Mutual openness is actually reinforced despite the content of the discussion. Most partners have little difficulty communicating positive information to one another, but many tend to have problems dealing with controversial matter. This may include accepting or delivering constructive criticism, allowing a partner to vent without personalizing it, or simply discussing a problem in the relationship. To me, the ability to discuss uncomfortable material in a civil, rational manner is particularly indicative of intimacy, and true intimacy facilitates emotional, physical, and sexual closeness.

Intimacy is also spiritual in nature. In an intimate relationship, partners may feel as if they have met their "soul mates." That is, when partners assess their lives in retrospect, they may feel as if they made very smart choices. They may feel lucky, perhaps humbled, to have found their particular mates. This is not about perfection; it is a very special connection that cannot be easily replaced. The pursuit of intimacy can be a very scary endeavor, but, at the same time, it can also promote a great deal of relational satisfaction and provide a sense of security. Suffice it to say that intimate partners are emotionally, physically, spiritually, and sexually close; therefore, intimacy is not the mere existence or survival of a relationship. It represents much more.

How does one achieve this state of relationship nirvana? In tune with Schnarch (1997), I believe that in order to achieve intimacy each partner must be adequately differentiated from the influences of their respective families of origin. By differentiation, I mean becoming as emotionally autonomous as possible from the confounding influences that have surrounded and saturated them while growing up (see "The Family Systems Movement: The Work of Murray Bowen" section, below). It is these influences that have led to internalized conflicts with intimacy, thus directly affecting each partner's sensitivity and, in turn, their ability to communicate appropriately and to problem solve. The powerful influences from one's family background, the conflicts they may have helped to create, and the life experiences that have reinforced these internalized conflicts can make it extremely difficult to be intimate as an adult for an individual who grew up in a home where little intimacy was exhibited. Simply put, if our parents did not teach or demonstrate it, we have to work that much harder to get it.

Finally, differentiation does not simply represent a certain physical distance. I often hear couples say: "If we moved away we could escape our in-law problem." Well, maybe, but family-of-origin problems are portable — they can be taken anywhere. When I would speak professionally on the family of origin, I would leave two empty folding chairs on the stage to symbolize that both my parents were always with me. I say this because no one can ever completely differentiate.

The Pursuer–Distancer Dynamic as a Vehicle To Avoid Intimacy

The *pursuer–distancer* (p–d) dynamic is one of the most common, yet challenging, dynamics that, when "fixed," is prominently representative of a conflict with intimacy. Fogarty (1976, 1979) is credited in the marriage and family therapy literature with defining and developing an understanding of this interaction. He contended that all people want closeness; they want to be cared for, to be accepted. However, he felt that people took the ability to become close too lightly. In fact, he suggested, when two people begin to move toward one another with the expectation of closeness, the emotionality or intensity that accompanies this process may result in fusion followed by a desperate need for space or distance. To achieve this degree of space, one partner may become the pursuer and the other the distancer. In this way, the couple fixes the distance between them with the pursuer pursuing and the distancer distancing. The more the pursuer pursues, the more the distancer distances and *vice versa*.

Peter and Janet were a couple in their early forties who had been married for 15 years. In their first session, Janet couldn't seem to control herself. She levied a barrage of loud, verbal attacks against Peter. She stated that he rarely initiated conversations with her, failed to show any passion for sex, and often forgot her birthdays and their anniversaries. She said living with Peter was like living alone. Moreover, she said that he could be in the room with her and still make her feel lonely.

Peter sat quietly throughout his wife's tirade. On several occasions I observed him staring out of my office window. At one point, he stretched his body out on his chair and closed his eyes as if he were drifting off to sleep. Initially, Janet didn't seem to notice Peter's behavior and continued to register complaint after complaint about him; however, when she caught him with his eyes closed, she leaned toward him and scolded, "Are you listening to me?" Peter opened his eyes slowly but soon drifted off again.

While Janet brought up numerous examples of Peter's inattentiveness, what she and Peter failed to realize was that they were both contributing equally to the p–d dynamic — a potentially destructive interaction that could worsen with time and ultimately cause irreparable damage to their relationship. Specifically, Janet did not realize that Peter's distancing behavior was in direct proportion to her complaining. She passionately proclaimed to desire more affection and attention from him but was unaware that her barrage of complaints only served to push him further and further away from her. It took several minutes for her to even notice that Peter had shut his eyes in the session. And, rather than express disappointment or hurt (feelings that would be less likely to enable his distance) regarding his behavior, she increased the level and tone of her anger.

Peter's obvious passivity contributed greatly to his wife's irritation with him. He admitted that he often forgot her birthdays, and he stated that, while he usually intended to get her something for Valentine's Day, something always seemed to deter him. He couldn't actually provide a rational explanation for this phenomenon but made it sound as if some cosmic power intervened, rendering it impossible for him to follow through with his plans. Peter was a far more active contributor to the dynamic in that he seemed to increase his distancing behavior the more stressful things became. His *coup de grâce* came when he actually appeared to have fallen asleep during a session. Peter complained that his wife was consistently demanding, and that she expected far too much of him. His message was that he only wished his wife to become a more agreeable person and curb her demands somewhat, particularly in the relational arena. Given Janet's behavior, one could not blame Peter for his attitude; however, rather than contributing to the achievement of his objectives by calming her and reinforcing his desire of her, he exacerbated the relational dynamic via distancing.

If Janet wanted more intimacy why, then, did she relentlessly pursue Peter, particularly given the evidence that her behavior only served to chase him away? If Peter wanted Janet to pressure him less why, then, did he not make her more of a priority in his life? It is obvious that Peter's distancing failed to quench Janet's thirst for him. The fact is that the protection this dynamic provides is greater than the risk required to solve one's internal conflicts in order to achieve intimacy. The underlying anxiety associated with intimacy specifically enables the pursuer to be chronically dissatisfied and, therefore, to consistently pressure the distancer. This keeps the distancer at a distance. The distancer, rather than taking a stand, runs away. The distancer cannot be open and honest with his or her feelings, and the pursuer most likely would not tolerate this anyway.

The Pursuer and Distancer in Context

The pursuer and distancer can utilize many different contexts in their effort to avert intimacy. In the preceding example, Janet and Peter argued over emotional connection and relational presence; however, couples routinely present p–d struggles within the specific contexts of sex, work, or hobbies, as well as other areas of content, with the unstated, underlying objective being to avoid intimacy. It is believed that gender conditioning exerts some influence not only in terms of which sex tends to pursue and which tends to distance (*e.g.*, women may be more prone to pursue and men more prone to distance), but also with regard to the context in which an individual chooses to pursue or distance (*e.g.*, men pursue sports or job-related activities and distance themselves from emotional encounters). These issues are addressed more extensively in subsequent chapters.

All couples pursue and distance. It is a natural dynamic that does not necessarily translate into relational dysfunction or severe marital discord.

For example, a wife might pursue her husband to go shopping with her and the husband may prefer to watch television. As an isolated incident or one restricted to a particular context of relative insignificance (*e.g.*, shopping), the marriage might not suffer. After all, nobody gets everything they want, particularly when living with another individual. However, if the dynamic cuts across many different contexts (*e.g.*, wife also pursues for sex and the husband prefers to watch television) or is fixed in a way that renders emotional closeness impossible, trouble may be inevitable.

The importance individual partners attribute to a particular context also affects the potential impact of the dynamic on the relationship. While the value of these contexts exists on a subjective continuum, certain transgressions, such as affairs, as well as nodal events, such as births and deaths, can carry greater weight and are therefore potentially more toxic if utilized in the p–d dynamic. For example, rather than heeding his wife, if a husband chooses to attend a business meeting (even if it is of some importance) over attending his father-in-law's funeral, irreparable marital problems may occur. Certain thresholds cannot be crossed without severe consequences to a relationship. In this case, the wife may never forgive her husband for the distance he imposed on the day of the funeral. Certainly, many couples have never recovered from distancers using the context of infidelity to create space in their relationships.

The Pursuer and Distancer in Process

I tend to view the pursuer–distancer dynamic as a process and the specific subject matter presented as the content or context of this process. This is a vital distinction in the model presented herein because couples tend to focus on one topic and see it as the problem that must be addressed at all times in the therapeutic process. They rarely separate process from content or context, and this, in my opinion, enables them to replicate their problematic patterns. I believe that, no matter what the content, if a couple has a faulty process they will find it extremely difficult if not impossible to problem solve. But, if their process is a good one, then almost any content issue can be worked through. Of course, some content issues may be too large to remedy.

Caitlin and Ethan were a couple in their early twenties who were to marry in six weeks. The invitations were out and a huge, expensive wedding was planned; however, the two partners disagreed on where to live after marriage. Caitlin wanted to stay on the East Coast near her close-knit ethnic family and Ethan wanted to move to the West Coast, not only for the climate but also because he thought the job market for his profession was much healthier there. Both partners gave compelling arguments for their stances, but neither would budge. It certainly wasn't a matter of right or wrong — it was simply two people who couldn't agree. In this case, the couple's process was fine. They explored the issue in an unemotional, relatively intellectual manner. They calmly made their arguments but could not resolve the issue. In essence, they had a fine process but a severe content problem. In the end, the couple canceled their immediate plans to marry, but Caitlin did decide to try a trial run on the West Coast, with the provision that she would be able to visit home at certain times of the year. If this arrangement worked out, she would entertain marriage plans. If it didn't however, she would end the relationship and move back to the East Coast. With a severe process problem (*e.g.*, one partner pursues to discuss the issue and the other distances from the discussion) the couple might never have been able to address the issue.

A Review of the Literature

During my search of the professional literature on the p–d dynamic, I found it to be, like most other concepts, linked over time and across different fields. I discovered the need to consider, for example, the fields of psychoanalysis, communications theory, and family systems theory in order to obtain an understanding of the roots of the concept in the psychotherapy profession. As will soon be made evident, the dynamic has been described by a wide variety of authors and clinicians in the literature. And, even though the majority of these individuals have referred to the interaction by different names (*e.g.*, nag–withdraw interaction), there is little doubt that they were talking about the pursuer–distancer dynamic — it is that pervasive in the lives of couples.

The Psychoanalytic Influence: 1930s to 1950s

While Freud is not generally associated with systems thinking and, in particular, marital therapy, he did recognize the impact of family relationships on an individual's personality development. The classical analytic approach to treating marital problems, however, was for the partner who was designated as the patient to undergo psychoanalysis. Rarely, if ever, were both parties seen together. If an analysand's partner seemed to be in need of psychological help as well, analysis might have been offered to that person also but most likely with a different analyst.

Some followers of Freud, however, began to think more systemically. Psychoanalyst C. P. Oberndorf (1938), for example, who is considered a pioneer in marital therapy, was one of the first to note that the neuroses of husband and wife complement one another and that the unconscious objectives of some of these complementary reactions actually served to perpetuate the pathological relational reactions. True to classical psychoanalytic technique, however, Oberndorf did not see the two spouses together in treatment; instead, he chose to analyze them consecutively.

Psychoanalyst Bela Mittelmann (1944) was heavily influenced by Oberndorf's (1938) work. In Mittelmann's classic paper, "Complementary Neurotic Reactions in Intimate Relationships," the author described the "common pattern" of an emotionally detached partner (usually the man) and a mate who craves affection (usually the woman). Advocating for concurrent treatment of the partners when the level of relational neurosis merited it, Mittelmann was in a better position than his famous predecessor to witness this dynamic style. He wrote the following:

> When the woman's violent demand for love and support arouses the man's fears, he becomes more detached while she evaluates this detachment as a humiliating rejection. Her guilt and fear of abandonment keep pace with the violence of her demand. Concomitantly, the man, who is warding off his desire for dependency and submission, becomes afraid of being completely dominated by these excessive demands for affection and defends himself by increasing his detachment. (p. 484)

In the 1950s, psychoanalysts continued to explore neurotic marital patterns. One such pattern that was strikingly similar to the p–d interaction was referred to as the "lovesick" wife and the "cold, sick" husband (Bird & Martin, 1959; Martin & Bird, 1959). The authors found that the wife in this combination appeared somewhat hysterical and often presented with a host of symptoms for which she incessantly blamed her distant husband. She complained, for example, that he simply didn't care about what she wanted or felt, and she described him as cold, unsympathetic, and unable to be intimate. She believed that only she had a deep capacity to love, thus the only solution was to change her husband. In contrast, the husband presented as rational and intelligent, albeit less assertive and sociable. His traumatic background enabled him to endure his wife's constant demands and criticisms and to defensively respond with coldness even though there was a deep capacity for warmth underneath. While both partners were recommended for treatment, they had their own individual analysts who consulted with one another on a somewhat regular basis.

The Family Systems Movement: The Work of Murray Bowen

Considered by many to be an extension of psychoanalysis, the family systems movement began to gather steam in the 1950s. At that time, many clinical researchers and theoreticians in different parts of the United States were concerned with schizophrenia and preferred to study the family system rather than the individual patient in an effort to unlock the origin of the disease. Perhaps the most prominent individual in this undertaking was Murray Bowen (1959). Also a psychoanalyst, Bowen believed that unresolved symbiotic attachment (or extreme fusion) between mother and child, actively or passively supported by the father, could lead to schizophrenia in the child. (This has been refuted by more current medical models of schizophrenia.)

Bowen (1966) contended that children grew up with varying degrees of autonomy or differentiation from what he referred to as the *undifferentiated family ego mass* (*i.e.*, family emotional oneness). At the higher end of the differentiation continuum were those who were more autonomous or independent and had a clearer sense of individual identity. They were said to have a higher level of *differentiation of self*. Those at the extreme low end of the continuum (*e.g.*, schizophrenics) were thought to be fused to the family ego mass and thus had very little sense of self.

Most germane to the p–d dynamic, Bowen (1966) discovered that all the parents of the families he had been studying alternated between periods of overcloseness and overdistance and eventually settled into a more fixed, less emotional distance with one another. He believed that this process, which he termed *emotional divorce*, began very early in their marriages. Bowen (1978) explained this behavior by suggesting that in the new husband–wife undifferentiated family ego mass, both partners longed for closeness. When this closeness was achieved, however, "their individual 'selfs' fused together into an emotional oneness with a 'common self'" (p. 93). This resulted in the loss of individual identity and created emotional difficulty. The partners therefore retreated to a sufficient distance from one another to preserve as much of their individual identities and autonomy as possible. The lower the level of differentiation in each partner the greater the risk of losing oneself in the marital process.

Fogarty (1979) trained at Georgetown University Medical Center, where Bowen was a clinical professor and director of the Georgetown University Family Center. Fogarty seemed heavily influenced by Bowen's theories of closeness and distance which no doubt helped him to lay the groundwork for his conceptualization of the p–d relationship dynamic as a way to combat the fusion or avert the discomfort of closeness.

The Communication Theorists: Palo Alto in the 1950s and 1960s

In contrast to the psychoanalytic/psychodynamic perspective, communication theorists in the early 1950s were examining the potential correlation between schizophrenia and faulty family communicational interactions (Bateson, Jackson, Haley, & Weakland, 1956). Largely as a result of the research conducted at the Mental Research Institute (MRI) in Palo Alto, California, this work was later expanded to include the impact of communicational dynamics on other areas of relationship functioning. For example, Bateson and Jackson (1964) contended that people engaged in a lengthy sequence of interchange will "punctuate the sequence so that it will appear that one or the other has initiative, dominance, dependency or the like" (p. 274). This can be demonstrated, for example, by a certain facial expression, a pause, the speed or tone at which one communicates, or hand or body signals.

Building upon this work, Watzlawick *et al.* (1967) described a couple's inability to punctuate the sequence of events by depicting a *nag–withdraw* dynamic in which the wife nagged and the husband withdrew. The more the wife nagged, the more the husband withdrew and *vice versa*. Neither partner took responsibility for his or her actions and reactions. The husband believed that he withdrew only because his wife nagged him, and the wife believed she nagged only because her husband withdrew. The authors described this process as a never-ending dynamic in which neither partner could assume control or punctuate the sequence of events of their interaction — an interaction strikingly similar to the p–d dynamic.

Fogarty and Others: The 1970s and 1980s

About the same time Fogarty (1976, 1979) published some of his most influential work on the pursuer–distancer dynamic, Napier (1978) described a similar interaction in his classic paper, "The Rejection–Intrusion Pattern: A Central Family Dynamic." Influenced by Kantor and Lehr's (1975) work on "emotional distance regulation" (p. 47) within families, Napier offered his conception of the "struggle over interpersonal distance" (p. 11) between married partners. In the *rejection–intrusion pattern*, one partner (usually the female) is depicted as the "type I" intruder, who seeks closeness and reassurance, and the other (usually the male) as the "type II" rejecter, who seeks separateness and fears being intruded upon. Napier contended that both individuals chose one another because of a covert similarity — a mutual fear of intimacy.

Guerin *et al.* (1987), colleagues of Fogarty at the Center for Family Learning in Rye Brook, New York (which Fogarty cofounded along with psychiatrist and fellow Bowenian Philip Guerin), demonstrated a five-step program that they referred to as the "interactional sequence." Building directly on Fogarty's work, the authors demonstrated that when the distancer does attempt to move closer, it is the pursuer who then elicits the distance in the relationship. The pursuer achieves this by attempting to close all the distance in the relationship or by exhibiting an angry or critical attitude that conveys the message: "Too little too late." This important contribution provided clear evidence that the pursuer had just as much difficulty with intimacy as the distancer.

The Popular Literature

Several authors brought the pursuer–distancer dynamic into the mainstream and popular literature with surprising success. Mornell (1979) published *Passive Men, Wild Women*, a book focused on husbands who perceived their wives' need for togetherness as added pressure on their already demanding work schedules. As this pressure is exerted, the husbands retreat or lapse into passivity, which in turn drives their wives wild. Mornell aptly stated that this dynamic could last years, even "lifetimes." In *Getting the Love You Want*, Hendrix (1988), developer of Imago Relationship Therapy, discussed the *fuser–isolater* dynamic. The fuser, like the pursuer, was described as the partner "who grew up with an unsatisfied need for attachment" (pp. 106–107) which manifested in a longing for security and stability in a relationship. The isolater, much like the distancer, has a "fear of absorption" and an "unsatisfied need for autonomy" (p. 107). Lerner (1989) discussed the p–d dynamic at length in her bestseller, *The Dance of Intimacy*. Although intended for women, the book became hugely successful with men as well. More recently, in *The Solo Partner*, Deluca (2002) offered practical advice and a variety of clinical techniques to help the general readership cope and strategize effectively when "one" partner in the p–d cycle refuses to acknowledge that a problem exists or to accept responsibility for contributing to the problem.

Behavioral and Physiological Marital Research: The 1980s

Also in the 1980s, marital researchers examined communication patterns between husbands and wives that proved similar to the pursuer–distancer dynamic. Gottman and Levenson (1988), for example, discussed *critical, complaining wives* and *withdrawing, stonewalling husbands*. Interestingly, the authors found that the husbands' autonomic and endocrine responses to negative marital interactions were greater and longer lasting than those of the wives. Husbands were thus found to avoid negative interactions while their wives confronted them. Influenced by Fogarty's (1976) ideas, Christensen (1988) referred to the *demand–withdraw* pattern. The author contended that this pattern can be assessed reliably via his questionnaire (*i.e.*, Communication Patterns Questionnaire), that the dynamic is strongly associated with marital unhappiness, and that the pattern is predictable based on the gender of the subjects and the independence and intimacy needs each brings to the relationship.

Same-Sex Couples and the Pursuer–Distancer Dynamic

The professional literature on same-sex couples supports the notion that gay male and lesbian couples are not exempt from experiencing p–d dynamics. Loulan (1984), for example, identified *close/far polarization* in lesbian couples. The author focused on the problems with sexual intimacy that can develop as a result of this type of dynamic. Burch (1986) contended that lesbian couples are the closest of all couple types and are, therefore, prone to experiencing difficulty in balancing or regulating their closeness. The author described a p–d-like dynamic in lesbian couples in which one partner attempts to escape the so-called enmeshment or fusion of the relationship by distancing. According to the author, the distancer may withdraw, be overly critical, or have an affair as a way to escape her partner.

Carl (1990) reported that the *pursuer–distancer syndrome* was, in fact, a common dynamic among gay male and lesbian couples. While he felt it was vital to consider the differences and difficulties idiosyncratic of these populations (*e.g.*, absence of boundary benefits because others may not know about or recognize the significance of their relationships, lack of clear role expectations partly because they are not as sex typed and sex differentiated in their behavior as heterosexual couples, lack of societal sanctioning of their relationships), he basically treated the dynamic within gay couples the same way he did for heterosexual couples; that is, he backed the pursuer off and brought the distancer in. Clunis and Green (2000) focused primarily on lesbian couples and the importance of balancing closeness and separateness in order to achieve intimacy. The authors also discussed the potential for a p–d-like polarity in the sex lives of lesbian couples.

Integrating Couples and Sex Therapy: The 1990s

The concept of integrating couples and sex therapy began to gather some much needed momentum in the minds of many systems therapists in the 1990s. Those considering the pursuer–distancer dynamic were interested in its correlation to sexual difficulty. Betchen (1991), for example, studied how the dynamic could be used as a vehicle for sexual distance. He found that some husbands preferred solo masturbation to having intercourse with their wives. The more these men masturbated, the more their wives pursued for sex and *vice versa*. Schnarch (1991), one of the leaders of the integration movement, discussed the dynamic in relation to *other-validated intimacy* as opposed to the healthier, more preferred *self-validated intimacy*. Influenced by the work of Bowen (1978), Schnarch contended that the pursuer pursues out of a need to be valued for his or her ability to self-disclose, and the distancer provokes this pursuit out of a need to feel wanted. Demanding that each partner work toward self-validation places pressure on them, much like their being in a "crucible." Schnarch believed, however, that this pressure is vital in order for couples to achieve long-lasting sexual intimacy.

Additions and Advances: 1990s to the Present

Several authors demonstrated the timelessness of the pursuer–distancer dynamic as an important concept in couples work throughout the 1990s and 2000s by continuing to build upon it. Wile (1993) developed a treatment plan for the interaction based on reducing blame. He preferred to call the dynamic *demanding–withdrawn polarization*. Following his earlier marital research in this area, Gottman (1994) re-examined "critical" wives and "stonewalling" husbands. Proof that he recognized the potentially damaging circularity of this marital combination, he wrote the following:

> I consider these spousal differences as having the potential to produce a vicious cycle in those marriages that are characterized by high levels of conflict: The more the wives complain and criticize, the more husbands withdraw and stonewall; the more husbands withdraw and stonewall, the more wives complain and criticize. How to break out of this cycle of criticism and withdrawal is likely to be a central problem that must be solved if conflict-engaging marriages are to avoid dissolution. (p. 260)

Influenced by Christensen's (1988) work on the demand–withdraw pattern, Gottman later joined others in applying the interaction to marital violence (Berns, Jacobson, & Gottman, 1999). This research is addressed more extensively in chapter 11.

Guerin *et al.* (1996) emphasized the importance of thinking about the p–d dance as a triangular dynamic emanating from the family of origin as opposed to simply a dyadic interaction. When Betchen (1996) examined the relationship between parentification and infantilization in the p–d dynamic, he found that the pursuer was parentified in his or her family of origin and that the distancer was infantilized. The unconscious complementary choosing of one another helped to ensure the development of a "parentified pursuer–childlike distancer" interaction, similar to Bowen's (1978) concept of *overadequate–inadequate reciprocity*, Bepko and Krestan's (1985) *overresponsible–underresponsible* marriage combination, and Sager and Hunt's (1979) *parental–childlike* union.

Schnarch (1997) introduced the concept of *critical mass* to describe the emotionally charged stage a couple must contend with in order to alleviate the p–d dynamic. In this phase of treatment, each partner must confront the anxiety and depression that may underlie each partner's contributions to the interactional dance. He believed that reaching this critical point is necessary in order to achieve a "passionate marriage." Shaddock (1998) discussed mergers and distancers. He believed that eventually these two individual types would evolve into a *pursuit–avoidance script* as a defensive way of coping with their "childhood issues of abandonment and intrusion" (p. 98). He wrote that mergers (pursuers) "replace intimacy with emotional drama," and "distancers replace it with a power struggle" (p. 94).

Sharpe (2000) discussed the *pursuer–pursued collusion* and presented a developmental approach based on object relations theory. She viewed the dynamic as an unconscious collusion in which "the partners try to solve their shared anxieties through projection of one side of the conflict onto the partner who receives and acts out the projection" (p. 194). In essence, the conflict is split so that one partner expresses the couple's need for closeness and the fear of distance, while the other expresses their joint need for distance and fear of closeness.

The Emergence of the Male Pursuer–Female Distancer Dynamic

While this topic is addressed extensively in chapter 2, suffice it to say that a change in the social climate toward greater educational and economic equality has, in part, enabled more women to be emotionally and financially independent of men. Some authors believed that this cultural shift has led to a proliferation of the once considered rare male pursuer–female distancer relationship. Wexler (1992, 1993), for example, contended that social changes — in particular, the call for women to own more power and men to seek emotional intimacy — have been a major contributing factor in this relationship shift. Others (Betchen, 2002; Betchen & Ross, 2000) have provided clinical and theoretical examinations of the male pursuer–female distancer dynamic and have noted an increase in power and control struggles between couples, as well as role confusion on the part of men.

CHAPTER 1

Traits and Tendencies of the Pursuer and the Distancer

Fogarty (1979) was adamant about the fact that pursuing and distancing were tendencies, not fixed developmental or personality characteristics. He wrote, "Inside of every distancer is a pursuer, and inside every pursuer is a distancer" (p. 47). While I generally agree, I have seen many pursuers and distancers remain in character outside their relationships and/or across different contexts. In fact, many pursuers seem to demonstrate somewhat anxious, histrionic, and/or obsessive–compulsive traits or tendencies, while many distancers tend to exhibit avoidant, depressive, and/or passive–aggressive traits or tendencies. I believe that one tendency is dominant, but in most cases a little of the other also exists simultaneously with the underlying issue having to do with a conflict around intimacy. It is as if pursuing and distancing exist on a continuum with the pursuer at one end and the distancer at the other end and graded levels of each in between; however, no pure or prototypical pursuer and no pure or prototypical distancer exist — just individuals who are closer to one end of the continuum. As shown in Figure 1.1, Sue is the pursuer and Joe is the distancer.

In support of the dynamism of the interaction, when two predominant pursuers get together one (the one who has more of a tendency to distance, or is closest to the extreme end of the distancer's side of the continuum) takes on the distancer role in the relationship. And, if two predominant distancers match up, the one who is closest to the pursuer's end of the continuum will take on the role of the pursuer. As shown in Figure 1.2, Sue remains the pursuer to Joe but the distancer to Sam. Joe is the pursuer to Jane.

Fig. 1.1 Continuum of pursuer–distancer interaction.

A list of some of the general traits and tendencies that pursuers and distancers may exhibit is shown in Table 1.1. These characteristics tend to vary in number and intensity depending on where an individual is on the pursuer–distancer continuum. For example, an individual closest to the extreme end of the pursuer side of the continuum would most likely exhibit more pursuing traits and tendencies or more intense versions of them than an individual who is further away.

Although these traits and tendencies have been described in the professional literature (Betchen, 1991, 1996; Fogarty, 1979; Guerin *et al.*, 1987; Napier, 1978), it is conceded that not all may resonate with every couple's therapist or to the same extent; rather, they will most likely be perceived somewhat differently from clinician to clinician depending upon their clinical experiences, and possibly even their specific therapeutic and theoretical orientations. Suffice it to say that the following list reflects my own experiences with pursuers and distancers, as well as the experiences of the authors cited above.

1. Pursuers express their thoughts and feelings freely; distancers keep their thoughts and feelings to themselves.

Pursuers are open with their thoughts and feelings. They are very verbal and can easily maintain a conversation. This, in part, makes them particularly important in terms of keeping the therapeutic process moving. Distancers, on the other hand, keep to themselves. Their thoughts and feelings are tightly contained, giving the false impression that they have none. Because they portray themselves as blank slates, or *tabula rasas*, it is difficult to know what they are thinking. Any insecurity on the pursuer's part may in fact be projected onto the distancer.

Yale and Olivia were a couple in their late thirties. Olivia was a very verbal and outgoing individual who did almost all of the talking in treatment. Yale appeared shy and seemed content to let Olivia carry the conversation.

Fig. 1.2 Dynamism of pursuer–distancer interaction.

TABLE 1.1 Traits and Tendencies of the Pursuer and the Distancer

	Pursuer	Distancer
1	Expresses thoughts and feelings	Keeps thoughts and feelings to self
2	Social	Asocial
3	Verbal and body language seems aggressive	Verbal and body language is passive
4	Appears anxious and very focused	Appears depressed or disinterested
5	Very impatient	Very patient
6	Truthful and confronting	Vague and indirect
7	Trusting	Distrusting and somewhat paranoid
8	Initiates action	Procrastinates
9	Devours self-help books	Avoids guidance
10	Loose boundaries	Closed and difficult to get close to
11	Parental	Childlike
12	Righteous	No cause is worth the fight
13	Responsible	Can be irresponsible
14	Optimistic	Pessimistic
15	Trouble with endings	No apparent trouble with endings

When Yale did want to say something, he had to struggle to intervene; it seemed almost painful for him to speak. When I saw each partner individually, it was interesting to note the stark contrast. Olivia's session flew by, and it seemed as if she had a never-ending stream of things to talk about. While she focused primarily on Yale and the marital issues, she drifted off into her work, friends, movies, and life in general. She even tried to keep the conversation going after the session had formally ended and I had to open the office door to move her along so I could see my next couple. Yale's session seemed to last a lifetime. He had little to say, and the majority of the session consisted of silence. It seemed as if he wanted me to do all the work, as Olivia apparently did. It is interesting to note that Yale expressed very little criticism of his wife in his individual work with me; nevertheless, Olivia was sure that he told me that he hated her and that he wanted to leave her. She attempted to pump me for information to support this hypothesis, but I encouraged Yale to speak with her about the subject. When Yale finally admitted to Olivia that he did not hate her and had no intentions of leaving the relationship, she seemed puzzled. Apparently Olivia was projecting her own anxious thoughts and feelings onto her reticent partner.

2. Pursuers are social and move toward people; distancers are asocial and move toward inanimate objects.

People who take on the pursuer role in their relationships tend to be the social organizers. It is they who will arrange to get together with other couples or plan a night on the town. They tend to have friends for all occasions. In fact, one woman told me that she needed to have people in her house all the time. She said that it felt lonely without the constant interaction. Some of these individuals are what I refer to as "collectors" in that they gather as many friends as possible. People who distance tend to be loners. If it weren't for their pursuing paramours, they might not have much of a social life at all. In fact, the husband of the woman mentioned above told me that he "couldn't care less if anybody ever came over to the house." Distancers, however, will partake in individual-oriented activities or hobbies or ones that require little intimate interaction (*e.g.*, photography). They may play a sport but prefer one that is less team oriented, such as running or swimming. If they do participate on a team, they may find excuses to avoid getting together with their teammates after the activity. They tend to prefer objects such as computers, and the Internet makes them particularly dangerous to their counterparts because vehicles such as chat rooms allow them to connect with others at a distance rather than become closer to their mates.

Steve and Sheila, a couple in their late forties, had been married for approximately eight years. It was the second marriage for both, and they had sufficient funds to build a beautiful, spacious home that was perfect for entertaining. However, Sheila complained that Steve was a workaholic and rarely had time to socialize with anybody. Meanwhile, she had an assortment of friends with whom she constantly stayed in contact. For example, she regularly worked out at the gym with two of them and always kept a full itinerary of luncheon and dinner dates with them. Even when it came to Steve's business, Sheila was the social director, planning parties for his company employees. Steve, on the other hand, had no friends and did not seem to mind. He was an avid collector of gadgetry and was constantly on his computer. The final blow came when Sheila decided to throw a large party on Memorial Day for all of her best friends. Although Steve did not object, he spent the entire time on his computer in a locked room, only to emerge to grab a bite to eat. Sheila reported that at rather short intervals she would knock on the door to get Steve to come out and play host. This experience so enraged and embarrassed Sheila that she threatened to divorce Steve if he did not attend marital therapy with her.

3. Pursuers have verbal and body language that is aggressive or very assertive; distancers have verbal and body language that is passive and distant.

Pursuers tend to be scolding, so their voice may be angry in tone. Their speech tends to be pressured and their body language aggressive. For example, a pursuer may sit forward in the chair (on the edge of the seat), aimed at the distancer. If the pursuer's legs are crossed, they will be crossed toward the distancer (picture a missile ready to fire). On the other hand, the distancer's voice is often calm and quiet. Because they are sometimes inaudible, you may have to ask distancers to repeat what they are saying or to speak louder. A distancer's legs may be crossed away from the pursuer, or the distancer's entire body may be turned away from the pursuer. Distancers rarely raise their voices or scream.

From the minute he entered treatment, Riley complained about his wife's refusal to spend time with him as well as her recent reluctance to have sex with him. "She hardly ever speaks to me, and when she does she gives me one or two word answers." Emily was a quiet woman who sat with her legs crossed away from Riley. She kept her eyes fixed on me throughout the entire session as if Riley wasn't even there. She stated that she was confused with regard to her actions but wished that Riley wouldn't be so angry with her. Riley used his hands when he spoke and constantly pointed his finger at Emily to make a point and/or to threaten her. Emily did not respond to him directly. Compared to Riley, Emily was slow speaking.

4. Pursuers appear anxious and focused; distancers appear depressed, disinterested, or in a state of confusion.

Pursuers are hyperfocused on the relationship difficulties and are almost certain that the distancers are solely responsible. They talk about the problem constantly, and it seems to absorb them. They can experience a wave of excitement or a high; however, they are also prone to lows when they are feeling out of control. They tend to worry a lot about the present (*e.g.*, how they will pay the bills today) and often exhibit quite a bit of anxiety. Distancers have a flat rhythm to them (Christmas is like any other day); they do not vacillate. They also do not exhibit as much anxiety. Many distancers appear depressed or disinterested. They tend not to be perfectionistic and, in fact, many can live with very little.

Peter and Janet, a couple previously depicted in the introduction, exhibited these traits. If you recall, Janet was angrily pursuing Peter for a variety of reasons, while Peter almost seemed to fall asleep during the session. Janet was extremely focused on the relationship issues as well as on

Peter, while Peter seemed confused about why his partner was so upset. Peter was also often caught staring off into space.

As a male pursuer, Ricardo presented as extremely anxious. He stated that his wife Sybil was thinking about divorcing him and he didn't understand why. Sybil appeared quiet and had a bored look on her face. She said that divorcing Ricardo was on her mind, but she wasn't quite sure what to do with the relationship. Indecisive and confusing statements such as these had raised Ricardo's anxiety level to the point where he needed medication. Sybil did, however, make one statement that clearly resonated with Ricardo: "I know I can financially afford to live without him."

5. Pursuers are very impatient, move quickly, and change quickly; distancers are very patient, move slowly, and evolve rather than change quickly.

Pursuers appear impatient; they tend to want things done immediately and to their liking. Many pursuers exhibit perfectionistic traits that they as well as others can never live up to. They like change and expect quick results in the treatment process. They put pressure on the therapist and want to be guided through the therapeutic process. They change first and want others, particularly the distancer, to keep up. Distancers are slow moving. They evolve rather than change quickly. They also hate being pushed around; it is one of the few things that will evoke overt anger in them. They generally don't like change.

Donna and Ted were a couple in their early forties. Donna was very anxious to begin treatment; in fact, she must have called me at least once or twice every day for a week before an appointment was scheduled. When treatment began, Donna continued to exhibit impatience. She wanted to know how long the treatment would last (but what she was really asking was how long it would take to fix Ted). She also wanted to know if I could recommend any exercises they could do at home and if I could suggest anything to read on the subject. At one point, Donna wondered whether Ted could take medication for his distancing behavior. Ted, on the other hand, appeared calm and reserved. He was clearly the slower moving of the two, not just emotionally but physically as well. Over the course of their treatment, Donna was in fact, making clear progress, but this was a blessing and a curse in that she constantly put pressure on Ted to keep up with her. Ted did progress, but to Donna's dismay it was at a much slower rate. Every concept that Donna saw as an exciting revelation Ted took twice as long to grasp. Donna had to get used to the fact that treatment was going to last a lot longer than her impatient nature had envisioned; she needed to learn to accept that Ted functioned at a different pace.

6. Pursuers are truthful and confronting even if it hurts; distancers are vague and indirect.

Pursuers tell it like it is. Sometimes they may not be very tactful, but you almost always know what is on their minds. Many pursuers could use lessons in "interpersonal finesse." They are usually unaware, for example, of the impact their truthfulness may have and, in fact, can be rather startled to realize the severity of the pain that they may inflict on others. While therapists understand that the timing of an intervention is just as important as the intervention itself, the pursuer doesn't quite get this. If something is on the pursuer's mind, it will likely come out.

Gabrielle and Drew, a couple in their early thirties, were in treatment at Gabrielle's urging. Gabrielle specifically complained that Drew hardly ever interacted with her. As evidence she said that they recently drove to North Carolina to buy furniture from a manufacturer and that Drew hardly spoke the entire trip. Gabrielle said he was always like this. Indeed, taking a history from Drew was like pulling teeth, but after a time he began to open up a little and tell me about his family. When he appeared finished, all was quiet until Gabrielle suddenly yelled out to him, "Well, aren't you going to tell him about your brother's suicide?" Drew and I both were stunned.

Distancers, on the other hand, are often difficult to read because they tend to be vague and indirect. I once saw a man who answered any and all questions with a question. I could never get a straight answer out of him, and when I pointed this out he seemed to have no idea what I needed from him. Distancers are like this in part because they cannot seem to explain things. To them, life is a "crapshoot," and external events rule; therefore, things that go on in their lives are most often unexplainable and out of their control.

7. Pursuers are trusting of others; distancers are somewhat paranoid (e.g., people are out to get them).

Pursuers tend to be optimistic and to see the good in people. They are more likely to give to charities and to empathize with the pain of others. They trust others and will often tell all their problems to several different individuals. Distancers generally have a skeptical view of the world. Their biggest fear seems to be that they will be trapped in a situation that they can't get out of — a metaphor for their fear of intimate relationships. They tend to view all relationships as somewhat dangerous. Rather than giving freely to charities, distancers seriously question where the money is really going and who is going to get it. There can be a paranoid-like quality to them. If they do invest, they may do so in a crazy venture that the pursuer will try in vain to stop. The venture will appear ill thought out and out of character for the normally cautious, somewhat stingy distancer. When the venture fails (which is most likely to happen), it seems as if the main purpose of the investment was to reinforce the distancer's belief that others are out to get him and that he should be even more cautious and suspicious. Pursuers tend to be more easily impressed, particularly by those with professional credentials. They will consult the best doctors they can and trust their judgments. Distancers are far too suspicious for this type of adulation and trust. They tend to wait until a crisis point to consult a professional authority. Even at this point they are not too impressed and may view with skepticism even the most skillful professional who has come with the highest recommendation.

Charles and Katherine were in their late fifties. They had been married for over twenty years and had saved plenty of money in that time, thanks in large part to their thriftiness. Charles, a very suspicious man, refused to invest his money in mutual funds because he thought they were too risky and because he believed that finance managers would only move his money to make commissions. One day, as if by a miracle, Charles decided to invest in an athletic facility (*i.e.*, gym). Although two other large gyms were located in close proximity, Charles bought into this venture at the urging of someone at his place of employment. Katherine thought the concept was financially suicidal, but Charles was forceful. He invested several thousands of his hard-earned dollars, but the venture failed. Instead of taking responsibility for his uncharacteristic impulsiveness, however, Charles blamed the other men involved in the investment of "probably running off with his money." Following this experience, he swore off all future investments with the exception of U.S. Savings Bonds.

8. Pursuers initiate action; distancers procrastinate and can be passive–aggressive.

Pursuers are motivators and can also be obsessive–compulsive in nature. They seek and love solutions; they are problem solvers. It is they who will initiate treatment of any kind. Oftentimes they will drag the distancer in for therapy by threatening divorce. They even have to plead with the distancer to seek timely medical attention. Distancers may procrastinate and avoid treatment. They can also easily end therapy if the pursuer decides to stop. As noted, distancers generally tend to wait until a crisis point to consult anyone of authority.

Bart's marriage had been in trouble for some time. He had low sexual desire for his wife, Pamela, and had not initiated sex with her in three years. Pamela told Bart that she was becoming more and more frustrated with him. She expressed concern that he was no longer attracted to her and that she felt like a glorified housekeeper. At one point, she even told him that she was considering an affair, but Bart still did nothing. Finally, Pamela contacted an attorney, who sent Bart a threatening letter. Bart suddenly woke up and decided to attend marital sessions with Pamela. In treatment, he explained his passive behavior by saying that he truly "didn't think the marriage was in that bad of shape."

9. Pursuers devour self-help books; distancers avoid outside guidance.

In line with their love of therapy and their respect for professional guidance, pursuers may collect a plethora of self-help books and attempt to enlist the distancer and, in some cases, the therapist to read the material. The distancer may read one or two pages and put the book down, never to return to it again. While this angers the pursuer, it doesn't necessarily stop him or her from continuing to bring in the "book of the week."

Len was a man in his late fifties living with Susan, a woman in her early forties. Len complained that Susan didn't seem as invested in the relationship as much as he was. She spent a lot of time at work and refused to marry him. Susan was a quiet woman who seemed to enjoy her independence. She and Len were each married twice before, and she wasn't anxious to remarry. She was also financially independent. Len was pressuring Susan to give more, and the more he pressured the more avoidant and passive–aggressive she became. On several occasions, Susan didn't show up for luncheon dates with Len. While she blamed her work, she rarely called to let him know that she wouldn't be able to make these appointments. Rather than seeing that pressure was not improving Susan's behavior, Len decided to go on a self-help binge. At one session he brought in a particular book and insisted that both Susan and I read it. Susan, as she usually did, rolled her eyes and admitted she had no intention of reading it. I told Len that I was familiar with the book but that it wasn't my orientation. Frustrated, Len stopped treatment two weeks later to seek out a therapist more in tune with the book he was advocating. Susan made it clear that she was happy with our treatment and that it probably wouldn't matter if the couple saw Freud himself. Len didn't pay attention to what she said and transferred the treatment.

10. Pursuers are very open but lose their boundaries; distancers are very closed and difficult to get close to.

As mentioned, pursuers are very verbal. Their lives are an open book. They also like to help others in need. In fact, they can be the neighborhood therapist. In contrast, distancers are difficult to get to know. They appear mysterious, and I believe that this is, in part, why many pursuers find them attractive. Sometimes pursuers can be intrusive and get into messy situations. Distancers stay out of other people's business and keep them out of their own. Because pursuers get involved, they tend to get drawn into more altercations with others. In fact, they may get into trouble and look to the distancer to protect them or to stick up for them, but distancers do not like involvement and prefer peace at all costs.

Barbara, a very gregarious woman, decided to help her dying neighbor with some household chores. Nick, her husband, had always kept to himself and insisted that the best way to stay on friendly terms with neighbors was to avoid getting too close to them. Regardless, Barbara proceeded to become heavily involved with the dying woman, and when this woman passed away she left some of her inheritance to Barbara. Initially, Barbara felt reciprocated for all that she had put into the relationship. Eventually, however, the deceased woman's children took exception to their mother's gift, and a nasty court battle ensued. Although Barbara received a significant amount of abuse from these individuals, Nick refused to help her in any way. He distanced himself from the entire process.

11. Pursuers are parental; distancers are childlike.

As previously stated in the introduction, the pursuer–distancer dynamic may resemble Sager and Hunt's (1979) parental–childlike relationship. The pursuer will most likely play the role of the parent and the distancer the role of the child. This is especially true if the pursuer was parentified and the distancer infantilized in their respective families of origin (Betchen, 1996). The concept of parentification was originally defined by Boszormenyi-Nagy (1965) as the molding of a child or an adult into a parental-like figure, thus burdening them with age-inappropriate responsibility. Boszormenyi-Nagy and Krasner (1986) reported that transactional, rather than fixed, parentification could be used to teach responsibility; however, from a contextual perspective, parentification is harmful when it serves to deplete someone's resources and trust reserves. It is the imposition of one person's needs on another person who is expected to assume responsibility for meeting those needs. Boszormenyi-Nagy and Spark (1973) stated that, "Marital choice is often based on a covert fantasy of attaching oneself to someone who will be like a wish-fulfilling parent. In a well-balanced marriage, mutual parentification expectations tend to form a more or less symmetrical pattern" (p. 154). Conversely, when one partner parentifies another on a consistent basis, the relationship becomes unbalanced and difficulties often ensue. According to the authors, if one mate parentifies another, "the distortion usually occurs through a fantasied, often unconscious regression of the self to a childlike position" (p. 152).

I believe that, by the act of distancing, the distancer may unconsciously choose the childlike position in the relationship and thus parentify the pursuer. The pursuer, possibly having been severely parentified in his or her family of origin, may be all too ready to take on the job of caretaking the distancer. Eventually, however, the pursuer may become the angry, overworked, critical parent. In response, the distancer may run from the pursuing parent, whom he or she perceives as trying to totally dominate the relationship. The two roles reveal themselves early in the treatment process, with the pursuer registering a significant number of complaints against the distancer, primarily about unfulfilled responsibilities. The distancer allows the pursuer to do most of the talking and/or scolding but may react like a disinterested teenager.

Christina was the eldest of nine children. She reported that her father died young and her mother was too "infantile" to assume sole responsibility of the family. Christina was the main cook, therapist, and all-around "go-to" person in her family. She was constantly bailing her younger siblings out of trouble and getting them the appropriate professional attention they needed. James was the youngest of four siblings. His father also died young, and this set James up to be overprotected by his intrusive mother. Christina brought James in for treatment and proceeded to scold him for everything from forgetting birthday presents to forgetting to take out the trash. Her tone clearly indicated to me that she considered James a "bad little boy." James sat with his hand over his mouth and had a bashful look on his face. He hardly ever spoke back and indeed seemed intimidated by Christina. He eventually admitted that he preferred to play golf and softball rather than participate more fully in the marriage. Not only did Christina make more money than James but she also paid the bills and fixed things around the house that broke down.

12. Pursuers are righteously indignant; distancers believe that no cause is worth the fight.

Particularly if parentified in their family of origin, pursuers can acquire a strong sense of injustice from which they can further develop a special sensitivity about feeling victimized by distancers as well as others. Distancers are not interested in taking up any causes; they don't seem to think that any are worth the battle. Even if they are being blatantly taken advantage of and feel the indignation, they might still choose distance over confrontation.

Sally and Rob were a couple in their early forties. Rob was always extremely conservative with their money, but when he invented a device that he was certain would succeed he sought financial backing to make his dream come true. He decided to enlist two of his friends in the project, but they stole the project from Rob and sold it to a major corporation. The product was very successful and made his two (former) friends very wealthy. This experience enraged Sally, and she begged Rob to sue the men. Rob, however, refused to take legal action. He said the situation was over and "that's the way things go." He said he should have known better than to get involved in a situation like that and he just wanted to forget about it. One evening, however, the couple bumped into one of these former partners at a restaurant. Sally was so angry that she had to hold herself back from creating a scene. Rob, on the other hand, went up to this man and shook his hand. This made Sally even "crazier." She just couldn't understand Rob's position. She said she was even angrier with Rob for his passivity than she was at his former business associate.

13. Pursuers are very responsible and prone to guilt; distancers can be irresponsible.

Correlated with parentification, the pursuer appears very responsible. The therapist need not worry about a pursuer canceling a session at the last minute or failing to pay the fee. Pursuers can also be depended upon to return a borrowed book; they would feel too badly if they didn't meet their responsibilities. Distancers would never ask to borrow a book, but if they did, they might lose it or keep it for an inordinate amount of time. Often, the pursuer may have to return it for the distancer.

Jeffrey and Michelle were a married couple in their early thirties. Prior to marriage, Michelle held a good job and had her own apartment. She was meticulous about paying all her bills on time and was proud of the fact that she had very little in the way of credit card debt. Moreover, she had amassed a sizable savings and retirement plan, which gave her a real sense of security. Jeffrey, on the other hand, had over $10,000 in credit card debt, a poor credit rating, and a history of paying his bills late. Interestingly, after their marriage, Jeffery took over the bill paying and trouble quickly ensued. Michelle was unaccustomed to collection agencies calling her; she found it both embarrassing and humiliating. She also did not relish paying high interest rates and penalties simply because Jeffrey took his time paying the bills. Michelle relentlessly pursued Jeffery to pay the bills on time, to no avail. This put her in the double bind of not wanting to pay the bills herself and adding to her already enormous work load but also wanting to preserve her credit.

14. Pursuers are optimistic; distancers are pessimistic.

Pursuers like to try new things and be creative. They are always thinking about getting into some new venture. Life is exciting to them. They are active organisms — they act on the environment. They also enjoy the moment rather than dwell on the future. They don't mind taking risks and are not very cautious. In fact, they can be overly optimistic at times, which can cause the distancer to view the pursuer's latest scheme with skepticism. Sometimes pursuers appear to have a magical quality about them, as if they can accomplish anything. Distancers are opposite in that they like routine. They don't have to experience new things because they are skeptical about life in general. They take few risks, if any, and are passive organisms. They don't live in the moment; in fact, some would say they don't live at all. Instead, they focus on the future (*e.g.*, what might go wrong next). As mentioned, they believe that they have little control in the world so they might as well sit back and see what happens next. Few things shock them. They tend to rationalize that it makes no sense to waste energy trying to assume responsibility because they have no control. Again, the environment and/or external forces are in control. This belief system allows distancers to be somewhat irresponsible and to let things erode around them. They can easily give up on life and expect little, if anything, from it.

Matt and Joan were a classic example of this dynamic. Joan was very gregarious. She had several hobbies and constantly added more to her life. She worked full time as a nurse. She also played a musical instrument, painted, and made crafts. She had a large family and social network. She loved traveling to exotic places and was constantly on the go. Matt worked and only recently took up golf (which Joan pushed him to do). He had no friends and rarely interacted with his family. Matt would reluctantly accompany Joan on trips if she forced him to, but he preferred to stay at home; he preferred routine. Matt expressed that life was dangerous and that anything could happen at any time. He said there was no use fighting this concept. Matt was a chain smoker, and when asked why he didn't quit smoking (given that his father died of a heart attack at an early age) he responded: "Everyone has to die sometime — it's inevitable. Besides, I'm only thirty-eight years old. By the time I'm at the age when cancer is more prevalent, I'm sure the researchers will have found a cure." This was an astounding philosophy. Notice the perceived lack of control and the reliance on outside forces to fix the situation. Matt wouldn't consider taking charge even though his father died at a young age. Joan thought this point of view was so absurd that she vacillated between anger and laughter when she heard it.

15. Pursuers have trouble with goodbyes and endings; distancers have no apparent problem with goodbyes and endings.

Although it is generally more difficult for pursuers to let go and move on, at a certain point they are more likely to end the treatment and relationship. (This is more true of female pursuers and females in general; see the chapter 4 section on "Termination.") Much of their threatening posture (*e.g.*, "I want a divorce if you don't change") throughout the marriage and treatment process is an attempt to change the distancer — to get the distancer to acknowledge that he or she cares. The distancer cannot seem to get the magic words (*e.g.*, "I care for you") out, and the pursuer may eventually be forced to seriously consider ending the relationship. It is, however, at this time that the pursuer truly begins to appear depleted and depressed. Much of the pursuer's natural energy and optimism have dissipated, in stark contrast to their initial demeanor. This is a serious sign that the marriage is in real jeopardy and that the pursuer is no longer posturing simply to maintain the dynamic. Despite their apparent lack of anxiety, distancers may in fact overreact if and when pursuers truly decide to end the relationship. It is as if a huge balloon suddenly bursts. This reaction dispels the myth that the distancer feels nothing, but it is, in fact, consistent with Lerner's (1989) point that "*distancing is actually a way of managing very intense feelings*" (p. 34). Many years ago, as I was watching a television broadcast of "Monday Night Football" (Arledge, 1970), I was struck by announcer Don Meredith's description of a quarterback who in a crucial situation seemed rather calm: "He's like a duck, calm on the outside but paddling like hell underneath." Some distancers have been known to become suicidal when they sense that their pursuers are through with them. Sometimes a strong enough reaction can postpone the loss of the relationship, but oftentimes it is too late.

Jake and his wife Audrey were a couple in their late thirties who had been married for ten years. Jake had been emotionally, verbally, and sexually distant in the relationship for many years. The couple had been to three marriage counselors but nothing changed. One day, Audrey decided to call it quits. While Jake didn't believe her (he thought it was her usual threat), Audrey began dating someone else and had her lawyer send Jake a letter demanding a divorce. When Jake received Audrey's divorce letter he began to take the whole situation seriously. First, he begged Audrey to attend marital sessions with him again (Jake had been the one resisting treatment in the past). Although Audrey came to one or two sessions, it was obvious that Jake had run out of chances and he knew it. With this realization, he became so distraught that he attempted suicide by swallowing an assortment of pills. A friend found him and took him to the hospital. From that point, Jake requested that he be seen by a psychiatrist three times a week — amazing for a man who previously would attend treatment sessions only once a month. He also took his medication regularly. Interestingly enough, however, the psychiatrist called me in disbelief. He said he had never seen such an amazing turnaround in a patient's life. Apparently Jake had found another woman within six weeks and acted as if nothing had ever happened to him. No doubt he was initiating the pursuer–distancer dynamic yet again.

CHAPTER 2

Gender Roles and the Pursuer–Distancer Dynamic

A point of controversy that has been raised in the marriage and family therapy literature regarding the pursuer–distancer interaction has to do with whether pursuers tend to be female and distancers male (Betchen, 1996). Many of the previously cited authors (Fogarty, 1979; Napier, 1978; Shaddock, 1998) stated that the pursuer–distancer roles were "gender flexible"; that is, males and females can be pursuers or distancers. However, these authors also agreed that females are more likely to be pursuers and males distancers — an assertion that correlates with various feminist theories (Chodorow, 1978; Gilligan, 1982). Feminist family therapists (Walters, Carter, Papp, & Silverstein, 1988) have contended that cultural conditioning plays a part in determining p–d roles because females are raised to be affiliative, expressive, and dependent and men independent and nonverbal. Lerner (1989) wrote that women, not men, were the relationship experts. She attributed this to a traditional cultural rule: "Men were to seek their fortune, and women were to seek men" (p. 5).

Biological Determinants

There are those in the professional literature (Fisher, 1992; Gurian, 1996, 2002) who purport that women are biologically predisposed to seek closer, more intimate relationships than men, and men, by nature, are prone to seek independence. Hormonal differences, as well as differences in the size, structure, and activity levels of the brain are believed to be accountable for

17

these differences. For example, the female hormones estrogen, progesterone, and prolactin are believed to play a part in a woman's ability to empathize, connect, and bond. The female brain has also proved to have a better developed left hemisphere, which contains a more advanced language center and allows for greater expression of emotions. The female brain also contains a larger cingulate gyrus, or "bonding gyrus," than does the male brain. Males, on the other hand, generally have higher testosterone levels than women and exhibit more aggressive behavior, are less empathic, and are more action or task oriented. Because they are predominantly right hemispheric, males tend to be more spatial than verbal.

While it is believed that biology may be a factor in determining p–d roles, particularly the female pursuer–male distancer combination, it does not necessarily account for the proliferation of male pursuer–female distancer dynamics in our society. I have, however, noticed that female distancers in general do tend to exhibit more typically masculine traits. They exhibit more independence, both emotionally and financially. It might prove interesting to measure the testosterone levels of female distancers, but for now two other factors help to explain this issue: societal/cultural changes toward greater gender equality and familial influences emanating from the family of origin.

Societal Influences and Changing Gender Roles

No doubt the differences in the way men and women express themselves have been exacerbated by a culture that has supported emotional development for women and discouraged it for men. In less complex times, women were limited to child rearing and domestic activities while their male counterparts embarked on hunting trips and fended off enemies and predators. Women were dependent on men for their survival and, in fact, were more attracted to the alpha male, or the male who was perceived as the strongest of his peer group. In an agrarian world, the physical strength and prowess of men make them the obvious evolutionary choice for performing such physical duties in a habitually dangerous, Darwinist environment.

While the brain prevails over brawn in post-industrial times and many significant changes have indeed occurred that have helped to balance the educational and economic power of the sexes, our society is still slow to give up past attitudes, roles, and values. While these attributes once helped to preserve the species, they now serve to stereotype the sexes, inhibit intimacy, and enable the p–d dynamic. Despite the increased number of dual-career marriages, for example, women still carry the bulk of the domestic responsibility. Women who earn as much if not more than their male counterparts often report a certain uneasiness. They tend to become more and more anxious as the gap in income widens because they fear their husbands will resent them (Drobnič & Blossfeld, 2001). At times, this resentment exhibits itself in two ways characteristic of males: violence or distance. One woman reported to me that the worst thing she could have done for her marriage (which did dissolve) was to go to graduate school. She believed that doing so drove her husband away. Interestingly enough, her mother agreed with her and tried to discourage her daughter's independence.

Too often significant others, such as athletic coaches, teachers, and parents, treat children according to traditional stereotypes. If these authority figures react to children in ways that support these stereotypes, the children may respond in kind. For example, many little boys are still chastised by coaches if they cry or show vulnerability. Male coaches have been known to cajole their athletes into playing harder by referring to them as "little girls" or "sissies." On the flip side, a mother I know of told her daughter (a high-school swimmer) that she was concerned that if she kept swimming competitively her shoulders would get too big and she would look too masculine. As a result, the girl refused to swim for her college.

Elium and Elium (2003) contended that girls are still rewarded for being feminine and less aggressive while boys are rewarded for aggressiveness. These authors also reported that teachers still give less attention and encouragement in the classroom to girls than boys, in part because they assume that the girls are quiet and conscientious. In fact, one of the reasons why attention-deficit disorder, predominantly inattentive type, goes undiagnosed among girls is because their quiet, introverted behavior is misconstrued as normal behavior expected of "little ladies" (Solden, 1995).

The media are also guilty of perpetuating sexist stereotypes. As a child, one of my favorite television shows was "Daniel Boone" (Spelling, 1964). At the opening of every show, Daniel (played by actor Fess Parker) was on his horse about to embark on some new and exciting adventure. His wife (played by Patricia Blair) was saying goodbye to him and offering some baked goods for the impending trip, while Daniel's young children were looking on knowing that they might not see their father for several months, if ever again. I distinctly remember feeling sorry for Mrs. Boone and her children, and I asked myself: Where is Daniel going? Is it a place that merits leaving his family alone in the wilderness for so long a time? How could his wife tolerate this behavior? Couldn't he hunt closer to home? How come he doesn't look sad or worried about his family?

In a similar vein, I recently saw a western film in which a man was trying to win over a certain woman almost the entire length of the movie. After he was finally able to capture her ardor, he, too, prepared to embark on another adventure. When the woman sadly asked him where he was going, he responded, "I don't rightly know." While the dynamic seemed almost ridiculous to me, it depicted the male need to distance in favor of a conquest to be named later.

According to Kindlon and Thompson (2000), boys who watch television sports are served a steady diet of commercials in which a man is not a man unless he is immune to pain, drives a big truck, and drinks lots of alcohol. Whereas boys used to emulate the likes of movie stars such as John Wayne, Fess Parker, and Clint Eastwood, the images they portrayed were eventually replaced by the super machismo of a single man capable of destroying an entire army by himself as the bullets and bombs drop around him (*e.g.*, Chuck Norris, Arnold Schwarzenegger, Sylvester Stallone). All of these characters are short on words and long on action.

Kindlon and Thompson (2000) wrote the following about boys:

> Pride and stoicism knot together in many boys, reinforcing each other. Not only is it difficult for these boys to express themselves; they take a certain pride in not doing so, in keeping their mouths shut. In psychological distress, they are like the captain of the *Titanic,* standing on the bridge gallantly going down with their ship. They want to look strong and brave. (p. 149)

The authors suggested that it is the need to be perceived as strong and independent "that makes boys wary of the mutual dependence and trust that are at the heart of any intimate relationship" (p. 196). Moreover, they believe that a boy longs for connection but at the same time feels the need to distance, and this opens up an emotional divide that renders most boys ill prepared to become emotionally healthy adults.

Women, on the other hand, can be seen in almost all of the domestic commercials, but even in this arena the heavy domestic work or "big jobs" go to a man — such as Mr. Clean. Television programs, in particular, tend to portray women as desiring to "capture a man," and the man is portrayed as more interested in beer, fast cars, competitive ventures, and, above all, avoiding the "marriage trap" as long as possible. Soap operas often depict women as sneaky, conniving, manipulative characters who are trying to trap a man (even when he is another woman's man).

Since the feminist movement, much social change has occurred in the form of greater gender equality. Women are clearly more independent thanks in part to improvements in their educational and economic status. For example, by 1999, women in the United States were completing high school and attending college at higher rates than men. Evidence suggests that within ten years more women will be seeking their bachelor's degrees than men. Women account for 37% of this country's MBAs, 43% of our MDs, and 41% of our JDs (Hales, 1999).

Women as a group are also working more and earning more. For the first time in our country's history, they are leading contributors to business and the professions (Rimm, 1999). In the United States, the number of female-owned and -operated small businesses has dramatically increased (Tiger, 1999), and women fill 48% of corporate managerial and professional positions and 33% of decision-making positions in government (Hales, 1999).

More and more households are headed by single mothers, and the percentage of employed married women with children is 77% (Hales, 1999). At one time, single mothers were often forced to remarry prematurely in order to survive, as if living in prehistoric times. Tiger (1999), however, reported that the advent of contraception and infertility technology has led many women to believe that they no longer need a man for anything, including reproduction. I have noticed in my clinical practice that many women now speak of men the way men used to speak of women — from a purely sexual standpoint. For example, an attractive female client earning a large six-figure income reported, "I was horny so I had sex with this guy last night. He was pretty good, but I was disappointed because he didn't give me an orgasm. Oh well, it doesn't matter because I don't have any interest in him — he met my immediate needs to some extent, but I won't go out with him again."

In my opinion, the societal changes that have allowed women more independence should be construed as positive, even for men. For example, men no longer need to carry the burden of responsibilities that have stressed them for centuries and probably contributed to their early deaths. (According to the U.S. Department of Health and Human Services [2004], women still outlive men by 5.4 years.) While this burden has served to keep men in a superior position to women, men have been paying for this so-called privilege with their emotional and physical lives.

Gurian (2002) wrote, "In the feminist logic of raising girls, there is a high emphasis on female independence and social status, but the reward of relational stability is downgraded" (pp. 12–13). Indeed, one consequence of gender equality is that more women can distance from men. While the ability to escape a bad marital situation is welcomed, it has also enabled women who have had a predisposed tendency to distance a way out of commitment or intimate relationships; this, in turn, has led to a proliferation of the male pursuer–female distancer dynamic (Betchen, 2002; Betchen & Ross, 2000; Wexler, 1992, 1993). As a result, many couples therapists are seeing more battles for power and control in relationships, more confusion on the part of men about their roles *vis-à-vis* women, an increase in the number of professional women having difficulty finding men who can tolerate their successes, and more and more people delaying marriage or avoiding it altogether.

Gary was always the head of the household and the dominant partner in many ways. Even his wife and children were somewhat intimidated by him. He made quick decisions and seemed to be right most of the time, although all members of his family felt that he was controlling and somewhat tyrannical. Gary was the distancer to his passive, needy wife, Jill, but as times got tougher economically Jill decided to attend night school. She graduated in about six years and accepted her first job. Although it was only part time, she obviously liked it and was bringing in some decent money. Gary struggled with Jill's newfound independence, her socializing, her new professional attire, and her distance as a result of the many activities in which she was now involved. She didn't have time to chase Gary and to look to him for sustenance. At times, Gary would criticize her and point out that her income was "grocery money," but, as finances became even tighter, Jill expanded her hours to full time. Gary's ambivalence grew, but he knew they needed the money. Just as his power base suffered, he made Jill suffer. One day, though, Gary lost his job. He was so overwrought that he fell apart. For the first time in his life he was forced to pursue his wife for help. He began to experience panic attacks and at one point could not even get out of bed.

Jill had plenty of pent-up hostility toward Gary, primarily because of the way he treated her prior to losing his job. She specifically resented the fact that Gary was now relentlessly pursuing her. (Gary even kept Jill up at night because he wanted to talk to her about his symptoms.) Jill needed to get Gary help so that he could give her some space. She got him to see a psychiatrist and to see me for marital therapy. Gary had suffered a major depressive episode which helped him to open up and declare that he had always been extremely attracted to his wife but was afraid to express this for fear of feeling vulnerable. Now, once clearly the distancer to his needy wife who craved affection, he was the pursuer.

Jill sought therapy in part because Gary was so anxious he was pursuing her and interfering with her work both professionally and domestically. As she became more confident and independent, Jill had become more of the distancer and Gary the disillusioned pursuer. Many older men had mothers who never completed junior high school and never earned their driver's licenses. If times had been different, Jill might not have been able to take over the family as she did.

Familial Influences

According to Toman (1976), "A person's family represents the most influential context of his life, and it exerts its influence more regularly, more exclusively, and earlier in a person's life than do any other life contexts" (p. 5). The author also wrote that it is the "early and more pervasive life contexts rather than contexts emerging relatively late and more sporadically that serve as a basis for generalizations of past experiences to new contexts" (p. 5). In tune with this thinking, I believe that gender differences are not alone in determining the existence or prevalence of pursuers and distancers. Like Shaddock (1998), I believe that certain emotional and psychological influences from the family of origin must not be underestimated when examining the origin of the pursuer–distancer dynamic.

A male colleague requested a consultation with me regarding a case that was particularly frustrating to him. A brilliant, young female professor (twenty-five years old) was desperately pursuing her much older (forty-one years old), equally brilliant husband to adopt a child with her. Years before the couple had met, the husband (who had two grown children from a previous marriage) had obtained a vasectomy that proved to be irreversible, so his wife saw the adoption process as an avenue to fulfilling her dream of having a child. The husband, however, was reluctant to adopt, primarily because he had had a number of negative experiences during his own life as an adoptee and father. But, his wife, unyielding in her position, relentlessly pursued him to join her in this endeavor, thus provoking a p–d relationship with the adoption issue as a vehicle.

In discussing the case, my colleague made what I believed to be an amazing statement. He said, "Aside from the issue of adoption they were a perfectly matched couple." I was astounded because this statement implied that if it weren't for the adoption issue the couple would not be in need of treatment and, in fact, would be in "marriage heaven." While it did sound to me that the couple was "perfectly matched," I considered it to be so from a neurotic perspective. Thus, I couldn't help but ask my colleague a series of questions: Did this desperate woman know prior to marriage that not all vasectomies are reversible? If she wanted a baby so badly, why did she choose a man who was so much older than she? Didn't his having a vasectomy tell her something about his desire to have more children? Did she know that her husband was adopted prior to marrying him, and, if so, did she know about his stance regarding adoptions? Did the husband know how badly his wife wanted a child prior to marrying her? If he knew her stance on this issue, as well as his own position on having more children and the concept of adoption, why then didn't he tell his wife directly how he felt? Why did he marry a woman in her twenties? The odds are great that a woman that young would want a child or two.

I strongly suspected that regardless of the apparent brilliance of these two individuals, neither had fully investigated this issue prior to marriage because they were unconsciously at work setting up a p–d dynamic, courtesy of the inner conflicts from their respective families of origin. By examining each partner's past, it might be determined specifically why, out of all the men in the world who could give her a baby, this woman chose an older man with a vasectomy and did not inquire about its reversibility. Likewise, the past might determine why this man, who clearly didn't want to adopt, would pick a younger woman desperate to have children.

To an objective observer, this investigative process might seem entirely logical, but to those directly involved in this collusive dynamic such thoughts may only reach the preconscious at best. In my opinion, by forgoing the appropriate premarital research, on a level beyond their awareness, the couple in question had achieved their desired goal — to get what they wanted … and didn't want: a p–d dynamic that would keep them at a certain distance, perhaps indefinitely. In this case, however, the p–d interaction could eventually end the marriage if a resolution is not reached before the woman's biological clock runs out.

While gender differences are indeed a major factor in determining the p–d roles chosen by men and women in our society, one could argue that in the preceding example it is perfectly understandable for a woman to pursue a man to have children or adopt because it fits with her biological and maternal nature. However, societal influences should not be overemphasized here, given that this couple could have found individuals who were more overtly syntonic about having children. The risk the couple took and the time wasted are symptomatic of personal conflicts that are rooted in their families of origin. No doubt this is a deterministic view as are most psychodynamic theories, but it is not without support, particularly with regard to the p–d dynamic (Betchen, 2002; Fogarty, 1976, 1979; Guerin, Fogarty, Fay, & Kautto, 1996; Shaddock, 1998; Wile, 1993). In the following chapter, these influences are examined more closely. The extent to which an individual reflects his or her pursuing and distancing traits and tendencies is considered to be directly correlated to the extent to which they were subjected to the dynamic in their family of origin and the strength of their subsequent conflicts regarding the dynamic.

CHAPTER 3

Family of Origin

The Emotional and Psychological Development of Pursuers and Distancers

While it may be expected that pursuers and distancers emanate from different dynamics in their respective families of origin, the same can be said for male pursuers and female pursuers and male and female distancers. Understanding specifically how these individuals develop and join together from a psychological perspective is considered key in the overall comprehension and treatment of this interaction. Borrowing from psychoanalytic and psychodynamic systems theories, it is my contention that, on an unconscious level, individuals can choose one another for long-term relationships and/or marriage because they possess similar intrapsychic conflicts that stem from their respective families of origin. When the partnerships are formed, couples can then collude to balance these conflicts so that neither partner has to choose one side of a conflict over the other or integrate both sides (which would still entail some loss because of the compromise required for integration). According to Waelder (1960), the conflicts are repressed or expelled from consciousness, but, because the repression has been unsuccessful, the conflicts are not rendered innocuous and return via "conscious manifestations in disguised form" (p. 37).

Freud (1910/1957) said that accepting an incompatible wish or living with prolonged conflict produces "a high degree of unpleasure" (p. 24). (He was referring to the conflict between instinctual (sexual) drives and opposing forces.) However, this discomfort apparently outweighs the anxiety associated with making a choice. As a result, the very symptoms the couple presents (in this case, the p–d dynamic in various contexts) may continue to exist. Perhaps Waelder (1960) put it best when he wrote that "people usually accept the inevitable and that the greatest strain seems to come from the need to make decisions" (p. 39). The great philosopher Sir Isaiah Berlin (1958) referred to this essential human dilemma as the "necessity and agony of choice" (p. 54). He contended that the "world that we encounter in ordinary experience is one in which we are faced with choices between ends equally ultimate, the realization of some of which must inevitably involve the sacrifice of others" (p. 53). In my opinion, couples have difficulty accepting this reality and will sometimes go to great lengths to avoid making these choices.

In my thesis, I stop short of Freud's focus on the sexual nature of the origin of these conflicts, and I look exclusively at the conflicts arising from the dilemmas into which individuals were (and in many cases still are) triangulated in their families of origin. It is the internalization of this triangulation and the impact it still inflicts on current relationships that are of primary concern. For example, in the following profiles, the pursuers and distancers were found to have been triangulated (to varying degrees) by their parents' p–d relationships. This is consistent with Bowen's (1978) concept of the *family projection process* — the process by which parents project their problems (or, in Bowen's meaning, their lack of differentiation) onto their children. When a pattern of this transmission is established over many generations (which is often the case), it is referred to as the *multigenerational transmission process.*

Note that I am only offering one of the ways in which the p–d styles may have originated. It is not my intention to suggest that they cannot develop via other avenues. Also, I believe that the strength of the tendencies exhibited in each individual reflects the power and influence of his or her family of origin. As mentioned, all individuals pursue and distance and all couples exhibit the dynamic to some extent. Again, I do not view these individuals as having fixed personalities; rather, I consider them to be individuals whose pursuing and distancing behaviors exist on a continuum depending on their past experiences (context, gender differences, and societal influences are also factors) and current partners.

Female Pursuers

As a young girl, the female pursuer may have been triangulated by her parents into a mediating role. In this case, one parent uses the daughter as a buffer against what is perceived to be the onslaught of his or her partner's neediness; the other parent needs support to engage his or her mate. Realizing how difficult it is to engage the distant parent, the daughter eventually becomes angry with him or her (oftentimes the father) and feels sorry for the abandoned parent (oftentimes the mother). She may even settle into a role that replaces the distant parent in the marriage, thereby fixing her triangulation.

The pain, rejection, and abandonment that the potential female pursuer experiences in this dynamic may result in a deep-seated insecurity regarding her attractiveness or value to future partners, thus producing a powerful intrapsychic conflict: As an adult, she desperately needs a mate to validate her, but she can't get too close to one for fear of being hurt again. Her unconscious compromise to resolve this conflict is to select someone who distances (*i.e.*, someone like her distant parent). This provides her with a buffer against her anxiety with intimacy (*i.e.*, she protects her "real-self" from being rejected), enables her to remain loyal to the abandoned parent (by insisting that she is the only victim in the dynamic), and allows her to vent her anger toward the distancing parent (which is achieved by consistently pointing out the incompetence of her partner). All of this is accomplished in a way that allows her to avoid any responsibility for her contribution to her current relationship strife. While the secondary gains are relatively enormous for the female pursuer, her solution to the problem or psychic compromise is not satisfactory to her because she remains caught between two worlds, never being able to get exactly what it is she so dearly missed — a close, trusting relationship as a child with her distancing parent; thus, her misery continues.

Watching the female pursuer systematically eliminate partners who want to be close to her is an interesting phenomenon that baffles the woman's friends, relatives, and, of course, the men in question, who claim to have good intentions toward her. When asked about this dynamic, she may claim to have felt bored, trapped, or even suffocated by the men in question. She may even convey this with disgust as if a relatively nice man is an aversion to her. Many female pursuers report that they think of these men as "weaklings." They are weak because she perceives them as needing her. Even if they only *want* her, she cannot tell the difference between the two concepts because they look and feel the same to her. If the female pursuer is particularly attractive, sexy, or dynamic, she may have left a trail of bewildered men behind her in her travels. It is the man who demonstrates only a fleeting interest or a certain passivity that will pique her curiosity. It is the "passive organism" that attracts her — others stand very little chance with her beyond a fling.

Case 1. Jennifer: Female Pursuer

Jennifer was a married woman in her middle forties when she presented for marital therapy with her husband, Seth. The couple had been married for thirteen years and had agreed not to have children. It was Jennifer's idea to seek treatment. She claimed that Seth was extremely passive and took little initiative in any phase of his life. She was particularly annoyed that she had to constantly press him to converse with her, set up social events, and initiate sex with her. But, as it turned out, this was not Jennifer's first experience with a distancer.

Jennifer was the second oldest of four siblings (one older sister and two younger brothers). She described her mother as demanding, yet somewhat incompetent and dependent. She described her father as an irresponsible, philandering man who was rarely home — business travels and numerous sexual affairs were priorities for him. Although Jennifer's mother pleaded with her husband to change his lifestyle, according to Jennifer, she was far too weak to set appropriate limits. Given her distancing father and her needy mother, Jennifer could barely help from becoming triangulated into a mediating role in her parent's p–d relationship. Coming to the aid of her mother and younger siblings, she would beg and cajole her father to commit more to his family, but to no avail. To make matters worse, each time her father left, her mother's demanding neediness served to parentify Jennifer, who accommodated because she felt sorry for her mother and siblings.

Suffice it to say, Jennifer felt a great deal of anger and disappointment with regard to her father. He had abandoned her, and by choosing his lovers over her and her mother he damaged her sense of self-worth. As an adult, Jennifer distrusted men yet needed them to validate her. Marrying a distancer such as Seth was an unconscious compromise to resolve her conflict. She was able to remain the victim, continue her quest to change her father, seek validation, reparentify herself, and maintain a certain distance without taking conscious responsibility for her behavior.

Male Distancers

As a young boy, the distancer may have also become triangulated by a demanding, needy parent and a distant parent; however, rather than feeling sorry for the needy parent for not getting enough attention from his or her partner, the son generally becomes annoyed with the constant attention the needy parent showers on him as a replacement. Although the needy parent is the child's primary nurturer, this parent has trouble setting boundaries, thus the son comes to view the parent as controlling and intrusive — a major force in his life to be reckoned with. As an adult, he may develop a deep-seated view of himself as inadequate in terms of being able to satisfy a mate.

Despite the distant parent's behavior, the future male distancer sees him or her in a positive light, as the "good" one. (If this parent is the father, the budding male distancer may grow up feeling more comfortable in the company of men.) His belief is skewed in that he views the distancing behavior solely as a "reaction" to intrusiveness (this he can empathize with) rather than as a flaw that has left a void in his life. The following conflict may result: As an adult he may need a partner to serve as his nurturer, but he will have to keep this person at a safe distance in order to avoid being dominated the way his so-intrusive parent attempted to do to both him and his distancing parent. This sets him up to choose someone with the tendency to pursue. A passive partner will not fulfill this type of man. He tends to be more attracted to an assertive, even aggressive individual who would demonstrate a certain tenacity and initiative.

Case 2. Andy: Male Distancer

Andy presented for marital therapy with his wife, Cindy. They were in their early forties and had been married for fifteen years; they had two children. Andy and Cindy were in treatment because Cindy was threatening to divorce Andy unless he would be willing to engage more in their marriage. Andy was the oldest of four siblings (two younger brothers and one younger sister). He described his mother as caring but intrusive and overbearing. He said that she was never satisfied with anything her husband had accomplished and, in fact, placed consistent pressure on him to meet her needs. Andy reported that his father was away from home quite often, in part to escape his wife. With his father away, his mother put more pressure on Andy to meet her "bottomless" need for attention and nurturing. Andy stated that, although his mother met most of his basic needs, he grew to dislike her. Interestingly, he felt sorry for his father, despite the fact that he had relatively little contact with him. When his father died, Andy blamed his mother. He said she "nagged him to death."

Following the death of his father, Andy said that his mother was particularly unbearable to live with. Her intrusiveness was such that he did not feel as if he had his own life. Andy was finally able to escape home by going to college. He never returned to live at home again, but he did call his mother frequently, despite being scolded for his distancing every time he contacted her. In adult relationships, Andy tried hard to avoid commitment; however, he needed to be in a relationship. After years of playing a seduction–abandonment game with women, he married Cindy, an assertive caretaker who he has spent his married life trying to dodge.

Male Pursuers

As a child, the male pursuer may have been triangulated between a powerful parent whom he found distasteful and a passive parent with whom he may have identified or whom he perceived as a victim (perhaps perceiving the more assertive parent as overly dominating or a bully). Herein lies his conflict: As an adult he may model the victim. To think of himself as dominating may be aversive to him and could threaten to break the psychological bond with his victimized parent. Nevertheless, he does long to have the approval of the powerful parent. Becoming involved with a female distancer allows him to strive for this approval but leaves him at the mercy of this distancing partner. The distancing partner's power, of course, is in the distancing. Despite how anxiety-provoking this makes the male pursuer feel, the fantasy that he will achieve his conscious or unconscious goal is worth it to him.

Case 3. Neil: Male Pursuer

Neil and Carol were in their early forties and married for fourteen years. Neil initiated marital therapy because he felt that Carol paid little attention to him. He said she clearly seemed more interested in her career, and at times he felt as if he were living alone. Neil claimed that he had loved Carol from the first time he laid eyes on her, but even early in their dating process he had to pursue her. He continued to beg Carol throughout the marriage to spend more time with him and to engage him in activities and conversation; however, he admitted to having trouble setting limits with her distancing behavior because he feared she would leave him — which she threatened to do on more than one occasion.

Neil was the middle of three siblings (one older and one younger sister). He reported that his father was an abusive man who often bullied his wife both physically and emotionally. In contrast, his mother was a very sweet woman who could barely defend herself. Neil loved his mother dearly but pitied her. Because of his gender (only male sibling), his father's disposition, and his mother's weakness, Neil was triangulated into a coalition with his mother that at times put him in a position to challenge his father's behavior. Neil loved his father and tried to avoid these confrontations because he desperately wanted a good relationship with this man and, above all, peace in the house. In support of this, Neil often fantasized about a friend's father whom he viewed as a wonderful man. He admitted he was somewhat envious of his friend for having such a close, congenial father–son relationship.

Neil was a very nice man who would do anything within his conscious power to gain his distancing wife's love. By all accounts, his wife was a very bright, beautiful woman and a financially successful individual; however, for a man like Neil to have chosen her is intriguing — one would think that he would have found someone more responsive to his needs. The problem, however, is Neil's internalized conflict. Neil admitted to being a "pleaser of women." This, of course, came from sticking up for his mother (and his sisters) throughout his youth. He gave everything he was capable of giving to the women in his life, and his wife, Carol, was the current recipient of this devotion. However, this unconditional caring brings with it a certain impotence on Neil's part — an inability to set limits on his wife's behavior, just as he had difficulty doing with his father.

Neil feared the loss of Carol the same way he feared the loss of his father; therefore, he was powerless to get what he needed from her. He continued to pity himself (relate to his mother), but he only challenged Carol in an emergency (the way he challenged his father when the man became physically abusive). Neil was riddled with anxiety. He pursued hard to gain Carol's love and approval and lived in constant fear that he would fail. To challenge Carol more directly was far too frightening a prospect. Not only might he enable her to leave him (which would tap into the loss of his father), but it would also signify a new strength and power that would make him believe that he himself had become a bully; this would ultimately relate him to his father and threaten the empathic, psychological bond with his mother.

Female Distancers

As a child, the budding female distancer may have been triangulated by a distant, passive, or rejecting parent and a pursuing, controlling parent. In her adult years, she may have decided that being in control of her significant relationships helps to protect her from rejection or domination, but it also prevents her from achieving the closeness and intimacy she was deprived of in her family of origin. Therefore, her conflict dictates that, while she may have the need to connect with a significant other, she can only tolerate this connection at a distance. The female distancer's unconscious compromise to resolve this internalized conflict is to choose a partner with a similar conflict regarding closeness but who gives the illusion, via pursuit, that he or she is able to be close. This way, the distancer feels wanted, yet never has to put her vulnerability to the test by actually getting close.

Case 4. Lara: Female Distancer

Lara and Chip were in their early thirties. They had been married for ten years and had one child. It was Chip's idea to seek marital therapy; Lara had made it very clear that seeking professional help for their marital problems was "ridiculous." She stated that she could handle her own problems, but that her "wimpy husband" couldn't. Despite her toughness, Lara was a likable woman who was extremely successful in her career. It was rather obvious from her demeanor and the way she carried herself that she belonged in the high-level executive position she occupied. She was, in fact, the major breadwinner in the marriage. Nevertheless, while her positive attributes were undeniable, Chip claimed that she was "cold" when it came to him. He reported that she demonstrated little affection and that he had to pursue her for attention, sexual and otherwise. He also stated that Lara cared far more about her career than about him and that she could spend endless hours at her job. Lara countered that Chip was too needy and that he should focus on becoming more emotionally and financially independent.

Lara was the eldest of two sisters. She described her father as an aggressive, controlling individual with a bad temper. She also said that he was extremely demanding and that he despised weakness. He tended to be very critical of family members if they complained about anything, particularly physical illness; he referred to them as wimps or whiners (as Lara does to Chip) if they did complain. Lara described her mother as emotionally and physically weak.

Lara was much like her father and sided with him on various familial issues against her mother and sister. She was aware of his negative traits but admitted that it was better to be tough and "on top" than weak like her mother; however, Lara missed the empathy and nurturing that her mother could provide. This conflict became manifest in her marriage. While she needed Chip for his nurturing ability, expressing this need or allowing herself to get too close would render her vulnerable or weak (like her mother). Her unconscious compromise was to marry Chip for his nurturing, yet keep him at such a distance that the relationship would not cause her anxiety or threaten her power.

CHAPTER 4
Treatment Model

The objective of the model presented in this book is to uncover and resolve the unconscious conflicts that are believed to be rooted in each partner's family of origin in an effort to alleviate their pursuer–distancer dynamic and any symptoms that may accompany it. As noted previously, the model integrates psychoanalytic conflict theory (Freud, 1910/1957) and psychodynamic systems work (Boszormenyi-Nagy, 1965; Bowen, 1978) into one treatment approach. Like psychoanalysis, it attempts to undo the repression of the present and the past and to bring the conflicts, present and past, to consciousness. This approach offers couples the possibility of achieving a high enough level of differentiation and, in turn, the ability to work out a viable solution. Although each partner is required to work toward discovering his or her respective conflicts, both must also come to realize on both intellectual and emotional levels how these underlying conflicts contribute to the interactional dynamic (p–d relationship). Each partner must also become cognizant of how they collude in symptom maintenance. The model, in essence, is constructed to contend with the fiercest struggle a couple can wage in order to avoid dealing with the anxiety that comes from the agony of choice regarding their individual and collective conflicts.

While the model is obviously psychodynamic in nature, behavioral exercises are sometimes utilized to alleviate various symptoms (or content) within the p–d interaction. This is most true of the couple presenting with a sexual symptom. As will be discussed later, to ignore an overt symptom of the magnitude of a sexual problem at the expense of the psychodynamic process might only prove fatal to the overall therapeutic endeavor.

Moreover, the late, great sex therapist Helen Singer Kaplan (1974) was less than optimistic about the success of treating a sexual symptom primarily via psychoanalytic and psychodynamic therapies. She instead advocated for the use of psychodynamic interventions if and when behavioral interventions were first met with overwhelming resistance. The model herein, however, is more integrative in nature. While I often incorporate Kaplan's recommended exercises (and in some cases others as well) into the treatment process when sexual symptoms are presented within the p–d dynamic (see chapters 5 to 8), they are not always considered a first line of treatment; rather, I recommend that the application and timing of these exercises be left up to the therapist pending a determination as to when they can be applied successfully. Sometimes they are utilized simultaneously along with the psychodynamic work. As will be demonstrated in chapter 6, in some cases the psychodynamic work is at the forefront of the treatment even when a sexual disorder is presented within the p–d dynamic.

Assessment

While the traits and tendencies listed in Table 1.1 (see chapter 1) can be used to assess the pursuer and distancer from an individual perspective, it is relatively easy for the therapist to spot the pursuer–distancer dynamic because the couple usually presents in interactional mode, or in the process of pursuing and distancing. The couple may present the interaction either as the symptom (*e.g.*, "He never talks to me") or within the context in which it is being played out (*e.g.*, "She won't have sex with me"). Nevertheless, it almost always entails one partner complaining that "more is less" and the other complaining that "less is more."

As discussed in chapter 1, the pursuer, in general, may appear angry and assertive and the distancer indifferent and passive. (This is not to suggest that distancers do not get angry, only that they usually do not express their feelings directly.) The pursuer will most often be the one to first contact the therapist. On occasion, however, the distancer will make the initial contact under pressure from the pursuer. During the first meeting, it will appear that the pursuer is more invested in the therapeutic process.

One difference between male and female pursuers is that the female may express more hostility whereas the male pursuer may be more affable and avoid attacking his distancing counterpart. While the female pursuer usually drags the male distancer in for treatment, under the threat of divorce, the male pursuer may use gentle persuasion on the female distancer. Beginning treatment may, in fact, take months or even years to accomplish. Given this ordeal, the therapist shouldn't be surprised to sense relief on the part of the male pursuer if the therapist finally manages to connect with the female distancer.

Mode and Frequency of Treatment

Berman (1982) believed that the best way to begin conjoint treatment is to see the couple. Seeing both partners together serves to balance the treatment, helps to ensure that the therapist is viewed as neutral, and increases the chance that the couple will envision their problem as systemic in nature. It is also recommended that, if one partner shows up before the other, the therapist may want to wait to initiate the session until both parties can enter the office together. While this might agitate the pursuer, who cannot seem to wait to join with the therapist against the distancer (as if assuming the role of co-therapist), it might be a good idea to follow this rule for the sake of neutrality. If necessary, the therapist might be able to get away with seeing the pursuer ahead of the distancer, unless, of course, doing so would tap into any paranoid tendencies the distancer may have (e.g., "They're both plotting to change me"). But, seeing the distancer without first allowing the pursuer to have his or her say, particularly the female pursuer (because of the amount of hostility she may be carrying), could result in premature termination of the treatment. A male therapist might especially be in jeopardy if he is perceived by the female pursuer as siding with her male counterpart.

In some instances, one partner may insist on coming to the first meeting alone (this would generally be a pursuer). If the therapist senses that he or she has no choice in the matter, then an individual session with the other partner should follow. Whenever individual sessions are requested (even at intake), I insist that the non-initiating partner be told.

Following the first conjoint session, it is proposed that each partner be seen individually at least once. According to Berman (1982), individual sessions may be useful in conjoint treatment to resolve certain therapeutic blocks. These may occur when the therapist feels that vital information is being withheld (e.g., an affair), when a sexual disorder exists that proves too embarrassing to discuss in the conjoint setting, when countertransference issues must be processed, or when internalized conflicts result in an especially rigid relational system. In order to maintain the structural integrity of the relationship system, however, Berman believed that it is best not to utilize more than two consecutive individual sessions at one time. If more than this are needed, the therapist might want to consider referring each partner to respective individual therapists. Couples treatment may or may not continue in this case, depending on the needs of the couple.

When conducting individual sessions in a primarily conjoint treatment process, the therapist must take extra care to hold what each partner reveals in the strictest of confidence. While some therapists have a "no secrets" policy, I find that this actually enables secrets and, in turn, hinders treatment. In fact, at the onset of therapy I will tell the couple that whatever is said to me in an individual session is not open to the couple unless the partner who reveals the information wants to discuss the issue openly. It will then be left to this individual to bring the subject up in the conjoint sessions. This also holds true if an affair is revealed to me; however, I tend to refuse to treat a couple when one partner is having an affair and the other isn't consciously aware of it. To do so, I believe, only further contributes to the lack of intimacy in the relationship; therefore, the partner who reveals this information to me has the option of confessing the affair to his or her partner or seeking individual therapy. Regardless, conjoint therapy is terminated unless the affair stops or the victimized partner is told about it.

In individual sessions it is also important for the therapist to avoid becoming trapped in a situation in which the partners use these sessions as weapons against one another; rather, the therapist should encourage each partner to focus on him- or herself. Given the pursuer's anxiety to change the frustrating distancer as soon as possible, the pursuer is not beyond trying to enlist all the help possible to change the distancer. This would include triangulating not only the therapist, but also friends or family as well. Utilizing willing in-laws (particularly a mother-in-law) is most common. The distancer is usually not as anxious to condemn the pursuer and triangulate others. He or she may, however, participate very little in individual sessions, leaving the therapist frustrated. Coping with this situation is discussed at length in a later section, but it is important to note here that the therapist should gently place the onus of therapeutic change on the distancer and learn to tolerate silence rather than overwork as the pursuer does.

Individual sessions may be added at the discretion of the therapist as long as each partner receives approximately the same number of sessions. (As mentioned, I have also found that it is a good idea to ensure, if possible, that both parties are aware that they will participate in individual sessions.) However, the therapist should be aware that individual sessions offered or granted in the middle of conjoint treatment may have consequences. The following is a somewhat rare example of a case in which a distancer became unnerved because his wife insisted on an individual session in the middle of treatment, even though he initially sanctioned it. The case also happens to depict how easy it is for triangulation to occur when individual sessions are used in a predominantly conjoint mode of treatment.

Elizabeth and Marty were a couple in their late thirties. Elizabeth had insisted that Marty attend counseling with her or she would leave him. It would be the couple's third try at marital therapy. On two previous occasions, Marty had complained so much about having to go for treatment that Elizabeth gave up, having decided that it wasn't worth the struggle; however, when Elizabeth began to seriously consider divorce, Marty decided to give therapy another try. It was clear from the onset of treatment that the couple was engaged in a p–d cycle. Marty worked very long hours and Elizabeth constantly pleaded with him to reduce his work load and help her with household chores and their four young children, one of whom was developmentally challenged. Elizabeth said that she felt like a "single mother." Sporadically, Marty would lend Elizabeth a hand. This encouraging behavior would lead Elizabeth to think that this particular problem had been resolved, but as soon as she appeared relatively satisfied (*i.e.*, stopped her pursuing), Marty reverted back to his distancing behavior. By her own admittance, Elizabeth could become extremely angry and critical of Marty, thus giving him more reason to stay out of the house.

The couple was seen together on a weekly basis with the exception of one individual session each (second and third sessions). After approximately two months of treatment, Elizabeth called to request an individual session. She said that she was at her wit's end with Marty and would like to explore a way that she could better handle herself. Elizabeth's sincere desperation convinced me that it would be a good idea to see her alone to support her and to help refocus on her own issues; therefore, I granted the session under one condition: Elizabeth must tell Marty about the session beforehand. In order to ensure that this would take place, I suggested she bring it up in the following conjoint session. Elizabeth agreed and Marty seemed fine with the idea. Of course, I told him that he would have to follow with his own session; he was less enthusiastic about this but agreed to honor my condition.

Although Elizabeth did not discuss the issue of divorce in her individual session, Marty could not be convinced otherwise. He implied that I was helping his wife carry out her evil plot, but his view was that it was predominantly her doing and that I was "under her spell" or being manipulated by her in her effort to end the relationship. Elizabeth called Marty "paranoid" but did admit to him that she was skeptical about the future of the relationship; nevertheless, Elizabeth was able to convince Marty that she was not going to seek a divorce, which calmed him down.

Within the next two sessions, Elizabeth eventually became conscious of the fact that she triangulated me and the individual session to put pressure on Marty to change. This maneuver is commonly experienced by professionals who split couples up for individual sessions. This is why it is vital for a couples therapist to be very careful about protecting the confidentiality of each partner and to focus the treatment on the person being seen rather than get caught saying something that could be used against that person's partner. In this case, Marty's panic was used to point out to each participant, particularly the pursuing Elizabeth, that in fact he really did value the relationship. His panic was also reframed as a pursuing technique, which was surprising. Marty was still required to follow up with an individual session in which we explored, via his family of origin, his reaction to Elizabeth's session.

Given the psychodynamic nature of the model, sessions are held weekly. In the case of a financial impediment largely unrelated to the couple's defensive structure, an alternative is for the therapist to hold biweekly treatment sessions or consider offering a fee reduction. I do not think it is in the best interests of the couple to be seen less often than biweekly. While couples vary in their ability to help themselves, on the average the p–d couple may require months, even years, to complete the treatment offered in this approach. It is recommended that they be told this soon after the assessment is made.

Joining

Minuchin and Fishman (1981) highlighted the value of "joining" or forming a partnership with the client–system in order to achieve the common goals of eliminating symptoms, reducing stress and conflict, and improving coping skills. In this vein, when a prospective client first contacts the therapist by telephone, it is recommended that the therapist donate a few minutes of time to the client. It is my opinion that this act could help the therapist to join with the client. The therapist can simply ask the client to give a "thumbnail sketch" of the problem (along with the usual business and identifying data). In our fast-paced society, where time is an important commodity, this offering gives clients the feeling that the therapist really cares about their problems. Nevertheless, the therapist must set an appropriate time limit on the conversation in order to avoid unbalancing the couple's future work. It is also vital that interventions not be offered — this clearly would be premature on the therapist's part. The main objective at this point in time is for the therapist to join with the client and convene the couple for treatment. I have had numerous clients tell me that other therapists they have called did not extend the courtesy of spending a minute with them on the telephone. One woman told me that she was made to feel like someone in a "delicatessen line."

While it would be wise for the therapist to apply this joining approach to all initial client contacts, it works exceptionally well for individuals with pursuing traits. Pursuers are anxious and do well with therapists whom they see as being energetic and engaging. This may feed into their fantasy of finding someone with whom they can join to "cure" the distancer, but when initiating treatment is on the line, to some extent the end justifies the means. Pursuers also look for someone to listen to them. They may have an intimacy problem, but at this point the therapist should take the pursuer at face value and offer a little time and empathy rather than rush the client into an appointment time and then off the telephone. This is especially important when a male therapist is contacted by a female pursuer.

Joining with the Female Pursuer

During the actual treatment process, the therapist must continue to support the pursuer regardless of gender; however, the female pursuer may demonstrate a significant amount of anger and frustration. She may appear critical and begin to immediately pressure the therapist to change the distancer. One way to connect with her is to realize that without her there will be no treatment. She is the "lifeline" to the therapy. Investing in the male distancer against the female pursuer may only result in premature termination. The therapist must keep in mind that the distancer will not stand up for the therapist if he or she challenges the female pursuer. The distancer's passivity will not allow him to challenge his mate. Without a doubt, therapists who side with distancers will have to fend for themselves — a daunting task when facing determined pursuers. Therapists who have difficulty with a female pursuer may want to offer her one or two individual sessions. During these sessions, the therapist can empathize with the pursuer's frustration, as well as provide support and positive reinforcement. It might also be wise to discuss the pursuer's commitment to treatment and the therapist's commitment to her.

The therapist must walk the fine line of empathizing with the female pursuer while gently giving her responsibility for her contribution to the relational difficulties. One technique I use is to tell her that our goals are similar but not necessarily the way in which we may go about reaching them. I also tell her that, to this point, her technique of relentless pursuit has not worked so an alternative should be welcome if she truly wants change; this usually seems to resonate with the pursuer. The therapist must always keep in mind that the female pursuer holds the power to terminate the treatment process. If she does not like the therapist, therapy is over. The male distancer has already lost the overt struggle to avoid treatment. From this point forward he will have to passive–aggressively challenge the therapist and the pursuer, but only rarely will he end the treatment. If the therapist is able to join with the female pursuer, the treatment process can last as long as needed.

Joining with the Male Distancer

Joining with the male distancer is not as vital or threatening as with the female pursuer, but it is no easy task. First of all, if the distancer could connect he probably would not be in treatment in the first place; therefore, the therapist must accept this distance and allow any connection to evolve slowly. As long as the therapist gently pursues the distancer and knows when to back off, he or she will give the distancer the appropriate amount of connection and distance that he needs to eventually trust the therapist. The therapist can join with the distancer by acknowledging that the distancer is under intense pressure from the pursuer and is trying to work on the relationship in his own way. Also, the therapist who demonstrates early in the treatment process that he or she is able to successfully challenge the female pursuer will gain the distancer's confidence that the therapist will eventually be able to balance the treatment process.

Humor is also an easy way to connect with the male distancer. He usually does not present quite as seriously as his female counterpart so he will be more amenable to a reference to the absurdity of life (*e.g.*, how ironic or tough life can be). He can relate to this type of reference given his perception of himself as a passive organism and victim of society and because of his somewhat paranoid distrust of life in general. If the therapist judges that the distancer is evolving far too slowly and that the therapeutic process or marriage is in jeopardy, one or two individual sessions can be offered to the male distancer. In these sessions, the distancer can be encouraged to work harder under the guise that the therapist is seriously concerned about the prognosis of the relationship.

Joining with the Male Pursuer

The male pursuer does not necessarily hold the power to end treatment or the relationship in the same way the female pursuer does. The anxiety that will be demonstrated on his part may be more pure, with much less anger and frustration accompanying it. While he, too, needs to be told that the therapist shares his treatment goals, the best way to calm him is to demonstrate that the female distancer can be controlled without dire consequences. One male pursuer was so anxious about his first conjoint session that he had his individual therapist call to warn me about the man's wife and to stress the importance of my connecting to her. If it is perceived that the male pursuer is overly anxious, one or two individual sessions can be offered. In these sessions, the pursuer can be allowed to vent his feelings without the fear of consequences from his female counterpart. He can also be offered encouragement and positive reinforcement, but the therapist must be careful not to pity the male pursuer. While he may need help building his own personal power, this power should not be lent to him by the therapist.

Joining with the Female Distancer

Because the male pursuer is concerned with angering or displeasing the female distancer, she (like the female pursuer) holds the power in her hands to end treatment. If she wishes to terminate therapy, the male pursuer (like the male distancer) will tend to oblige her. He will not stand up to her or rescue the therapist; therefore, it is particularly important to join with the female distancer in order to preserve the therapeutic process. If the distancer threatens to end therapy, the therapist should gently confront her about her distancing herself from treatment and offer her encouragement to continue. (One or two individual sessions may be required to join with the distancer and discuss her commitment to treatment.) However, the therapist must not get into a control struggle with the distancer or pursue her beyond this point. If the therapist pursues as the distancer's pursuing counterpart does, the female distancer will most likely distance herself from the therapist, as well, and the chances of losing the couple are greater. This may also kill any chance of the couple returning to the therapist at a later date. This is not to say that the therapist should exhibit a fear of the distancer. In fact, as mentioned, the female distancer disrespects weakness, and if she perceives the therapist as anxious then treatment could be jeopardized. The therapist must strike a delicate balance between showing strength and being careful not to challenge the distancer's power position prematurely.

The female distancer has power, but she does not need as much of it as she may think. If she discovers that she can afford to lose some of it without being traumatized, a more balanced relationship may emerge. The therapist should positively reinforce the distancer's power but let her know that the amount she carries may be an indication of an underlying anxiety (similar to that of the pursuer) that has yet to be discovered.

Encouraging Individual Responsibility

As mentioned, the mode of treatment utilized in this model is predominately conjoint; however, in this approach it is hypothesized that each individual brings his or her personal intrapsychic conflicts to the relationship dynamic, so it is vital that the therapist examine each partner from this perspective throughout the treatment process. It is as if individual treatment is given equal weight within a conjoint systems model. To this end, both the pursuer and the distancer are given individual responsibility for what each brings to the p–d interaction. The pursuer must be encouraged to take responsibility for pursuing, the distancer for distancing.

The therapist can take significant steps toward accomplishing this objective in the initial session by interrupting the p–d dance and asking each partner questions about his or her family of origin. There is no need to separate the partners at this point. The therapist may simply interview each mate one at a time while both are present. By forcing each partner to concentrate on the self rather than focusing on his or her mate, the therapist is sending the following strong message: Each of you is responsible for the relationship symptoms, and each of you will be held accountable accordingly. In some cases, the person whose turn it is to speak will get stuck or block something important; therefore, it should be conveyed to the couple that the other partner is allowed to intervene briefly as long as doing so does not disrupt the interviewing process.

Some therapists have questioned me as to whether it is good couples therapy to interview one partner at a time. They have expressed particular concern that leaving one person out of the ongoing dialogue for several minutes may serve to unbalance the treatment process and possibly lead to premature termination of the treatment. In my experience, therapists can take as long as they want to interview each partner. This style of interviewing offers one of the few opportunities for the partners to sit still for any extended period of time in order to actually listen to one another. Moreover, because of the sensitive nature of the information put forth, partners may develop empathy for one another after hearing a particularly moving event or history (*e.g.*, a female pursuer may painfully discuss the premature death of her father).

The extensive questioning of each partner may turn out to be a pleasant surprise for the distancer, who is all too familiar with being blamed for the ills of the relationship. The pursuer, on the other hand, may react quite differently. Because the pursuer is anxious to focus on the distancer, he or she may become angry or grow inpatient with this style. Nevertheless, the therapist should stick to the model. The pursuer can be calmed and told that an extensive evaluation is common in all cases. I have found that most pursuers can tolerate this process.

Constructing the Genogram

When interviewing the couple, the therapist can utilize a genogram (Bowen, 1980; DeMaria, Weeks, & Hof, 1999; Guerin & Pendagast, 1976; McGoldrick & Gerson, 1985) as an intake tool in order to uncover various conflicts, interactions, patterns, triangles, and unbalanced ledgers (Boszormenyi-Nagy & Spark, 1973) in the family of origin. The therapist may simply draw a genogram in his or her notes and fill it in as the session proceeds. While this evaluation can be completed in the initial session, a second conjoint session may be necessary depending on the amount of data the couple has to share, as well as the complexity and cooperation of the couple. With such data, the therapist can help the partners connect their personal histories to the interactional dynamic (in this case, the p–d dynamic).

I pose a specific list of questions to the couple during the intake process. It is the answers to these questions that I record on the genogram in order to develop an accurate and expedient framework for the treatment process. Some of the questions are asked of the couple and others are asked specifically of each partner. While I ask the questions in the exact order presented, this is left to the discretion of the therapist.

I try to put as much information as possible on the genogram, but it may not be large enough to record all the answers to the following questions; therefore, I may attach separate note pages to the genogram. If a couple presents with a sexual problem, I will add several specific questions of a sexual nature to the evaluation, as is discussed at length in the following chapter.

Presenting Problem(s)
   What brings the two of you to treatment? [Obtain each partner's opinion.]
   Was there a time when you didn't have this problem?
   Did either of you ever have this type of problem in a previous relationship?

Relationship Data
   How long have you been together as a couple?
   Are the two of you married? If not, do you live together?
   How long did you date before marriage?

Did either of you experience any problems when dating or living together?

How did each of you feel on the day of your marriage?

How did each of your parents feel about your marriage or relationship?

If either of you was married before, can you describe your previous partner and tell me what ultimately happened to the relationship?

Can either of you describe any other previous long-term relationships you have had?

How did each of your prior relationships end?

Children

Do you have any children?

What are the ages and sex of your children?

How do your children seem to be doing?

Do any of your children have special needs?

Do any of your children seem particularly close to either of you?

Psychological and Medical Issues

Have you ever experienced any anxiety or depression?

Have either of you been hospitalized or institutionalized for any problem?

Have you ever been in any type of counseling before? If so, for what reason?

Why was your previous treatment stopped?

Do either of you have any physical health problems?

Are either of you taking any type of medication? If so, for what reason and who prescribed it?

Do any members of your families of origin have mental or physical health problems? If so, do they take any medication for these problems?

Siblings

Do you have any siblings?

Starting with the oldest sibling, can you describe each of their personalities?

Where do each of your siblings live?

Are your siblings married?

Are these your siblings' first marriages? If not, what happened to their first marriages?

What does each of your siblings do for a living?

What does each of your sibling's spouses or paramours do for a living?

If your siblings are in current relationships, what is your opinion as to how the relationships are doing?

What do you think of your siblings' mates?

Do you maintain contact with your siblings? If not, why?

How do you think your siblings are viewed by your parents?

What role did each sibling play in the family of origin?

Did you feel that any of your siblings were favored by a particular parent?

In your opinion, do any of your siblings have any problems?

Client's Individual Personal Data

How old are you?

Where did you grow up?

Where did you go to high school?

Did you participate in any activities?

How were your grades?

Did you have any friends?

What did you do after completing high school?

If you went to college, where did you go and how did you do academically and socially?

What do you do for a living?

Parents

Can you describe the personalities of each of your parents?

How did you view their marriage when growing up?

Did you witness any open affection between your parents?

Did your parents spend time together?

Did either of your parents spend alone time with you?

Did either of your parents attend any of your activities?

Did your parents fight (verbally or physically)? If so, what did they tend to fight about?

Did your parents ever separate or divorce?

If your parents separated or divorced, how old were you when they did so? How did you feel about the experience?

If there was a separation, how long did it last?

If there was a reconciliation, which parent do you think requested it?

If there was a divorce, what were the new living arrangements?

Did you hold a particular parent responsible for the separation or divorce?

If you were angry, who did you express this to when growing up?

Were you closer to one particular parent?

Did you feel sorry for either parent when growing up?
Did you ever serve as a mediator in your parents' marriage?
What did/does your father do for a living?
What did/does your mother do for a living?

Addictive Behaviors (Alcohol, Drugs, Gambling)
Do either of you drink alcohol? If so, what type and how much per week?
Do either of you take recreational drugs? If so, what kind and how often?
Do either of you gamble? If so, how often?
Do any members of your families of origin drink, take recreational drugs, or gamble? If so, can you provide details about this behavior?

Sexual Data
How would you rate your current sex life on a scale of 1 to 5 (1 = very poor; 5 = excellent)?
Do either of you have specific issues with the frequency or quality of your sex life together?
Do either of you have any sexual functioning problems (*e.g.*, erectile disorder)?
Did either of you ever have any abusive or provocative sexual experiences?
Has either of you participated in any extramarital affairs or cheating behavior? [This may be asked again in individual sessions.]
If either of you cheated, how long did you do so and with whom did you have the affair? [This may be asked again in individual sessions.]
Has either of your parents ever had any affairs?

Some of the therapists I have supervised or consulted with over the years have delayed carrying out a comprehensive evaluation in exchange for allowing the couple to obsess about their problems. In my opinion, this behavior fails to give the therapist a framework for evaluating the couple accurately and efficiently and may enable the therapist to avoid the evaluative process entirely. The latter is true because it is more difficult to ask many of the preceding questions once the couple becomes fully engaged in the interactional treatment process.

When I am serving as a consultant or supervisor, if I do not have what I consider to be a sufficient amount of information from which to draw a working hypothesis, I strongly recommend that the colleague or supervisee involved work with the couple to complete a genogram as soon as possible.

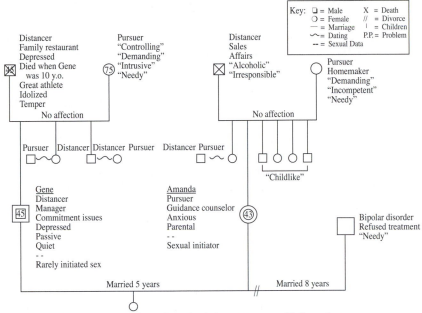

P.P. Amanda was threatening to divorce Gene unless he became more engaged in the marriage.

Fig. 4.1 Gene and Amanda

It is recognized that the evaluation process is ongoing and that the geno-gram can be modified as the treatment progresses, but having an initial framework gives all those involved a distinct advantage in the treatment process.

Gene and Amanda's genogram (see Figure 4.1) indicates that they were a couple in their middle forties. Gene was employed as a manager of a department store and Amanda was a high school guidance counselor. Both held college degrees and had done relatively well academically. Gene went to college on an athletic scholarship. The couple had been married for five years and had one child (a daughter). It was Gene's first marriage and Amanda's second. She was first married to a man who was diagnosed with bipolar disorder. This marriage lasted approximately eight years and pro-duced no children. Amanda claimed she finally left her first husband because of his "exhaustive mood swings." Apparently her ex-husband refused medical treatment and his behavior became intolerable. Amanda reported that she had a history of dating men who she perceived as need-ing help in some way.

Gene had several relationships with women, but as the relationships deepened and moved toward marriage, he was able to escape either by cheating or disappearing. Gene almost escaped Amanda and had put off marriage to her several times. At one point, the couple split up for close to a year, but when Amanda pursued Gene he fell back into the relationship and eventually married her. When asked how he felt on his wedding day, Gene sounded as if he had given in and married Amanda because he was worn down by the dating process and his long struggle with her. Amanda reported that she was happy on her wedding day, but nervous given Gene's issues with commitment.

Amanda dragged Gene into marital therapy under the threat of divorce. She specifically reported that Gene took very little initiative in the marriage and at times acted as if he didn't care about her. She said he never initiated sex with her, often forgot to celebrate her birthday, and rarely held conversations with her. She said she might as well be "living with a dead man." Indeed, Gene appeared very quiet and passive, somewhat distant, and even a little depressed, with a relatively flat affect.

Gene reported that he cared for Amanda and that she was "over-exaggerating" the problem. He said that other than his wife's bickering and nagging, he was satisfied with the relationship. He said life isn't perfect and that his wife needed to accept this fact in order to be happy and to leave him alone. He felt she was too anxious and couldn't set limits on her high-energy activity level. He doubted that anything could satisfy his wife. In the session, Amanda did appear quite anxious and angry with Gene. She was very talkative and almost authoritative and parental at times. She was clearly pressuring Gene to change "or else."

Gene was the oldest of three siblings. His father died at age forty-five when Gene was ten years old. He and his siblings feared yet idolized their quick tempered father, who was a tremendous athlete with a great future in his youth but was a sad character in his adult life. At the time of his death, he was running a family restaurant that he had owned for many years. Prior to her husband's death, Gene's mother also worked in the family restaurant. Gene and Amanda described her as "needy, intrusive, demanding, overbearing, and manipulatively controlling." Gene admitted that he did his best to stay as far away from his mother as his guilt would allow. He felt that his mother was always in pursuit of his father and far too demanding of his time. Gene actually believed that his father died at such a young age because his wife killed his spirit and worked him to death. Gene rarely saw any affection between his parents. It is interesting to note that neither of Gene's siblings (a brother and sister) was married, but both had long-term, live-in lovers who had relentlessly pressured them for marriage, to no avail.

Amanda is the second oldest of six siblings. Her deceased father was an alcoholic who had numerous extramarital affairs and was away from home a lot because of his job as a traveling salesman. Amanda's mother was a homemaker whom she described as "needy, demanding, and somewhat incompetent." She rarely saw any affection between her parents and reported that her mother was constantly trying to keep her husband at home, at times even enlisting her children in this endeavor. Amanda described all but her older sibling (an older sister) as "childlike." Amanda considered herself the mother of the family.

Uncovering Conflicts and Facilitating Differentiation

As mentioned earlier, this model aims to help the partners become aware of the underlying conflicts they may be experiencing. Becoming conscious of these conflicts allows each client to choose one side of their conflict over the other (or reach an emotionally palatable compromise between the two sides) in an effort to alleviate their respective symptoms. Unlike classical psychoanalytic theory, which proposes that the conflicts are between instinctual (sexual) urges and opposing forces, this model contends that they are cast between urges or desires to take certain actions and various opposing forces emanating from each partner's family of origin.

The act of unveiling and working on these conflicts contributes to an increased level of differentiation from the families of origin which in turn allows for a smoother resolution of the conflicts and reduction in individual and interactional symptoms (in this case, pursuing and distancing). Akin to psychoanalytic treatment, in order to uncover these conflicts the couple's therapist must recognize and point out the various contradictions that each partner exhibits. As Waelder (1960) put it, it is the job of the therapist "to open the area of conflict widely and clearly, with a view to discovering possible unconscious elements, ultimately to help the patient to 'make peace with himself'" (p. 220). While finding contradictions that lead to inner conflicts may seem easier said than done, I can assure you that the contradictions are plentiful. When the couples therapist begins to watch for these contradictions, he or she will be astounded by their abundance and absurdity.

Exposing Contradictions and Conflicts on the Interactional Level

As you may recall, Amanda said that she brought Gene into treatment in part because he wouldn't speak to her or initiate conversation. She was considering divorcing him if he did not attend sessions with her in an effort to become more engaged in the marriage. Gene did demonstrate his passivity in the first conjoint session, but with patience I was able to help him open up and he gave me quite an elaborate portrait of his family of origin.

I mentioned to Gene that he did well in communicating with me, but I wondered if he didn't have something of significance to tell his wife. Gathering his courage, Gene began to tell Amanda about something in the marriage that had been bothering him for some time, but before he could get out a full sentence, Amanda cut him off with an angry, verbal barrage. Gene's first reaction was to immediately shut down, but I encouraged him to continue. Amanda, however, would not let him get a word in and Gene became far too reliant on me, so I let him retreat.

Soon after Gene disappeared, Amanda then began accusing him of "clamming up." At first I thought that it was perhaps only negative comments that Amanda could not tolerate, but when I tested this out I soon discovered that Amanda would not allow Gene to finish *any* thought, positive or negative, and Gene didn't seem to have the strength to insist on finishing his thoughts. The following excerpt demonstrates how I helped the couple see their conflicts and contradictions:

Dr. B: Amanda, you claimed to have brought Gene in for treatment because he doesn't communicate with you, but I've been watching you for about 35 minutes and you have shut him down every time he has tried to say something to you, whether it is of a positive or negative nature. What's up?

Amanda: [*somewhat embarrassed*] Have I done that?

Dr. B: What do you think, Gene?

Gene: She does this to me all the time. It's as if I don't have a mind of my own.

Dr. B: Well, Gene, if that's the way you feel, I would think that you would stand up for your point of view.

Gene: She won't let me. I'm a manager at work, and I don't seem to have any trouble expressing my feelings to the men under me. [*Amanda attempts to interrupt but I stop her with a hand signal.*]

Dr. B: Well, then, why do you have such a hard time stopping Amanda from interrupting you?

Gene: It does no good. She wears me down.

Dr. B: You don't look very weak to me, Gene. Something else must be operating. Are you interested in getting closer to Amanda?

Gene: Yes. Well, except when she verbally assaults me. Then I admit that I want to get as far away from her as possible.

Dr. B: So, from your perspective, you only feel the need to distance or retreat when your wife is on the attack?

Gene: Yes.

Amanda: That's not true. You rarely initiate any interaction with me. Most of the time you leave the room before I even get a word out.

Dr. B: What about that, Gene?

Gene: I guess. I don't know. Maybe I'm trained to keep my mouth shut.

Dr. B: You mean you used to be an outgoing guy who took a lot of initiative but Amanda has turned you into a shell of a man?

Gene: Nah, I guess I've always been laid back, but she makes me worse.

Dr. B: I need clarification on something, Amanda. Am I correct in thinking that you don't seem to believe that your pursuing style of behavior chases Gene away under any circumstances?

Amanda: [*after a long pause*] Right. Well, I know I can be tough, but I think Gene brings out the worst in me. I'm not like this with my friends. I don't have to beg my friends to speak to me or to go places with me, but I had to drag Gene here. I had to threaten to divorce him to get him here.

Dr. B: Good point. Gene, why did you give in and show up for treatment?

Gene: [*long pause*] I came here because I don't want a divorce.

Dr. B: So, Gene, can we assume for now that a large part of you wants to be in this marriage and to be connected to Amanda?

Gene: Sure.

Amanda: [*to Gene*] Oh, I know you don't want a divorce. Why should you? You get breakfast and dinner served to you, and you get to have a clean house while you're watching sports on television. And God forbid you should have to split up any of the money you've been hoarding over the years. Your wanting to stay married to me is not evidence that you want me. It's evidence that you don't want to disturb your comfort zone.

Dr. B: Is she right, Gene?

Gene: No. Well, yes. Life is comfortable with the exception of Amanda's behavior, and, besides, Amanda is once again overreacting.

Dr. B: What do you mean?

Gene: I have on occasion brought her flowers and taken her to movies and to dinner, but she critiques everything. I just don't think she can be satisfied.

Dr. B: You have done some of those things?

Gene: Yes.

Amanda: [*to Gene*] When?

Gene: The birthday before last I bought you flowers and took you out to a seafood restaurant, but because you didn't like the flowers you bitched the whole night.

Amanda: [*exasperated*] I was angry because you know what kind of flowers I like, but instead you got me some ratty looking yellow things that looked as if you pulled them from our neighbor's yard.

Gene: Forget it.

Dr. B: Gene, what kind of flowers does Amanda prefer?

Gene: It doesn't matter.

Dr. B: So, let me get this straight, Gene. You want to stay married to Amanda and make her happy, yet you allow her to verbally dominate you so you can then distance from her. You buy her the wrong flowers, and you want to have sex with her but you rarely if ever initiate it. Wow, if there ever was a way to woo a woman …

Gene: [*chuckles*] Now that you put it that way it does sound crazy.

Dr. B: Actually, I don't think you're crazy, but it does sound to me as if you're in conflict.

Gene: You mean like I don't know what I want?

Dr. B: Could you be more specific?

Gene: I'm not sure.

Dr. B: Well, it may be that you want to get close but you don't. It's as if there are two opposing sides within in you playing a tug of war.

Amanda: I rarely get to see the side that wants to connect.

Dr. B: Oh, I disagree. I think you see it but you can't appreciate or reinforce it because of your own conflict about closeness.

Amanda: How?

Dr. B: Gene, can you help her?

Gene: I guess by never giving me credit for anything good I do for you.

Dr. B: Can you think of anything else, Gene?

Gene: Not right now.

Dr. B: Amanda, I think your conflict is exhibited by not allowing Gene a point of view, by failing to reinforce any efforts toward intimacy that he does make (miniscule as they may seem) or by upping the ante so that he eventually gives up. I do think a part of you desires the closeness you say you're craving, but it seems to me that another side of you throws up road blocks. [*addressing both partners*] Marrying satisfies one side of each of you. It is like connecting at a distance. If you wish to get closer, however, each of you will have to determine where these conflicts emanate from and then resolve them in order to achieve an increased level of intimacy. Otherwise, you both will continue to collude in this never-ending dance. In essence, you are both feeding this problem as if watering a plant.

Examining the Origin of the Conflicts on a Psychodynamic Level

Utilizing the genogram constructed at intake, the therapist can also help each partner look for points of conflict that may be contributing to the current conflict in their lives. This exploration should continue throughout the treatment process and be tied to the pursuer–distancer interaction. I will continue to use the case of Gene and Amanda to demonstrate this examination.

Dr. B: Gene, you reported that your mother was controlling. Can you give examples of this?

Gene: She ruined my father's athletic career. He was in training camp, and she made him come home to her. He ended up working in a restaurant the rest of his life. He could have been a pro ball player if it weren't for her.

Dr. B: Did your father complain about this?

Gene: Not really, but everyone in the family could tell he was depressed because of it. He didn't live much longer after that.

Dr. B: Are you implying that your mother killed him?

Gene: Yeah. I think she did. I think she not only made him quit playing sports, but she was so demanding of him when he was around that the combination killed him.

Dr. B: She sounds like a dangerous woman.

Gene: Yeah. She can drive you crazy.

Dr. B: Was she controlling of you directly?

Gene: She constantly watched over me and my siblings. I can remember that she set her bedroom up so that my brother and I couldn't leave our rooms without walking through hers. She knew where we were and where we were going all the time. After my father died it got even worse. She wanted me to take his place and I really didn't want to work in the restaurant the rest of my life.

Amanda: His mother is very difficult. She uses guilt and anger to bully Gene, but I don't think his father was as wonderful as Gene makes him out to be.

Dr. B: What do you mean?

Amanda: Well, his father worked two jobs and never had time for any of the kids.

Dr. B: What was his second job?

Gene: He sold insurance at night after the restaurant closed.

Dr. B: It sounds as if he really wasn't that involved in your life, Gene.

Gene: He was busy.

Dr. B: So, you had a dangerous mother and a distant father.

Gene: [*laughs*] Yeah.

Dr. B: Tell me, Gene, when you had a problem to whom did you go?

Gene: Well, I tried not to go to either one of them, but my mother was a better listener. She did want to be involved in my life — just too much.

Dr. B: So, a dangerous, pursuing woman was at times more helpful than an angry, distant man?

Gene: It sounds pitiful, doesn't it?

Dr. B: Well, it could help to explain the origin of your conflict. Do you know what I mean?

Gene: That in some crazy way I need my mother also ... because she was my caretaker.

Dr. B: Yes. Your father was distant, so it is possible that your only source of comfort was a dangerous woman (your mother). Because of this internalized past, perhaps you developed a need for a caring mother figure (such as your wife) but consider her to be dangerous.

Gene: So, my wife is like my mother — dangerous to me?

Dr. B: Yes, it could be. Does it feel that way to you?

Gene: Yeah, definitely.

Dr. B: Given the danger, the only compromise or solution might be for you to marry such a woman and keep her at a safe distance so she doesn't harm you. If in any way she begins to remind you of a bad or dangerous woman, you would be more likely to run from her. Of course, this is only a preliminary hypothesis, but you can imagine the havoc these feelings could wreak on intimacy.

Amanda: Wow. Gene, you do see me as dangerous, but there's no way I'm as bad as your mother.

Gene: That's what you think.

Dr. B: Gene, I noted in the history that I took in our first session that your brother and sister are still single. They both seem to be dodging marriage and to be involved in p–d relationships. Any comment on this?

Gene: I never thought of that. We all have the same disease.

Dr. B: Amanda, in the first session you described your father as being irresponsible and said that he would leave home for long periods of time. Can you elaborate?

Amanda: Well, he drank a lot and would run off with different women. When these affairs would end, he would come back home. I could never understand why my mother would take him back. I guess she was too infantile to kick him out for good. God, she used to beg him to stay home with us, but it didn't matter ... he still left. Part of it was his sales job, but he wouldn't come home for months. He finally came home to die. It was the longest we had him.

Dr. B: Did you miss not having him around?

Amanda: [*tears up*] Yes, I particularly missed him around the holidays, but Christmas is still painful to me. When he was home for the holidays he was usually drunk. Once he knocked our tree over because he was so drunk. Then he cried the rest of the night.

Dr. B: You said you were the mother of the family or the responsible one ...

Amanda: My mother was too needy. She was a big baby. I raised my younger siblings. My big sister went off to graduate school. She escaped and I can't really blame her.

Dr. B: You said your mother tried to get you to keep your father home. Give me an example of this.

Amanda: She would call me at college and ask me to call my dad and convince him to go home. Once I had to leave college to take his place for awhile. Luckily, I went back and finished. She also wanted me to cater to him so that life would be easier for him when he was at home — so he would be less likely to leave. He left anyway.

Dr. B: How did you feel about having to work to keep your dad at home?

Amanda: Very frustrated. If it worked it would have been worth it, but nothing worked. Nobody could keep Dad home or sober.

Dr. B: I asked you that question because it seems you're in a similar position in your marriage.

Amanda: What do you mean?

Dr. B: Well, you seem to be trying very hard to get Gene to be engaged in your life, but from your perspective you have failed.

Amanda: It is similar, isn't it?

Dr. B: Yes. I wonder if you haven't quite given up on Dad yet. That is, by marrying someone like Gene you are able to continue the struggle to engage a man to be in your life. This enables you to avoid the pain of letting go of Dad or dealing directly with the void he left in you. There is, however, a flip side.

Amanda: I continue to fail and frustrate myself which also leaves me angry with Gene ... and Dad.

Dr. B: Probably.

Examining the Options

In classical psychoanalysis, the neurotic process includes three steps: the conflict over a sexual urge, (unsuccessful) repression, and the return of the repressed conflict. Traditional psychoanalytic treatment, however, only addresses the second of these steps. It does not aim to eradicate the existence of inner conflict. It tries to undo the repressions and make them conscious so the individual in question can face them (Waelder, 1960). As noted earlier, the model presented here takes things a bit further. It makes a concerted effort to help clients expose as well as resolve their respective conflicts in order to increase differentiation and alleviate the p–d interaction. The difficulty with the latter objective, however, is that the real solution of a conflict involves frustration on both sides of the conflict. Simply put, the gain of one side is the loss of the other.

Freud (1910/1957) contended that the solution of a conflict between instinctual drives and opposing forces can be in favor of either or can be a compromise between the two. Again, the solution involves the frustration of one of these forces at the expense of the other. Clients, however, do not seem to accept this notion very well and will spend inordinate amounts of energy trying to find a way to "have it all," even after their conflicts are made clear to them. To the therapist, it may look as if the client insists on living in a fantasy world; however, making this kind of choice can be extremely difficult and most often depends on the degree of anxiety in the client or on his or her ability to bear frustration.

Waelder (1960) wrote:

> A solution in favor of the instinctual drive will usually occur if the adult feels his opposition to the drive is no longer justified or no longer necessary; perhaps, opposition had been due to fear of dangers which frighten us no longer. Such a solution reflects, for better or worse, increased *courage*. In a great many instances, the decision will fall against the gratification of the instinctual drive. The drive, no longer repressed but received into the ego, *i.e.*, recognized as part of oneself, is then, as Freud put it, condemned, *i.e.*, consciously denied gratification. This, of course, causes unpleasure. What usually happens is that over a certain period of time a wish that is persistently denied satisfaction is gradually given up; just as people forced to follow a diet, or to give up smoking, after a time — usually not a very short time — lose their craving. Such people may search for, and find, new gratification. The situation is comparable to all weaning processes and to the process of mourning. (pp. 225–226)

The following excerpt demonstrates how I helped Gene and Amanda understand their options in terms of resolving their conflicts. Notice that I must challenge each partner to see that they are in a no-win situation and that they will ultimately have to make choices that will not completely fulfill them. In fact, they will have to settle for something less than expected, and a grieving or mourning process will have to take place no matter which choice they make. This process often takes a great deal of time and requires both an intellectual understanding of their dilemma as well as an emotional readiness to conquer it.

Gene: Dr. B., I wanted to play golf this past weekend and Amanda was all over me. I rarely hang out with anybody, and all I asked for was one day to enjoy myself.

Dr. B: It sounds as if you want me to get Amanda off your back.

Gene: Yeah. I don't think it's fair that she constantly harasses me.

Amanda: Yeah. He thinks he's Garbo; he wants to be left alone.

Dr. B: Gene, I suspect you can do something about that. You have more power than I do.

Gene: She won't listen to me.

Dr. B: Think about it. What can you do to help reduce her pursuit?

Gene: I'm telling you nothing will work.

Dr. B: I'm not saying that you can cure this marriage of its woes on your own, but you have to take care of your own contributions to the marital problems; Amanda will have to examine herself.

Gene: I guess I don't have to play golf … but I also don't think I should have to give it up.

Dr. B: Maybe not, but perhaps if you engage in other contexts golf will not be such an issue.

Gene: I think she'll always have a problem with me no matter what I want to do because enough is never enough for her. She wants to own me.

Amanda: I don't want to own you!

Dr. B: But, Gene, you have already admitted that you're a distancer to begin with. Amanda could say that, no matter how much space she gives you, you will want more. Now where do we go?

Gene: Yeah. I get it. I guess I can try harder to be there for her.

Amanda: [*sarcastically*] Right.

Dr. B: Well, Gene, that sounds good in theory, but what about that conflict we spoke of? I suspect that it will interfere with your ability to follow through.

Gene: You mean because I see Amanda as behaving like my mother?

Dr. B: Something like that. I know it may sound like psychobabble to you, but we have determined that both are clearly pursuers.

Gene: Yeah. I can see the similarities. So what can I do, then?

Dr. B: Well, what do think the options are? I do know that one of them is to stay the same and let the p–d dynamic ultimately ruin your marriage. Or, you can completely give into your wife and let her totally dominate you. You can also pull the ultimate distancing act and leave the marriage. Anything else?

Gene: I guess I can take a risk and move in a little closer.

Dr. B: Yes. In that case, you will also have to give her time to get used to the increased level of intimacy. Can you think of any more options?

Gene: No, but the first three are unacceptable, and I'm pessimistic about the other one.

Dr. B: Well, it looks as if it's all we've got to work with. Apparently Amanda refuses to allow you to have your cake and eat it, too. Meaning, she will not let you stay peacefully married at a distance that is comfortable to you. In my opinion, you've been trying to pull this off, but I doubt very many partners on this planet would allow you this luxury — sorry.

Gene: Suppose we're incompatible. Maybe there is a woman out there who isn't as needy.

Dr. B: Well, you can look, but you said you didn't want a divorce and, more importantly, I suspect you'll end up in the same dynamic. You know, conflicts are portable — we can take them anywhere.

Amanda: I can't believe he called me needy when he gives so little. He could make any woman feel needy.

Dr. B: You also have options, Amanda.

Amanda: Yeah. I could divorce him, and believe me I'm considering it.

Dr. B: Can you identify any other options?

Amanda: Well, I can't live like this — it's as if I'm not really married. I don't know. If I back off of him he will disappear. I know him.

Dr. B: Well, it's your call, but you may have to risk backing off and seeing what happens.

Amanda: But, suppose I'm right and he distances even more?

Dr. B: You mean when you're in pursuit you at least have some contact with him?

Amanda: Yes.

Dr. B: That's a lot of work for so little isn't it?

Amanda: You can say that again.

Dr. B: Well, you may be right. Gene could try to take advantage of the new situation, but we won't know unless you can risk losing him further. If you can't, you'll have to reconsider your other options. For now, however, the compromise to your conflict has been unsuccessful. That is, you cannot maintain a healthy, peaceful marriage by constantly pursuing your husband the way you do. In fact, both of your behaviors have achieved distance from intimacy, but to the point where it is almost unlivable. Nevertheless, I suspect both of you will continue the dynamic because the options are not entirely acceptable [*said with paradoxical intent*].

Moving Toward the Resolution of Underlying Conflicts and Increased Differentiation

Understanding and accepting the limitations of their options is difficult enough, but partners must then make their choices in order to resolve their conflicts. In order for this to occur, the therapist must help the partners tie their conflicts to their respective families of origin. The following excerpt demonstrates how I moved Amanda and Gene toward resolving their conflicts and toward greater differentiation. The tying process may go on for several months or, in some cases, several years.

Amanda: I followed your advice and pulled back for a couple of weeks. Man, it's hard to do.

Dr. B: What did it feel like?

Amanda: It felt scary.

Dr. B: In what way?

Amanda: I felt anxious. I was chomping at the bit to go after Gene but I held off even though he didn't do his job and come in any closer.

Dr. B: Don't focus on Gene right now; let him worry about his own job. What do you think the anxiety was all about?

Amanda: I don't know. I just felt as if I was going to jump out of my skin. I was also angry. I think that had to do with letting Gene off the hook.

Dr. B: I find it interesting that after all we've talked about you still think that this treatment will let Gene off the hook. It sounds more like something deep-seated ... perhaps related to the family of origin.

Amanda: I can relate to anger. I was angry with my dad for his irresponsible behavior. He had children, for God's sake, and my pitiful mother kept taking him back — she infuriated me.

Dr. B: You also mentioned that you missed your father. Perhaps your anxiety could be related to being abandoned by Gene. If you stop pursuing, perhaps the anxiety is triggered.

Amanda: So, you're saying it's as if I'm losing Dad when Gene distances?

Dr. B: Perhaps.

Amanda: Wow. How do I get over that?

Dr. B: You might have a bit more grieving to do, and I suspect you will have to bury your dad, so to speak — only this time emotionally. I doubt Gene would ever be able to replace that loss anyway, so he's right when he suspects you will never be satisfied with him.

Gene: Amanda has been better lately.

Dr. B: I'm sure she appreciates the compliment, but how are you doing?

Gene: I'm trying, but I can't figure it out. I can't seem to finish off anything.

Dr. B: Can you give me an example of this?

Gene: I was planning a night out for me and Amanda, but I got sidetracked. I looked up a restaurant in the telephone book, but I never got around to calling it. I also initiated sex last week, and although it went well I just can't seem to follow up.

Dr. B: It sounds as if you run out of steam.

Gene: Yeah. [*laughs*]

Dr. B: Amanda usually goes after you when you run out of steam, doesn't she?

Gene: Oh, yeah, although as I've said she's been more restrained lately.

Dr. B: I'm wondering if you're unconsciously setting her up.

Gene: To chase me?

Dr. B: Well, you seem to be very skilled at getting women to come after you. Your mother chases you, past girlfriends have, and now your wife. I'd say you're gifted in this way.

Gene: [*laughs*] Yeah, I never thought of that.

Dr. B: But, they never seem to catch you ... at least completely.

Gene: And this has to do with my mother?

Dr. B: Do you have some thoughts about this?

Gene: I do distance from my mother.

Dr. B: Well, yes, but I also think you need her, that you want her to chase you because it lets you know she cares. I just don't think you want her to catch you.

Gene: If you're right, how do I stop?

Dr. B: I need your help in finding the answer to that.

Labeling

Systems therapists, in particular, believe that the act of labeling or diagnosing in the therapeutic process is in line with the medical model and is counter to circular thinking. It is suggested, however, that therapists label the pursuer–distancer dynamic for couples as soon as they feel confident with their assessment. In my opinion, labeling helps the couple see their problem as systemic in nature which in turn prevents partners from blaming one another. It also helps the couple to recognize their interactional pattern, gives them something tangible to work on in the therapeutic process, presents them with a clear objective to work toward, offers them a sense of control over their destiny, and increases the couple's level of self-confidence. It is recommended in this model that the therapist label the dynamic immediately after it is enacted and continue to do so throughout treatment until the couple demonstrates that they can detect it without assistance.

Assigned Readings

Occasionally, a partner will ask for something to read on the p–d topic. Most likely, the request will come from the anxious pursuer, who, as mentioned, may be a self-help "junkie." Lerner's (1989) book, *The Dance of Intimacy*, can be recommended. This book has a clear, easily understandable description of the p–d dynamic, and it is comprehendible to the general public. Deluca's (2002) book, *The Solo Partner*, can also serve as an excellent resource, especially for couples in which one partner is particularly resistant to improving the conditions of the p–d dynamic. Fogarty's (1979) article, "The Distancer and the Pursuer," may be recommended if the couple is deemed adequately sophisticated enough to understand it. The article provides a good description of the individual traits and tendencies of the pursuer and the distancer and a basic understanding of the dynamic; however, it focuses primarily on the female as the pursuer and the male as the distancer. If the therapist is in need of material concerning the male pursuer–female distancer combination, I would recommend Betchen and Ross's (2000) article, "Male Pursuers and Female Distancers in Couples Therapy." Again, the therapist will need to ascertain whether the couple can comprehend such an article.

Before any readings are assigned, it is important to assess whether the couple is emotionally strong enough to withstand the content; it is also important to assess the couple's level of dedication to the treatment process. The latter point is vital in that some couples may mistakenly take the assigned readings as a message that they can cure themselves. Partners can also use the material to support accusations against one another; in my experience, the pursuer is more likely to use the material in this way. Nevertheless, the burden falls on the therapist to assess, on a case-by-case basis, whether assigned readings would benefit a particular couple. All readings should be discussed and referred to in the treatment process when appropriate.

George, a classic male pursuer, requested readings. Given the couple's level of education (both had masters degrees) and a certain sophistication, I assigned Betchen and Ross' (2000) article. Typical of the pursuer, George immediately read the article, recommended it to friends, and used it to focus on the emotional unavailability of his wife, Beth. Typical of the distancer, Beth did not read the article until George complained in treatment. She then began to read it but never finished it. Interestingly, Beth didn't even have a legitimate excuse for not completing the article. When questioned by George, she simply shrugged her shoulders and murmured, "I don't have the time to read anything." To avoid becoming triangulated in a p–d dance, the therapist should not insist that the distancer read the material; rather, the pursuer's newfound knowledge should be used to help the couple.

Balancing Content and Process

As previously discussed, a couple will most often present with specific content that serves as a vehicle for their p–d dynamic. It is important, however, that the couple's therapist think of this dynamic as a communication style or process that contains content, or operates in different contexts. The therapist needs to observe this process and point out the many manifestations of it to the couple. A therapist who focuses too heavily on the symptomatic content may not pay enough attention to the process and little improvement will occur. If, however, the therapist concentrates too heavily on the process, the couple might feel their problem is being ignored. Even if the therapist thinks that the couple is in denial for ignoring the process, it is the couple's perception of reality that should take precedence at this point in time. To attack this defense too soon may result in premature termination of the couple's therapy. The therapist must balance discussion of the symptom with discussion of the process, giving them equal weight throughout the entire treatment process.

Wanda and Gerry were a couple in their early fifties who had been married for four years. It was the second marriage for both. Wanda was very angry with Gerry for not being able to achieve an erection with her as often as she would like. Although they had successful sex on the average of three times per week, Wanda expected it every night, and when Gerry couldn't seem to respond she threatened to end the marriage.

In my opinion, this didn't really qualify as a sex therapy case *per se*. I believed that the couple was having a p–d power struggle, with sex as the context or content issue. In support of my hypothesis, the evaluation revealed that Gerry was very angry with Wanda because of her demanding nature, but he had a great deal of difficulty confronting her. Instead, he vacillated between distancing from her and making vain attempts to sexually accommodate her. Wanda appeared to have a deep-seated conflict about being desired. She constantly pursued for sex, and whenever Gerry failed her the insecure side of her emerged and threatened the relationship.

Even though I pointed out to the couple that I believed they were having significant marital difficulties that should be addressed before assigning sex therapy exercises, they both disagreed, particularly Wanda. She warned that they had fired their previous couples therapist because the therapist told them the same thing and refused to treat the case as a sexual problem. Apparently, Wanda's friend, who happened to be a psychiatrist, had informed Wanda that sexual problems are often cured in a short period of time with the help of medication and sexual exercises. Because Gerry had a heart condition, however, both partners pressed for exercises rather than risk the side effects of medication.

To me, the demand for exercises represented part of the couple's defensive structure, and I strongly suspected that they would never complete the exercises successfully. Rather than risk sabotaging the treatment, however, I cooperated with the couple and integrated Sensate Focus I exercises (*i.e.*, nongenital, mutual caressing exercises developed by Masters and Johnson [1970]) as a prelude to more specific erectile dysfunction exercises. While it is not uncommon to lead erectile treatment with mutual caressing, in this case I assigned the most benign exercises primarily because I knew the odds for behavioral success at this point in time were slim and that this would be the least damaging way to prove to the couple that they in fact had process marital problems that transcended their sexual difficulty. (Kaplan [personal communication, 1987] contended that care should be taken when assigning sex therapy exercises in order to maximize the opportunity for clients to have a positive experience. The success of the first exercise assigned is most important for it sets the tone for the rest of the treatment.) My hypothesis was supported in that the couple could not even complete one set of caressing exercises. I therefore continued to address the sexual issue but integrated marital treatment as well. Exercises were assigned at a later date when it was determined that the couple had their p–d dynamic under control. More specific examples of how integration is achieved are demonstrated in the following chapters.

Another way to balance content and process is to augment or broaden the process so the couple comes to realize that the p–d process is pervasive and can therefore accommodate any content issue (*e.g.*, money, sex, work). To achieve this, the therapist should attempt to find the p–d dynamic by searching for it and pointing it out in other contexts of each partner's life that are separate and apart from the content issue they may have reported with. When both partners can recognize this process from a wider perspective, they are better able to own personal responsibility for their contributory roles. This acknowledgement also helps to greatly reduce blame, increase mutual understanding, and expose hidden commonality. Wile (1993) contended that these objectives are vital to promoting improvement of this type of dynamic.

Colin and Tara were a couple in their early forties who had been married for twelve years. The couple had two young children. Tara had demanded that Colin attend marital therapy with her under the threat of divorce. She claimed that Colin rarely engaged her in conversation and spent far too much time at work. At first, Tara's approach was to joke with Colin about his distance; however, her tone soon escalated to sarcasm, then to sarcasm in front of friends and family, and finally to yelling and screaming at Colin. As mentioned, she was now at the point of threatening to divorce him.

Colin admitted that he worked a lot. He claimed that his job was very demanding (he was a project manager in a large engineering firm) and that he felt a lot of pressure to perform as he was usually up against deadlines. Rather than resolve this issue with Tara directly, however, Colin retreated further into his work. Specifically, he began coming home later and later from the office and began working on Saturdays. True to the p–d dynamic, Tara reacted to Colin's every distancing maneuver with angry pursuit until the couple became engaged in a classic p–d process, with work as the vehicle for this process.

Only when the couple came to realize that their faulty process, not work *per se*, was a major culprit did they begin to improve their relationship. For example, Colin was eventually able to connect the fact that he was as inaccessible to his underlings at work as he was to his wife. He also connected his distancing behavior to his lack of friends and general social isolation. He was particularly emotional when he connected his distancing to his relationship with his children.

On the other hand, Tara admitted that she was her family's rescuer, as well as the "neighborhood therapist." She constantly pursued friends as well. Later chapters offer more specific examples of balancing process and content, but suffice it to say here that the therapist simply needs to explore each partner's relationships in other contexts and help the couple make the connections.

The Question of Intimacy

While I pointed out earlier that the couple who is engaged in a chronic p–d dynamic is attempting to avoid intimacy, it is the pursuer who believes that he or she is very capable of this type of closeness. In fact, the pursuer may make it a life goal to convince the distancer that the distancer is both the problem in and the solution to their relationship difficulty. This misguided focus only serves to distract the pursuer from his or her problems with closeness. The therapist must help the pursuer realize that he or she is demonstrating an intimacy problem by continuing to pursue even though it is obvious that this pursuit only chases the distancer further away. The pursuer must also realize that he or she tends to fail to notice or positively reinforce any effort on the distancer's part to become engaged in the relationship.

Guerin *et al.* (1987) contended that, when the distancer does move in, the pursuer either demands more closeness or finds a way to reject the distancer. This allows the couple to revert to their baseline interaction. As mentioned earlier, the authors referred to this pattern as the interactional sequence. The therapist should help the couple to become more aware of this pattern and help the pursuer to be patient with the distancer. The therapist also needs to positively reinforce both partners for any attempts to move toward intimacy. The following is a brief example of the interactional sequence.

Timothy and Stephanie were a couple in their early forties who had been married for fourteen years. They had three children together. Stephanie was a female distancer. Described as cold and robotic, she was employed as a high-powered CEO of a large corporation. Timothy, on the other hand, was a laid-back, affectively oriented man in human resources. He brought Stephanie in for treatment by nagging her about it for many years. After several months of therapy and Timothy pleading with Stephanie to show some interest in him, she responded one night by making a sincere effort to be with him both emotionally and physically. She planned a romantic dinner for the two of them, wore something very seductive, and proceeded to initiate sex with him. Because she didn't replicate the same behavior the following night, however, Timothy became irate and pronounced, "You haven't changed." In treatment, I gave Stephanie positive reinforcement for her attempt at intimacy. Timothy's response was questioned as an attempt to block it from entering the marriage. Even though Timothy made excuses for his behavior, I would not accept them and insisted that he in fact was demonstrating the very behavior he was accusing Stephanie of — distancing.

The Role of Medication

During a routine office visit, my physician confided in me that he had a dozen or so patients who refused medication even though their cholesterol levels were extremely high. He referred to these individuals as "human time bombs." This confidence, I believe, was a reaction to the patient who had preceded me. When I asked the doctor why he thought people were noncompliant given the potential severity of the consequences, he shook his head and said that he wasn't sure. He did, however, state that his male patients were less compliant than his female patients because, as he put it, "men in general have more difficulty being vulnerable."

While my physician stated the obvious, we can identify several reasons why individuals forsake medication despite being urged by their doctors to take it. First, it can be a burdensome experience. The medication, for example, may have to be taken at certain times and on a daily basis. Depending on the type of medication, it may also merit monitoring by regular blood work (*e.g.*, drugs that affect the liver). Some people will tell you that they would rather take their chances on something happening to them rather than upset their lifestyle. This is the ultimate existential decision. Second, many people worry about side effects, both short and long term. They will tell you that drug companies want to make money now and couldn't care less about the health and welfare of the people who will use their products. Third, the chronic need for medication can prove to be prohibitively expensive. This, of course, would be true for many thousands of people who have little or no medical insurance or have medical plans that do not adequately cover prescriptions. Fourth, taking the medication is a validation that something is wrong; they prefer to live in a state of denial. Fifth, because of the stigma attached to mental health problems in our society, the taking of psychotropic drugs, in particular, is even more of a taboo to many. And, sixth, taking medication makes them feel dependent and out of control.

While very few people relish being out of control, it is the individuals who tend to have anxious, controlling personalities that react more strongly to losing control. Pursuers, as mentioned, tend to err on the side of control. They are the caretakers, focused on their partners' problems as opposed to their own. While they will initiate treatment, they do so in order to get help for their partners, not necessarily for themselves. When pursuers do admit that they need help, it is help in coping with their partners' pathology. They simply do not like seeing themselves in the "patient" role. In their minds, this is a role better suited for the distancer.

Pursuers, in general, believe that they are fine. Taking any kind of medication, particularly psychotropic drugs, may make them feel defective. While their anxiety levels may be extremely high, it will be difficult to convince them to seek medical attention. They will, however, insist that their distancing counterparts seek help for what often appears to be depression and can be relentless toward this end. If pursuers do take medication, they might make a tremendous push to get the distancers to take it also. This is because pursuers cannot bear the fact that they might have to take it and the "sick" distancers don't — this is perceived as an injustice by most pursuers.

Distancers aren't interested in taking medication or following up with physicians, either. They can distance from anybody — doctors aren't treated any differently. As mentioned, distancers are suspicious by nature, so they don't necessarily trust physicians. A distancer might be the first one to insist that a doctor ordered a test solely out of fear of liability.

Because of their procrastination and passive–aggressive tendencies, many distancers will appease their partners and promise to seek medical advice, but it is unlikely that they will follow through. This, of course, drives pursuers crazy who feel compelled to seize upon the opportunity to harass their distancers to seek medical attention. It is not unusual for a pursuer to set up a physical exam for a distancer and the distancer to refuse or forget to show up.

Leslie was a classic female pursuer. She constantly complained about Geoff and was threatening to leave him if he didn't become more engaged in the relationship. She swore that Geoff was depressed and constantly pushed for him to seek out a psychiatric evaluation and to take medication. In fact, she was on the Internet regularly, offering Geoff facts about selective serotonin reuptake inhibitors (SSRIs), particularly those used commonly for depression, such as fluoxetine (Prozac®) and sertraline (Zoloft®). She was optimistic about these two drugs because she said that Geoff's mother had taken them with some success.

Leslie also constantly complained that Geoff never got physicals, which she said was crazy because his father died at such a young age (44 years old). She made a particular point about his smoking. She said he would only get help if an injury or ailment directly interfered with something he loved to do, such as play softball. Apparently, Geoff was quick to see an orthopedist when a sore foot made it impossible for him to play. Leslie joked, "My God, you would have thought he needed an emergency appendectomy."

While Leslie made some very good points, she was no better than Geoff when it came looking after her health. Believing that her anxiety level was extremely high (she was experiencing panic attacks), I tried for several months to have her evaluated by a psychiatrist. When she finally did give in and accept my referral, the treating psychiatrist told me that she was worried because she was having some difficulty getting Leslie's tachycardia under control. Even when Leslie was feeling better with the help of alprazolam (Xanax®), she prematurely stopped taking her medication but resumed taking it when her symptoms reappeared. When questioned about her resistance, Leslie stated that, if she was given enough time, she could cure her problems without assistance. She sounded as if she believed her expertise to be on par with that of the psychiatrist. I suspected that Leslie hated the fact that she was on Geoff's level (*i.e.*, they both needed medication).

Geoff appeared depressed, but he was far too suspicious of the medical establishment to take medication. At work, however, he was told by his boss that he wasn't paying attention and that he looked depressed. The boss was concerned that Geoff's mood would aversely affect customers — a real problem because Geoff was in the entertainment industry. Afraid of losing his job, Geoff sought help. Following up on a referral I offered, he was prescribed Prozac®, but he shook uncontrollably and was switched to Zoloft®. While his depression lifted somewhat, Geoff expressed sadness and disappointment that the medication did not prove to be an elixir for his depression and distancing. After several weeks of taking it, he got even more depressed. It was if he was replacing Leslie (the bad mother) with Zoloft® (the good mother) only to find that the good mother had let him down.

The therapist needs to warn the distancer that medication is not a cure for distancing; it is only an adjunct tool in the treatment of his or her mood disorder. The therapy treats the p–d dynamic and should be continued. It also is important that the therapist not refer a client for medication because of pressure from a partner. In this dynamic, it must be understood that the pursuer will pressure the therapist to view the distancer as being sick. The therapist who falls into this trap will unbalance the relationship. This is not to say that the distancer might not need medication, but the therapist should remain independent of the pressure.

The therapist should avoid a struggle with the pursuer concerning medication unless it is absolutely in the client's best interests. To get into a fight over the issue and jeopardize treatment for mild to moderate anxiety might not be worth it. I let the pursuer decide when he or she has experienced enough pain (as in Leslie's case). The same applies to the distancer, unless of course the distancer discusses or exhibits suicidal ideation or intent. In these cases, action must be taken and the therapist can enlist the aid of the all-too-ready pursuer.

At certain times during the treatment process, the pursuer or distancer may merit medication, and the therapist needs to be aware of these junctures. For example, if the pursuer leaves, the distancer can break down mentally and be in sudden need of extra care (refer to Jake and Audrey in chapter 1). Or, if either partner begins to focus on the personal losses experienced then depression might set in. In this case, the pursuer will be the one most likely to be caught off guard. In Leslie's case, she became very depressed at one point in the treatment — when she began to realize that she was chasing her father. It was during this mourning process that she finally agreed to take medication.

Transference and Countertransference

This model values the analysis and use of transference and countertransference in treating couples, particularly those engaged in the p–d dynamic. According to Siegel (1997), therapists who are able to recognize their own reactions and can question the ways in which they stem from or mirror the couple's relationship have an advantage, because the issues externalized onto the therapist are those that cause the couple the most conflict and tension. They are, in fact, precisely the issues that have brought the couple in for treatment. Pursuers, for example, will put enormous pressure on their therapists to align with them against the distancers. The projection of a pursuer's anxiety (regarding a conflict with intimacy) onto the therapist can be attributed to the pursuer's family of origin and reinforced by subsequent relational experiences, particularly with the distancing partner.

The therapist should anticipate and recognize the preceding transference behavior because it can trigger countertransference anger, anxiety, feelings of inadequacy, and ultimately, unbalanced therapeutic behavior on the therapist's part. For example, a therapist who has not yet resolved a personal conflict with intimacy may join with the pursuer in pursuing the distancer (reflecting, perhaps, the therapist's own family of origin and current relationship). This may cause the distancer to distance from the therapist as well as from the pursuer; it may also evoke shame and humiliation in the distancer. On the other hand, a therapist might align with the distancer because he or she has taken a disliking to the pursuer and empathizes with the seemingly embattled distancer because of prior experiences. This therapist may then be perceived by the pursuer as an advocate for the distancer or as the distancing parent or partner, thus replicating the couple's relational dynamic. Either way, the pursuer may become angry enough to prematurely terminate the treatment process.

Bill and Cheryl, a couple in their middle forties, were engaged in an extremely contentious p–d dynamic. Cheryl was enraged because Bill had paid very little attention to her during the course of their fifteen-year marriage. Bill, a passive man, spent much of the session trying to pacify Cheryl to no avail — she was inconsolable. From the very beginning of the first session, Cheryl edited and restricted my relatively nonconfrontive comments. Eventually, however, she turned on me full force while Bill remained silent. He was probably relieved that I was now bearing the brunt of her anger. Cheryl accused me of siding with Bill and minimizing his "neglectful" behavior.

As a result of Cheryl's hostility, I became angry and anxious. I began to see her husband as the "nice guy" who had to put up with this crazy woman's behavior. I desperately wanted to challenge Cheryl, but I feared that she would complain to the director of the clinic and I would lose my job. At one point, it seemed that any comment I made, no matter how benign, was met with anger (unless it supported Cheryl's position against her husband). My decision: Rather than continue to work, I shut down. I didn't say another word for the remaining 25 minutes of the session. I thought it might be better for me to distance than to challenge this woman and risk my job. In the end, however, it didn't matter because she complained to my immediate supervisor anyway. She told him that I acted as if I was afraid of her, and that I had stopped talking in the session.

Apparently, my response made Cheryl even angrier. I didn't realize it then, but my reaction reinforced her as being the horrible person her distancing husband made her feel like. Had I been able to handle my feelings, I would have dealt with Cheryl differently. I would have interpreted her transference and assured her that I shared her goal of helping her to get her husband to be more responsive to her. I would have also found a way to de-triangulate myself and re-engage Bill in the treatment process. Unfortunately, I allowed Cheryl to tap into unresolved issues from my family of origin with regard to a hard-to-please, demanding mother. When this occurred, I could not control my need to distance from Cheryl as I did my mother.

Schnarch (1991) recommended that couples therapists stay invested and involved, yet differentiated, in the therapeutic process. In order to remain objective and avoid deleterious countertransference effects, it is especially important for therapists to be conscious of their tendencies to pursue or distance and avoid becoming triangulated into a fixed pursuer–distancer dance. A therapist who has the tendency to distance should be especially careful not to run from the pursuer, especially the opposite-sex pursuer. The therapist who has a tendency to pursue should be especially cautious not to chase the distancer, particularly a distancer of the opposite sex.

While an attack by a pursuer is an unpleasant experience, it is not without value to the therapist, as the therapist may need to experience this direct pressure in order to empathize with the distancer; however, the therapist may also use the experience to empathize with the pursuer's anxiety and possible feelings related to rejection and abandonment. The therapist may also relate to how difficult it is under these conditions not to pursue the distancer. If I could have related to the anxiety and pain that my mother experienced (she lost her father at a very young age and lived with a distancing husband for many years), I might have been more empathetic with regard to Cheryl's plight. For this to have happened, however, I would have had to get in touch with the pain I experienced as a result of not having as much contact with my father as I would have liked.

As mentioned earlier in this book, the distancer can be extremely frustrating and slow moving. Therapists who are controlling, impatient, perfectionist, or insecure about their therapeutic skills may begin to feel like failures. The distancer is usually quiet, and on some occasions even silent for much of the treatment. A therapist who needs approval or positive feedback from the distancer may soon experience anxiety in the treatment process. The therapist must always remember that the distancer is not in the habit of "giving." The therapist may get some positive feedback from the pursuer but would do better to resolve his or her need for it or seek it from supervisors or contact with professional colleagues. The following case example displays how I dealt with insecure feelings prompted by a male distancer.

Al and Faith were a couple in their late fifties. Al was a surly-looking professional man with a skeptical attitude. Faith, an extroverted individual, did most of the talking. At one point in the treatment process, Faith questioned whether I was challenging Al enough to examine himself. She hypothesized that perhaps I was intimidated by Al and therefore let him off the hook. I thought about this, and it dawned on me that Al looked and acted much like my late, distancing father. In fact, his height, weight, and demeanor were strikingly similar; they were even in the same profession. I therefore determined that Faith was right; I had been letting Al get away with distancing in the treatment process primarily because the thought of challenging him stirred up anxiety in me the same way it did when I contemplated dealing with my cantankerous father. Moreover, I realized that the concept of getting closer to Al aroused the same feelings. It wasn't until I processed my countertransference that I was able to establish a much easier and more productive relationship with Al. To his credit, he let me in to the extent that he could and eventually improved in his ability to be intimate with Faith.

The therapist's use of self is an essential tool in working with all therapeutic modes but can be particularly valuable when working with couples, in part because the therapist's attention is already split between the two partners and the dyadic interaction (Siegel, 1997). By keeping a finger on his or her own pulse, the couples therapist can relate to the plight of both partners, thus helping to ensure balance in the treatment process. One of the benefits of couples work is that, if the therapist is open to it, a partner can be useful in pointing out a blind spot in the therapist. The therapist needs to consider the fact that each partner has his or her own agenda. (Sharpe [2000, p. 85] reported that "each partner expects the therapist to act as a narcissistic extension and magically fix the other partner who is, of course, the real problem.") However, this should not necessarily negate the fact that the partner may be offering some very valuable information that may be beyond the reach of the therapist. I listen very intently to what each partner has to say. I believe that partners are usually right about one another — it is the self they need clarification about so they can take responsibility for their contributions to the relational process.

As implied, a therapist listening to a p–d couple may experience different, perhaps conflicting, feelings about each mate. Solomon (1997) wrote the following:

> When the therapist observes the unfolding interaction — maintaining a receptive capacity to how he or she is used by each mate in the relational space between them — various needs, feelings, and defenses emerge and become available for examination and modification. In order to operate therapeutically within that relational space, the therapist must be able to maintain a stance of open-minded curiosity about what is occurring within the spouses as well as in him-/herself, listening for messages from within and making some determinations about their source. The internal experience of the therapist often reflects the emotional experience of the individual or partners in the interactional space of the relationship. (p. 25)

One of the ways to achieve this therapeutic attunement is by considering questions that are essential to the treatment process, such as: Who am I to the couple? Who does the couple represent to me? Who does each partner represent to me? Are my reactions unique to this particular couple or this p–d dynamic? Are my reactions unique to each partner? Do I feel differently in this particular session than I generally feel with this couple? Sometimes it might be profitable to share certain aspects of one's response with the couple. Other times, it is enough to know what an unusual therapeutic reaction may signify (Solomon, 1997). The therapist must decide when it would be helpful to reveal certain feelings to the couple.

In tune with Siegel (1997), I believe that clients can never become healthier than the therapist; however, all couples therapists will at one time or another participate in the craziness of the couple. As Solomon (1997) contended, for example, every therapist will experience a misalignment with a couple. It is when it happens repeatedly that consultation or supervision is required. Couples therapists can only take couples as deep within themselves as the therapists can go within themselves. For this reason alone I believe that couples therapists (other than perhaps behavioral couples therapists) should pursue their own personal psychodynamic psychotherapy or psychoanalysis.

Termination

Premature Termination

As previously hypothesized, female pursuers and female distancers are more likely to end treatment prematurely. This finding is consistent with the sociological literature, which indicates that females tend to be less tolerant of, and more likely to end, unsatisfactory relationships regardless of their economic and financial status (Diedrick, 1991). However, the ability of women to support themselves financially has made it even easier for them to initiate separation or divorce, and they are doing so with increasing frequency (Hales, 1999; Rimm, 1999; Tiger, 1999).

Men, on the other hand, have a more difficult time ending relationships. Men also suffer greater trauma following separation and divorce (Collins & Coltrane, 1995; Diedrick, 1991). Betchen and Ross (2000) contended that men might not be able to separate as easily as women because, as a group, they may be more emotionally dependent on women than women, as a group, are on men. Having been raised predominantly by their mothers might be the major contributing factor. Even the male distancers who thought highly of their fathers were ambivalent about losing their mothers. They did not seem to believe that their fathers cared as much about them and would maintain a physical or emotional connection (Betchen, 1996). The fact that male distancers tend to marry women like their mothers further supports this hypothesis.

While joining with the female pursuer and distancer is vital in order to combat premature termination, it is no guarantee for success. If the therapist senses or is warned that treatment is in jeopardy, he or she should take immediate action. A direct warning from a client may merit an individual session with that partner in order to calm, support, validate, and process that person's feelings. The therapist must be careful, however, not to become triangulated into the p–d interaction by cajoling the distancer to work harder or pleading with the pursuer to leave the distancer alone. Oftentimes, a client may use the threat of premature termination to manipulate both their partner and the therapist in order to control the treatment process. If the therapist is able to tolerate the anxiety that this maneuver can stir up, the couple may rescind the threat or end therapy only to return to it at a later point in time, having realized that the maneuver failed. In some cases, however, it may be better to allow the treatment to end, rather than take on the role of "triangulated caretaker." Simply put, it is wiser to live to fight another day.

At specific times in the treatment process the p–d couple may threaten to terminate prematurely even though the therapist has joined with them over a significant number of sessions: when the female pursuer begins to realize that she, too, has contributed to the interactional dynamic and her defenses require her to retreat; when the male pursuer fears that he or the therapist has pushed the female distancer too far and has placed the relationship in serious jeopardy; when a partner begins an affair. In each of these cases, the therapist should intervene immediately, and individual sessions might be useful in these situations. Wanting to terminate the sessions is often a sign that the treatment may be moving either too quickly or slowly for the couple which can generate more anxiety than they can tolerate. The therapist will have to adjust the speed of the treatment process to better match the anxiety level of the couple. The following case is an example of this.

Marie, an attractive woman in her middle thirties, was married to Ned, a sweet but rather homely man in his early fifties. It was Marie's first marriage and Ned's third (Ned's first two wives left him for other men.) Ned was both a pleaser and a pursuer. He appeared to be in a never-ending struggle to meet any and all of Marie's needs, but she never seemed to be satisfied. Marie could be verbally abusive at times and was in control of the couple's financial, social, and sexual lives. She also seemed to carefully but unpredictably ration her affection to Ned, while he couldn't seem to get close enough to her.

Following several months of treatment, Ned began to complain mildly about Marie's treatment of him in the conjoint sessions. In an individual session, however, which took place on a Friday afternoon (Marie was out of town), he was overtly angry. He said that he was tired of the abuse and the distance and that he couldn't take it anymore. Marie returned from her trip on Sunday and called my office that day in a panic. It seems she and Ned had a fight and he left the house abruptly. This was foreign behavior for him, and it took Marie completely by surprise — her anxiety level was extreme. While I calmed her, I hoped that Ned would be able to maintain this stance, as I saw it as much-needed limit-setting behavior and a balancing of power in their dynamic. By their Tuesday session, however, both partners were threatening to end the treatment. Ned had clearly scared himself with his assertive distancing and felt that I should have been able to stop him from reacting to Marie as he did. Marie was upset because she thought I was turning Ned into an irrational "monster." The couple had clearly regressed, and they were far too defensive for me to take advantage of Ned's anger. I decided to allow the couple to retreat into their dynamic in exchange for rescuing the case from premature termination. My hope was that another opportunity would eventually appear when the couple was in a better position to capitalize on it.

Treatment Goals

The goals of treatment are to alleviate any symptoms (*i.e.*, content) that the couple has presented with as well as address the dysfunctional p–d interaction (*i.e.*, process) being used as a vehicle for these symptoms. In order for these goals to be reached and for the couple to achieve intimacy, both partners must increase their respective levels of differentiation. In this way, their individual conflicts regarding closeness and intimacy may be resolved.

The conflict resolution that comes with greater differentiation is designed to alleviate anxiety in both parties. This reduction in anxiety enables distancers to relinquish some of the protectiveness and allows them to stay physically and emotionally present with their mates. It usually helps pursuers achieve a more solid sense of self which allows them to tolerate the level of distance required to form an intimate connection with their partners.

In tune with Goldberg (1987), I do not believe that it is the job of a couples therapist to judge levels of intimacy in couples. If, for example, a couple agrees to live in separate dwellings or to maintain separate bank accounts, so be it. To consider this behavior as nonintimate or as abnormal misses the point of couples work. If the couple has agreed to live this way, they do not merit treatment.

Some time ago I received a referral from a prominent gynecologist who insisted that I speak to him before I saw a couple he was sending to me (the wife was one of his patients); however, the couple's appointment time had arrived before the physician and I touched base. The couple, in their late twenties, had been married for about one year. When I asked them to tell me why they had decided to seek marital therapy, they looked at me and agreed that it was not their idea. They said that they were, in fact, quite pleased with their relationship and that it was the wife's referring physician who decided that they were in desperate need of help. When I inquired as to why they thought the physician might be alarmed, they told me that he was concerned because they had yet to consummate their relationship. I asked each partner whether they saw this as a problem; both answered with a resounding "no." I then asked whether they desired to have children and again, the answer was "no." Needless to say, the couple was kind enough to allow me to complete my evaluation, and as the hour neared its end, I gave them my blessing for a happy life together. Two days later the gynecologist finally contacted me. He was extremely angry. He said he was offended that I had seen the couple without first consulting him, and when he heard that I sent them on their way he was particularly enraged. He told me that the couple had serious problems and that he had spoken to a friend of his (a psychiatrist) who apparently diagnosed the wife as having a borderline personality disorder, without having seen her. He proceeded to tell me that the wife was sick because she had yet to consummate her marriage. I gently explained to the concerned physician how couples therapy works and that, while I did think the couple was in denial about certain issues, they did not merit treatment because they were in agreement about their sex life. I also assured him that the wife was not a borderline personality; I thanked him for his compassionate care of this couple, and I told him that regardless of what was operating the couple was not ready to deal with it. Whether this couple would be considered non-intimate by anybody else's standards really did not matter at that point. They certainly were not locked into a control struggle similar to the p–d dynamic.

Ending Treatment

Therapist and clients generally agree on when it is appropriate to terminate treatment; however, the therapist can rely upon certain signs to determine when termination is not far off. The pursuer will appear to be less anxious, will demonstrate a new ability to confront the distancer, and will become more interested in understanding his or her own intrapsychic conflicts. The pursuer will not appear as anxious to get the distancer into treatment every week. When the pursuer begins to bring up the subject of termination, he or she is clearly feeling safer, stronger, and better able to handle the distancer. The therapist who has remained neutral throughout the treatment process should begin to feel more relaxed and under less pressure to accommodate the pursuer. The distancer shows a definite interest in treatment and appears to be working harder — a sign that the distancer is becoming more engaged in the process and the relationship. The therapist will feel that he or she has come to know the distancer on a more personal rather than theoretical level. Near the end of successful treatment, a highlight is when the distancer prods the pursuer to continue to work on the relationship.

While the couple may in fact be more intimate as a result of treatment, the therapist might want to consider "predicting" that they will slip into their pursuer–distancer dance from time to time throughout the course of their relationship. This is especially likely during times of high stress. The therapist should assure the couple that this is normal and, as long as they are not fixed in their dance, they now possess the skills to address the problem before it proves fatal to the relationship.

CHAPTER **5**

Evaluating Sexual Dysfunction in the Pursuer–Distancer Dynamic

Sex: A Common Context for the Pursuer–Distancer Dynamic

According to McCarthy (1999), "When sexuality functions well in a marriage, it is 15 to 20% of the relationship, creating special feelings and energizing the bond. When sexuality is dysfunctional or nonexistent, it plays an inordinately powerful role, 50 to 75%, draining the marriage of intimacy and vitality" (p. 297). Couples who are engaged in pursuer–distancer dynamics often present with sexual symptoms. While these symptoms vary, the common denominator is that one seemingly desperate partner pursues the other in the context of a sexually related activity. The pursuer may pursue for any sex, more sex, a particular type of sex (*e.g.,* oral), more passionate sex, higher functioning sex (*e.g.,* firmer erection), or sex initiated by the distancing partner. The distancing partner tends to avoid giving the pursuer whatever he or she is after, and the dynamic ensues.

While both partners may agree that their sex life is lacking in terms of frequency or quality, I have found that they are rarely conscious of the fact that their sexual symptom may be correlated with a p–d dynamic that is lodged in a deeper, longer-standing conflict with intimacy. For example, a man who has little or no sex with his wife is usually aware that something is amiss; however, he might first think that there is something physically wrong with him or that he has lost attraction for his wife simply because of the many years they have spent together. On the other hand, the wife

79

may not believe that her pursuing behavior may cause or exacerbate her husband's sexual difficulty. She may fear that her husband has lost his attraction for her and respond with anxious, angry pursuit; it is highly unlikely that she views her reaction as symptomatic of an underlying problem with intimacy.

When sexual conflict does make up the content for the p–d interaction, couple strife often escalates beyond what it would if any other symptoms were presented (Betchen, 1997). Sex is so closely correlated with love and commitment that when there is problem in this area people tend to react very strongly. Earlier in my career I was astounded to learn that the majority of the male murderers at a jail at which I was working were incarcerated because of "acts of passion." That is, they found their wives with other men and in a fit of rage committed murder.

The reaction to being sexually pursued or distanced from is also quite subjective. Individuals who have been abandoned, cheated on, or made to feel unattractive in their families of origin or in prior relational experiences may react more strongly to being distanced from sexually. For example, if the distancing partner chooses television over sex with the sexually pursuing partner or refuses to have any sexual relations with the partner, does it mean that the distancing mate doesn't love the pursuing partner? Does it mean that he or she will abandon the pursuer?

If the pursuer pursues for sex and the distancer accommodates, does it then follow that the distancer will have to be at the pursuer's beck and call? Does it symbolize the beginning of the distancing individual's loss of freedom? Those individuals who have been sexually intruded upon in their past (*e.g.*, by an overbearing, intrusive parent with very little sense of personal boundaries) may react strongly to being sexually pursued. Someone who was molested, raped, or sexually traumatized in some way may even develop an aversion to pursuit. In this case, posttraumatic feelings of being controlled or trapped might be conjured up.

Integrating Sex and Couples Therapy

My experience at the Marriage Council of Philadelphia taught me that couples problems and sexual problems are usually intertwined, and it would be beneficial to relationship therapists and their clients if the therapists were skilled in treating both (Weeks & Hof, 1987). This is particularly true when a sexual symptom is the predominant reason for seeking treatment. While many clinicians in the professional literature support this notion (Berman & Hof, 1987; Lief, 1977; Sager, 1976; Scharff & Scharff, 1991; Schnarch, 1991, 1997), others continue to shy away from integration. Some sex therapists, for example, are not systems oriented; while they may see a couple, their main focus is still on the partner with the sexual symptom. On the other hand, many couples therapists feel uncomfortable dealing with sexual issues; in fact, I have found that some tend to avoid investigating this part of a couple's life altogether. A second reason for resistance to integration is that therapists may be averse to obtaining the extra years of training required to become competent in both specialties. Because it is so esoteric, obtaining sex therapy training can require travel and great expense. Also, some therapists simply do not think it is necessary to master two areas. These individuals believe they can consult a sex therapy text for guidance if a couple reports with a sexual problem or can refer them to someone skilled in the area. The following case example supports the need for training in both areas of specialization.

Bruce, a physician, brought his wife, Sarah, in for treatment because she could not achieve orgasm during sex with him or in his presence. She could, however, achieve a strong orgasm via self-stimulation either with her hand or with a vibrator if she was alone. While Sarah did not think that she had a major problem, Bruce clearly did. The couple eventually fell into a p–d dynamic: Bruce pursued Sarah to work on her orgasm and Sarah avoided sex with Bruce as often as possible. Bruce finally convinced Sarah to get treatment for her problem.

The center where I was working was not systems oriented, and I was advised to validate Bruce's feelings — it was his wife's problem, and everything would be fine if she would stop blocking herself and achieve orgasm with him. I had received training in integrating marital and sex therapy, and it was obvious to me that the best way to proceed was to integrate the two therapies into one treatment approach. In this case, Bruce was treating his wife like a patient (he even prescribed anti-anxiety medication for her); he clearly viewed her as having the problem, and he dropped her off at my office so that I could fix her. He did not view the situation systemically (*i.e.*, a p–d process with an orgasmic disorder as content) or as one that he and his wife were contributing to equally. Despite my training, however, I followed the center's philosophy and focused on sex therapy exercises to increase the chances of Sarah having an orgasm with her husband.

In the one session we had, Sarah let me know that, at best, she was ambivalent about having to go through treatment, particularly without her husband. On the one hand, she took some responsibility for her anorgasmia, yet she also seemed quite angry with her husband for his controlling, pursuing behavior. In my opinion, her decision to prematurely terminate treatment was a reflection of her anger toward her husband and our center. The center was not supporting her need to balance her marriage (in fact, it enabled the unbalancing of it), and the personal responsibility she took for her sexual symptom made it difficult for her to do so on her own. I am convinced to this day that if I had been allowed to involve Bruce in the treatment process then things might have turned out differently. But, for this to have occurred, the center would have had to view this case from an integrative and systemic perspective. Subsequent chapters demonstrate specifically how couples work is integrated with some of the major sexual disorders that are often presented in the context of a pursuer–distancer process.

Taking a Sexual History: The Sexual Genogram

Berman and Hof (1987) recommended the use of the genogram as a tool to record and "explore issues of sexuality in the structure and belief system of the client's family of origin" (p. 45). The authors contended that the sexual life of an adult is greatly impacted by family history and that the clinician needs to understand this in order to be effective in the therapeutic process. Moreover, they derided the lack of integration of sex and couples therapy and expressed concern that even though "sexuality is a central binding and organizing force in the life of a couple" (p. 37), it was often ignored by marriage and family therapists and left primarily to the sex therapists.

As indicated earlier, I always ask the couple presenting for treatment some basic questions about their sex lives and record the answers to these questions on their genograms. I do this even if the couple presents with nonsexual symptoms because the information may give an indication of a sexual problem that perhaps is not acknowledged by the couple or may simply provide a broader picture of the couple's relationship. As previously mentioned, however, if a couple presents with a specific sexual problem (*e.g.*, erectile disorder) that primarily accounts for their seeking therapy, I will inject a more extensive series of sexually related questions into the intake process and record as much as I can onto their genograms for later exploration.

While I usually complete the entire evaluation in one to two sessions, Berman and Hof (1987) suggested that sexual material should be explored *after* the initial evaluation is completed because sexual questions may stir up a significant amount of anxiety in a couple; therefore, this type of material is better addressed "when a climate exists in which therapeutic trust and rapport have been established, there is no acute marital crisis, and the couple has agreed to explore their sexual issues and problems" (p. 46). While I acknowledge that sex does seem to stir up significant anxiety or discomfort in many individuals, I prefer integrating the sexual and nonsexual information throughout the intake process. In this way, the material is somewhat normalized, which I find is actually more helpful in relieving anxiety. This style also obtains significant information more quickly and in certain cases appeases couples who expect inquiry into their sexual lives. In some situations, particularly those in which a client has a history of sexual abuse or one spouse does not wish to hear about a mate's previous sex life, I may choose to discuss the issue in the individual session that I conduct following the initial intake. Very few couples have ever reported problems with this style.

Following is a list of questions I integrate into the intake process when a couple presents with a sexual symptom. Some of this material is based on Kaplan's (1983) model of evaluating sexual disorders, an approach with which I am quite familiar as it was she who taught it to me several years ago. Notice that when doing a sexual evaluation great detail is sought, for several reasons. First, because behavioral and medical treatments are often integrated into the treatment process, an accurate diagnosis is that much more critical to a successful outcome. Failing to request a medical exam or prescribing the wrong sexual exercises can in some cases prove disastrous. Second, because each sexual disorder usually has more than one definition, it is important to know which definition the client is using. For example, if a man reports having an erection problem, does he mean that he is not as firm as he would like, he is not firm enough for penetration, he loses his erection prior to penetration, or he loses it after penetration? The client's definition of the problem is vital because it not only helps the therapist to obtain an accurate diagnosis but also indicates where to begin treatment. Getting the nonsymptomatic partner to validate the definition of the sexual problem is also important. For example, I have seen some men who have reported that their erections were much harder than they actually were. If it were not for their partner's input, I would have never been privy to this information. Third, because talking about sex may inhibit some clients or make them anxious, they may gloss over their problems and omit information that may be crucial to the treatment process. Slowing these individuals down by requesting detailed information may help the therapist to avoid errors in diagnosis and treatment.

The answers to the questions listed below are plugged into the general genogram. While most of the questions are posed directly to the symptom-bearer, the non-symptomatic partner may contribute at anytime. The exact types of questions asked will depend on the problem the couple is presenting (*e.g.*, premature ejaculation). Subsequent chapters address specific types of sexual problems and their treatment.

Presenting Problem

Can you describe your sexual problem to me in detail?

When did you first experience this problem?

What were the circumstances surrounding the problem?

Can you describe in detail what happened the first time you experienced this problem?

How were you feeling the first time you experienced this problem?

What were you thinking the first time you experienced this problem?

Can you describe the progression of the problem?

Current Sexual Dynamic

Can you give me a step-by-step or "video" description (Kaplan, 1995, p. 96) of your latest sexual experience?

How were you feeling during the experience?

What were you thinking during the experience?

How did your partner react?

Psychological and/or Medical Issues

Did you ever have a urological/gynecological examination?

If so, when was your last exam and what were the results?

Can you have a report from your physician sent to me?

Are you aware that some prescribed medications can interfere with your sexual functioning?

If you have or have had significant anxiety or depression would you say that it preceded or followed your sexual symptom?

Psychosexual History

Did your parents talk about sex?

What sexual messages did you get when growing up in your home?

Do you know anything about your parents' sex life?

Did your parents show any affection toward one another?

Did your parents sleep in the same bed?

Did you have your own bedroom?

When did you lose your virginity and how was the experience?

Have you ever been sexually attracted to or experienced a sexual encounter with a member of the same sex?

Did you ever fantasize about having sex with a member of the same sex?

Did you ever have or experience sex of any kind against your will?

General Sexual Data

Do you masturbate? If so, how often do you do so?

Are you orgasmic?

Do you fantasize about sex in general? If so, can you describe these fantasies to me?

How do you feel about your body image?

What is your preferred type of sexual activity?

Are you interested in any unusual sexual behaviors (*e.g.*, sadomasochistic sex [S/M])?

Do you use the Internet for sexual purposes?

Do you have any repeated sexual dreams or nightmares?

Relationship Data

How does your partner react to your sexual symptom?

How do you feel about your partner's reaction to your sexual symptom?

How do you [nonsymptomatic partner] feel about your partner's sexual symptom?

Have you [nonsymptomatic partner] ever experienced this problem before with any other partner?

After I have completed the entire evaluation, I give the couple some basic information on the particular sexual disorder they have reported. For example, I might tell them the incidence of the disorder. This information may provide some relief because people with sexual problems oftentimes feel they are alone and unusual in their suffering. I also explain how the disorder may be linked to their p–d dynamic and that underlying conflicts usually hold the p–d dynamic in place. Just as I might recommend some literature about the p–d dynamic, I might also recommend some readings on a particular disorder (see chapters 6 through 8 for these readings).

As noted earlier, some couples who present with sexual disorders may demand sexual exercises before they are ready. I usually recommend that they hold off until we get further into the treatment process; however, some couples do not like this approach, in which case I assign them the relatively benign Sensate Focus I exercise. Couples who are not ready for any exercises will inevitably fail, and when they do they may then be ready to admit that they have relationship issues that are linked to their sexual disorder. I tell them that we can always get back to the exercises if need be.

While many of the exercises described in the succeeding chapters are routine, the therapist must be able to determine when to assign them. In some instances, premature assignment may depress a couple; it may also lead to premature termination of the treatment process. The therapist must also know how to apply the exercises creatively. Not every couple possesses the same degree of symptom difficulty, level of resistance, and motivation to change.

CHAPTER 6

Male Sexual Disorders and the Pursuer–Distancer Dynamic

Male Erectile Disorder

The *Diagnostic and Statistical Manual of Mental Disorders* (DSM-IV) (APA, 1994) defines male erectile disorder as a "persistent or recurrent inability to attain, or to maintain until completion of the sexual activity, an adequate erection" (p. 502). Some men can feel excitement yet not have an erection, and others can ejaculate with a limp or flaccid penis. This is because the erectile and ejaculatory reflexes are two distinct processes. Thanks in large part to the work of Masters and Johnson (1966), we now have a clearer idea of what the male experiences physiologically during a cycle of sexual activity.

With regard to the physiology of the erectile process, Weeks and Gambescia (2000) wrote:

> … the "bottom line" for maintaining penile tumescence through-out the duration of sexual activity is a structurally and function-ally intact sexual system. That is, the central nervous system (brain and spinal cord) and both vascular and hormonal systems need to be operating optimally. Any disruption in the activity of any one of these systems will interfere with the quality of an erec-tion. (p. 15)

The erection process begins when the brain is sexually stimulated (mentally or physically). Nerve impulses then cause blood to be pumped into the penis and the spongy tissue cylinders (corpora cavernosa and corpus spongiosum). Once these cylinders are gorged or swollen with blood, they press up against the veins that normally would allow blood to drain from the penis. In essence, the blood is trapped in the penis and an erection results. The testicles are engorged, grow larger (at least 50% larger), and are pulled up into the sac until they press against the wall of the pelvis (anticipating ejaculation). The scrotal sac then becomes thicker in order to support the testicular elevation.

Ejaculation, on the other hand, is a spinal reflex in which blood drains away from the penis and other engorged areas. It occurs in two phases:

1. *Emission phase* — Prostate, seminal vesicles, and vas deferens contract, pouring their secretions into the prostatic urethra; the sperm then mix with the secretions to form the ejaculate. These contractions are the beginning of what Masters and Johnson (1966) referred to as the state of "ejaculatory inevitability."
2. *Ejaculation phase* — Contractions of the penis and urethra propel the ejaculate out through the tip of the penis.

According to the DSM-IV (APA, 1994), the subtypes of male erectile disorder are *lifelong* or *acquired*. Male erectile disorder, lifelong type, refers to the man who has never achieved an erection firm enough for penetration with anyone. With male erectile disorder, acquired type, the man has had successful intercourse at one time in his life. Kaplan (1974) referred to the lifelong type as "primary" and the acquired type as "secondary" male erectile disorders. She reported that secondary erectile disorder was the most common subtype and had the highest cure rates. Primary erectile disorder is thought to be more serious and difficult to treat. Male erectile disorder may also be classified as *generalized* or *situational*. Men with erectile disorder, generalized type, cannot sustain an erection with anyone. The man who has male erectile disorder, situational type, may have problems in certain situations or with a particular person, usually his mate; this is the more common type. The third classification is *due to psychological factors* or *due to combined psychological and medical factors* (APA, 1994).

In a review of the literature on erectile disorder, Simons and Carey (2001) found that the incidence reported by sexuality clinics varied from 1 to 53%. The researchers attributed this wide variation to the fact that the studies they examined did not have a uniform definition of the disorder. Because of the wide variations in the pattern of this problem, sex therapists tend to use the symptom-bearer's definition of the problem. As noted, some men report an inability to attain any semblance of an erection under any conditions; others can achieve an erection only via oral or autoerotic sex (self- or other masturbation) but cannot sustain one for intercourse. Some men report an erection firm enough for penetration but not as firm as they would like. Still others report losing a firm erection just prior to intercourse or soon after penetration.

Causes

Because erectile disorders have several organic causes, the first step of treatment should be to make sure the symptom-bearer obtains a complete workup or physical examination by a qualified urologist. Kaplan (1974) reported that some of the physical causes of male erectile disorder include diabetes, low androgen levels, multiple sclerosis (MS), and tumors of the lower cord. The prevalence of erectile disorders, however, has also been found to increase with age, history of heart disease, hypertension, ulcer, arthritis, allergies, and smoking (Simons & Carey, 2001). Various medications can produce the problem such as thiazides, beta-blockers, anti-androgens, and selective serotonin reuptake inhibitors (SSRIs). Alcohol and drug abuse can also be factors (Plaut, Graziottin, & Heaton, 2004). In my opinion, it is not safe to assume that just because a man, on occasion, has morning erections or sometimes achieves a healthy erection he does not have an organic basis for his problem; therefore, a physical exam is almost always required.

The psychological causes of male erectile disorder vary, depending on the perspective and orientation of the therapist. According to Kaplan (1974), psychoanalysts, for example, attribute the problem to castration anxiety; that is, between 3 and 5 years of age, a little boy wants to possess his mother and kill his father. When he approaches having sex as an adult male, a conflict surfaces: He wants to be with a woman sexually, but feelings of anxiety and guilt regarding his Oedipal problem emerge, rendering him impotent.

Cognitive-behavior therapists (McCabe, 2001; Metz & McCarthy, 2004) take into consideration the negative cognitions associated with experiencing difficulty gaining and maintaining an erection. Given the correlations found between erectile disorder and emotional problems such as depression (Strand, Wise, Fagan, & Schmidt, Jr., 2002), anxiety (Fagan, 2003), and panic disorder (Sbrocco, Weisberg, Barlow, & Carter, 1997), for example, cognitive-oriented sex therapy is the treatment of choice for some sex therapists.

Relationship and/or systems therapists may perceive the symptom as one to which both partners in the dyad are contributing because of unresolved anger, power or control struggles, or a fear of intimacy (Weeks &

Gambescia, 2000). This orientation is closest to those therapists who recognize the possibility that the erectile disorder could be providing a context in which the p–d process can thrive, and *vice versa*.

Treatment

While Kaplan (1974) acknowledged the perspectives of others in the treatment of erectile disorder, she believed that most often the "immediate cause" of the problem was performance anxiety, or fear of failure; that is, the male fails to achieve an erection suitable for intercourse because he worries to the point that he cannot relax and focus on his feelings. When he experiences failure, he may set in motion what some sex therapits refer to as a "worry cycle." Building on the work of Masters and Johnson (1970), Kaplan, along with other prominent sex therapists (*e.g.*, Zilbergeld, 1992), advocated the use of various sexual exercises to alleviate erectile disorder.

While the exercises assigned vary according to the training of the therapist and the level at which the client is functioning, the main objective of the process is to diminish the anxiety so the male can relax and perform. The couple is asked to refrain from having intercourse for four to seven days. Readings on erectile disorder are usually assigned immediately upon diagnosis of the problem (particularly to the male partner), primarily in an effort to help reduce anxiety, dispel any myths about sexual performance, and supplement the exercises assigned by the therapist. Zilbergeld's (1992) *The New Male Sexuality* or Metz and McCarthy's (2004) *Coping with Erectile Dysfunction* may be suggested.

If the male cannot achieve a good erection via solo stimulation or stroking, the therapist may initially assign individual exercises. Specifically, the male is to stroke himself with a dry hand while he relaxes and focuses on his feelings. "Spectatoring" (*i.e.*, obsessive self-observation) or worrying about achieving an erection is discouraged (Masters & Johnson, 1970). If this is a problem, the male is encouraged to use fantasy as an aid to divert his attention away from anxiety and increase stimulation. Initially, I suggest to the male that he fantasize about his partner; if this fails, however, I will ask him to use anything that excites him. When the male is finished with this exercise he is to repeat it using a water-based lubricant such as K-Y Jelly® or Astroglide® (lubrication better simulates the feeling of a vagina). All exercises are to be performed three to five times per week, fifteen to twenty minutes at a time.

If the individual exercises prove successful, then the nonsymptomatic partner is asked to join the process. Sensate Focus exercises are initially assigned to reduce the clients' anxiety and promote togetherness. During these exercises, the nonsymptomatic partner may be given the option of being brought to orgasm which helps to avoid any negative feelings (such as the feeling of being used). The individual exercises are then repeated but this time the partner strokes the male. When these exercises are completed, the partner mounts the male (female superior position) and rubs his penis on her vagina while the man relaxes and/or fantasizes. (Gay male couples can adapt this exercise accordingly.) Next, the partner mounts the male and inserts his erection but only moves enough to maintain the erection (quiet vagina or nondemand coitus). In the final exercise, full intercourse is allowed. Communication between the partners is encouraged during the entire conjoint exercise process.

The pharmacological treatment of male erectile disorder has evolved rapidly over the past decades. In 1997, the treatment of the disorder was revolutionized by the introduction of sildenafil citrate (Viagra®) (Segraves & Balon, 2003). With the advent of Viagra® and other medications such as the newer vardenafil HCl (Levitra®) and tadalafil (Cialis®), as well as various medical procedures introduced in the 1980s, such as the vacuum constriction pump and intracavernous injections (Milsten & Slowinski, 1999; Segraves & Balon, 2003; Weeks & Gambescia, 2000), it has been my clinical experience that sex therapists are treating far fewer erectile disorders than in the past. It is reasonable to suggest that this observation can most likely be attributed to the success of these medical interventions. Another reason, however, may be related to the fact that many general physicians and urologists seem to be prescribing these medications and procedures at an astounding rate, without attempting to find out if any relationship or psychosocial factors are contributing to the disorder and to what extent.

McCarthy (2001) wrote, "Both the general public and medical community now prefer use of a medical intervention first, and only if that is unsuccessful are psychological or sex therapy assessment and interventions considered" (p. 1). In the presence of significant psychosocial factors (Moore, Strauss, Herman, & Donatucci, 2003), however, these medical interventions may be ineffective. When low sexual desire underlies or is primary to an erection problem, for example, medical interventions will generally fail because they are specifically designed to cure erectile disorder, not low desire. Some men I have seen fail to fill their prescriptions or refuse to follow the medical advice. Others use the medicine or device prescribed successfully, but their relational difficulty continues — it has merely been covered over or camouflaged.

One example of this I can think of pertains to a separated man, forty-nine years old, who was experiencing difficulty achieving an erection with a woman he had been dating for approximately two months. In the very beginning of the relationship, the woman was concerned about but still somewhat patient with her date's sexual difficulty. Eventually, however, she began to complain about the situation and pursue for better sexual performance which, in turn, increased the man's anxiety level and compelled him to see a urologist. The urologist cleared the man of any organic problems and prescribed Viagra® for his erectile disorder. Interestingly, however, the man came to see me without ever having filled his prescription. Following my evaluation, it was clear that the man had little or no attraction for the woman he was dating. Rather than confront her, however, he tried to have sex with her and repeatedly failed. It was safe to say that the man's failed erections were speaking for him (or enabling him to distance from his pursuing date). When this man found a woman he was sexually attracted to, he began to experience firm erections and a pleasurable sex life. What is most germane here, however, is that the man's urologist did not even ask him about his relationship. The physician simply gave him a physical workup and prescribed medication.

The following case demonstrates specifically how erectile disorder and the p–d dynamic can be linked and how integrating sex and couples work can help to alleviate the symptom and dynamic simultaneously. While the remainder of the cases presented in this chapter demonstrate how sexual exercises are integrated with psychodynamic conflict work, the following case exhibits treatment of a sexual problem without exercises in the forefront of the treatment process. In this case, it is the pursuer who presents with erectile disorder.

Case 1. Anthony and Maria. Anthony and Maria (see Figure 6.1) were in their late fifties. Anthony was a business consultant and Maria was in marketing. They had been dating one another for approximately three years and had maintained separate residences. Anthony's first wife died five years prior to his meeting Maria, and Maria had been divorced and on her own for eleven years. They both had grown children. Anthony and Maria were referred for sex therapy because of Anthony's erection difficulties, which developed approximately one year prior to entering treatment. Before this, Anthony functioned fine. The couple could not pinpoint any particular event that may have resulted in this problem; they said it just began to appear "out of the blue." Anthony first went to his urologist, who astutely determined that his erectile problems were psychological. Because medication for erectile disorder had yet to be discovered, the urologist immediately referred the couple for sex therapy.

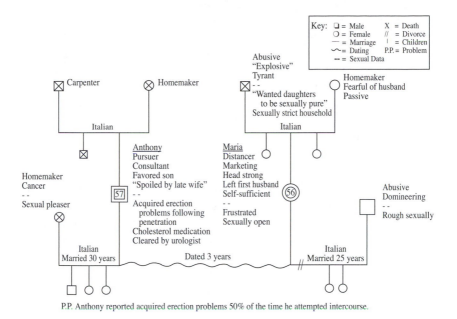

Fig. 6.1 Anthony and Maria.

Apparently, Anthony could achieve a firm erection approximately 50% of the time he attempted intercourse with Maria. On a scale of 1 to 10 in terms of firmness, Anthony rated his erection as a 9 or 10. On the days he failed, his erection would initially be hard but would turn flaccid soon after penetration. His ratio was the same when it came to manual and oral sex with Maria as well. He claimed that, although he rarely masturbated, when he did he fantasized exclusively about Maria and was relatively successful. Although Anthony achieved a healthy erection 50% of the time he attempted intercourse, most men with this problem have difficulty most of the time. Given his unusual success ratio, the fact that his problem was related to Maria (he had never experienced the problem before), the absence of organic problems, and the fact that the couple did exhibit a p–d dynamic, it was obvious that the erectile symptom was related to emotional and systemic problems.

While Anthony seemed motivated for couples/sex therapy, he had a difficult time convincing Maria to join him. In fact, it took him a year to get Maria in for treatment. She believed it was Anthony's responsibility to fix his problem and that she had little to do with it. Unlike many other women in her position, she said that she never personalized the problem; rather, she hypothesized that Anthony's erection problem was a direct result of being spoiled by his late wife, who attended to his every need. She stated, "Now that Anthony is involved with an experienced, liberated woman who wants to get her sexual needs met, he is having difficulty." Anthony was perplexed by his problem. He claimed that he achieved morning erections quite frequently, had no problem when he masturbated, and was very attracted to Maria and wished to have sex with her regularly. He also claimed that he had never had this kind of problem before.

Anthony agreed that his first marriage was traditional in a sense that he was the breadwinner and his wife was the homemaker. He also reported that his family of origin was very much the Italian family with the man in charge. Anthony stated that he got along fine with his parents and that he was somewhat spoiled. He had one older brother, and he believed that, being the younger of the two, he was somewhat favored by both parents. Maria, on the other hand, reported a very different experience. She said that she, too, grew up in a traditional Italian household, but her father was a tyrant and could be somewhat abusive if crossed. She also reported that her ex-husband was also very domineering and could be verbally and physically abusive, which is why she eventually left him. Maria did not find Anthony abusive, but she claimed that he always wanted his way and would pout or be passive–aggressive if he didn't get it.

Anthony and Maria reported somewhat uneventful sexual histories. Anthony claimed that sex wasn't really talked about in his family of origin but he didn't get the impression that anything was wrong with it. He reported that his parents slept in the same bed up until his father's death (his mother died a few years later), and that probably his parents had sex when his father wanted to. Anthony confirmed Maria's hypothesis about his sex life with his late wife. He reported that they had regular sex (*i.e.*, two to three times per week) and that it was geared toward pleasing him. He said he was interested in pleasing his wife, but "things turned out the way they did because she also grew up in a traditional Italian family that focused on pleasing the male." He said that his wife seemed happy and never complained about sex. Anthony denied having experienced any sexual abuse in his history, and reported no alcohol or drug use or abuse. He was on medication for high cholesterol, but his urologist did not believe this was a factor in Anthony's erectile difficulty.

Maria denied any sexual abuse in her family of origin but was afraid of her father's temper. Apparently, he could be explosive and her mother was unable to protect Maria and her siblings from his outbursts. Maria said that sex was not mentioned in her family, and, in fact, she and her sisters were expected to be "pure." They knew that if they did not dress and act conservatively their father would severely reprimand them. She reported that her parents slept in the same bed and had sex, but she wondered if her mother was too afraid to resist her husband's overtures. "I think it was her job and if she turned him down he probably would have hit her," she said.

Maria claimed that there was no history of drug or alcohol abuse in her family of origin, and that both parents were hard-working individuals who came to America from Italy when she was an infant. After high school, Maria married her boyfriend and settled into a marriage that lasted twenty-five years. She felt controlled and said that her husband would be very rough with her sexually, although she would not elaborate. It was obvious from her affect that she was ashamed that she took so long to end her marriage. Following her divorce Maria dated sporadically, but for the most part she was relieved to be in control of her own life. She stated that she would never be abused or controlled again, and although she is willing to please Anthony he will have to do his share of pleasing or the relationship will be over. Maria was not on any medication and appeared to be a strong, self-sufficient woman who would end the relationship if things didn't improve.

Interestingly, Maria seemed more concerned about being controlled by Anthony than she was bothered by his erection problem. He seemed like the anxious one, constantly pursuing Maria to continue to work with him on the problem. She was definitely more resistant to treatment than he was. She was also less verbal and more guarded in the sessions. I was not sure whether she would return from week to week, and in fact she refused to come in on more than one occasion. It seemed that for the last several years Maria had prepared herself to be independent of men. She even earned a master's degree in marketing and had established a lucrative career for herself. She once said, "I want Anthony, but I certainly don't need him. If things don't work out between us I'll survive — I have to this point."

The couple was not aware that they were engaged in a p–d dynamic nor were they conscious of the fact that the dynamic was connected to the erectile symptom. Nevertheless, because Anthony insisted on sex therapy exercises (which he read about prior to treatment), I started the couple on Sensate Focus I exercises. The hope was that these exercises would either expose their dynamic or prove successful so that we could move to more specific exercises for erectile disorder; however, the couple was not able to get through the Sensate Focus exercises. Maria was not very enthusiastic, and Anthony hounded her. The more he hounded, the less she tried. The couple was very frustrated when they returned to treatment.

From this point forward, I was able to more easily focus on integrating the p–d dynamic and erectile problem with little resistance from the couple. Moreover, I hypothesized that Anthony was upset with Maria's distance and thus unable to achieve an erection on a consistent basis. His partial impotence represented his partial resentment toward Maria's partial commitment to him. He did seem sincerely attracted and committed to her, but his feelings about her distance were missing; these he denied. The following session was a key turning point in the case. This exchange solidified the fact that both partners were in conflict, that the conflicts were reflected by their p–d dynamic, and that the erectile disorder was symptomatic of this dynamic.

Dr. B: Anthony, do you feel that Maria is as committed to the relationship as you are?

Anthony: No. I have to push her a bit.

Dr. B: What do you mean?

Anthony: Well, I had to drag her into therapy.

Dr. B: I noticed treatment was your idea. Do you pursue Maria for anything else?

Anthony: I didn't bring this up before, but I have been trying to get Maria to move in with me for some time. I proposed marriage as well, but she wants to keep things the way they are.

Maria: I just don't feel the need to live with him. Why can't he be satisfied with seeing me regularly? I'm not seeing anyone else, and we sleep over at one another's places all the time.

Dr. B: I didn't know this was such a big issue between the two of you.

Maria: Oh, it's big, but I just won't do it.

Dr. B: Not that I'm for or against it, but what are your reasons for not moving in with Anthony?

Maria: I've already been married and I want to stay independent.

Dr. B: Are you afraid of something?

Maria: Well, I never want to give any man total control of me. You know my history.

Anthony: I would never abuse you, you know that.

Maria: Forget it; it's not going to happen.

Dr. B: But, you do want to be in a relationship.

Maria: Yes.

Dr. B: So, you want to connect at a distance.

Maria: Now that you put it that way, yes.

Dr. B: You can't live with them, and you can't live without them.

Maria: I can live with them as long as they live around the corner. [*laughs*]

Dr. B: Can't you find a man who wants the same type of relationship that you do?

Maria: Apparently not. [*laughs*]

Dr. B: I'm just trying to understand why you might choose a man who relentlessly pursues you rather than one who agrees with your relationship philosophy.

Maria: I've tried, but they all seem to want to dominate me. Believe it or not, Anthony's the easiest going guy I've been out with since my divorce.

Dr. B: Hence, that's why he is still around.

Maria: You better believe it.

Dr. B: So, given what you have witnessed between your mom and dad and your experiences with your ex-husband, you've decided that it's better, or should I say safer, to be in control. By the way, did you feel sorry for your mother?

Maria: Yeah, I felt sorry for her, but I also thought she put up with way too much. I realize she didn't have the resources to leave my father, but I think I would rather have starved than put up with him.

Dr. B: Anthony, how do you feel about what you're hearing?

Anthony: I understand it, but I hate it. It's not the way to conduct a relationship.

Dr. B: Have you ever thought about ending the relationship?

Anthony: Yes, but I love Maria.

Dr. B: So, you live with your anxiety and pursue her to make more of a commitment to you.

Anthony: Yeah, I guess.

Dr. B: How have you been doing?

Anthony: Obviously terrible.

Dr. B: Well, not always.

Anthony: What do you mean?

Dr. B: We'll get to that, but first I'd like to know when you began to want Maria to move in with you.

Anthony: About a year ago.

Dr. B: Wasn't that about the time the sexual symptom appeared?

Anthony: I never thought of that. So, you really think there is a connection?

Dr. B: Well, I'm interested in what you think.

Maria: It makes sense to me. This has been a big issue for him — he won't let it go.

Anthony: I'm certainly not sabotaging my erection on purpose, but there is no other explanation for this problem. I have been angry and disappointed with Maria over this issue. She can be so stubborn.

Maria: Unlike your mother and wife, who catered to your every whim.

Anthony: Their lives weren't so bad.

Dr. B: Anthony, it's not easy to give up a life like the one you had with those women. I can understand your need to pursue it, but why with someone like Maria, who clearly will not give you what you want? It all seems contradictory to me. Are you into big challenges? [*laughs*]

Anthony: No, I just fell in love with Maria.

Dr. B: What was it about her that you fell in love with — aside from her intelligence and looks?

Anthony: Even though she can be stubborn, she can also be exiting. She's interested in many things, and she is experimental in bed as well.

Dr. B: More so than your late wife?

Anthony: Absolutely. My wife was very traditional. While she met my needs, she had her limitations. At times, I guess, she was somewhat predictable and boring — Maria is neither.

Dr. B: So, you're in a bit of a dilemma. You want someone as exciting and experimental as Maria, but she won't meet your need to live together or marry.

Anthony: Yes.

Maria: So, he's sabotaging his erection?

Dr. B: Possibly, but he is only partially upset with you. I do believe Anthony truly wants you — this is represented by his ability to achieve an erection half the time. I also believe, however, that he is upset with you, as well, so the other 50% of the time he fails.

Anthony: If you're right, then I have to resolve my issue about the live-in situation before I can achieve a more consistent erection.

Dr. B: If I'm right. Of course, it would be optimal if simultaneously Maria could resolve her conflict regarding control and closeness, as well.

Premature Ejaculation

Premature ejaculation (PE) has been found to be the most commonly reported male sexual disorder (Laumann, Gagnon, Michael, & Michaels, 1994). In a review of the research, Simons and Carey (2001) claimed that estimates of the disorder ranged from 4 to 31% and as high as 77%, depending on the setting (*e.g.*, sexuality clinic) in which it was reported. Masters and Johnson (1970) referred to a man as a premature ejaculator if he could delay ejaculation long enough for his partner to reach orgasm

50% of the time. Several sex therapists, however, have found this definition troublesome because most women do not achieve orgasms without clitoral stimulation (Kaplan, 1974, 1989; Polonsky, 2000; Reinisch, 1990; Zilbergeld, 1992). These therapists seem to agree that a man suffers from PE if he cannot voluntarily exert enough control over his ejaculatory reflex to enjoy a high degree of sexual arousal during intercourse. Kaplan (1974) believed this is the case, regardless of whether the male ejaculates "after two thrusts or five, whether it occurs before the female reaches orgasm or not" (p. 290). Reinisch (1990) added that the couple "shouldn't be watching a clock or counting strokes. No particular length of time is 'too quick' or 'too long' unless a couple finds it is a problem for them" (p. 206).

The DSM-IV (APA, 1994), which provides the most often used criteria for PE (Metz, Pryor, Nesvacil, Abuzzahab, & Koznar, 1997), defines the disorder as the "persistent or recurrent onset of orgasm and ejaculation with minimal sexual stimulation before, on, or shortly after penetration and before the person wishes it" (p. 509). Similar to erectile disorder, distinctions are made between lifelong and acquired type, generalized and situational type, and due to psychological or combined (*i.e.*, psychological and medical) factors. Age and the frequency of current sexual activity are also considered in the diagnosis of the disorder.

Causes

Metz *et al.* (1997) found that some of the physiological causes of PE include sexual infrequency, hypersensitivity of the glans penis, pelvic fractures, urological problems, diabetes, prostatitis, arteriosclerosis, and neurological disease. Again, the psychological causes attributed to PE depend on the theoretical and therapeutic orientation of the clinician. According to Kaplan (1974), some psychoanalysts view PE as symptomatic of unresolved Oedipal conflicts reflecting a sadistic attitude toward women; the man's objective is to quickly soil the woman and deprive her of pleasure. In her later research, however, Kaplan (1989) found that men with PE are no more or less hostile toward women than other men are.

Cognitive-behaviorists (McCabe, 2001; McCarthy, 1989; Metz & McCarthy, 2003) seek to change internalized negative cognitions and behavior associated with faulty learning or conditioning which may have reinforced shortened ejaculatory latency, negative learning and attitudes about sex, and various emotional problems such as anxiety and depression. Relationship or systemic causes include poor communication, unrealistic expectations about sexual performance, sexual performance anxiety generated by demands from a partner, power or control struggles, and the fear of intimacy (Betchen, 2001b).

Treatment

Those who examine PE from an organic perspective are most likely to look to medication for a cure (Segraves, Saran, Segraves, & Maguire, 1993; Strassberg, de Gouveia Brazao, Rowland, Tan, & Slob, 1999; Waldinger, 2003). Segraves and Balon (2003) wrote: "Treatment of premature ejaculation with pharmacological agents is feasible, practical, and well tolerated" (p. 281). Symonds *et al.* (2003) reported that, although no pharmacological agents are licensed to treat PE, "certain antidepressants (monoamine oxidase inhibitors [MAOIs], tricyclic antidepressants, selective serotonin reuptake inhibitors [SSRIs]) and other drug classes (topical anaesthesia, neuroleptics, α-blockers, β-blockers, anxiolytics, smooth muscle relaxants), as well as oral PDE5 inhibitor agents (*e.g.*, sildenafil) have been used" (p. 363).

Kaplan (1989) contended that "99% of premature ejaculation is purely psychogenic" (p. 27) and "90% of premature ejaculators can be cured within an average of 14 weeks of treatment" (p. 2). Her multimodal treatment approach is aimed at helping the PE sufferer to develop "full sexual sensory awareness" (p. 43) and, in turn, gain greater control over the ejaculatory reflex. Individual and partner exercises are utilized in this process, during which brief, psychodynamic psychotherapy sessions help to resolve deeper relationship issues.

Behavioral exercises are assigned to help the male get in touch with the sensations prior to the point of ejaculatory inevitability. While distraction is used in treating erectile disorder, focus is more important in treating PE; the objective is for the male to be able to enjoy himself, not numb himself so that he can last longer. In order to accomplish this, the male is first asked to lie on his back and stroke his penis with a dry hand while paying attention to the erotic feelings in his penis. When he feels near orgasm, but before the point of ejaculatory inevitability, he is to stop stroking and allow the erotic feelings to dissipate (but not long enough for him to lose his erection). This exercise is referred to as the stop–start technique and was developed by urologist James Semens (1956). Masters and Johnson (1970) developed a squeeze technique for the treatment of PE (squeezing the head or coronal ridge of the penis prior to the point of ejaculatory inevitability), but many sex therapists still believe this technique is too averse for some men. Men are asked to do the stop–start exercises three to five times per week.

When a male only has to stop two to three times over a fifteen-minute period, he may move on to the second exercise (stop–start using a water-based lubricant). As an adjunct exercise, I may ask each man to practice Kegel exercises (contracting the pelvic floor muscles) during the week and at the point before ejaculatory inevitability, which may result in better control. Gynecologist Arnold Kegel (1952) originally developed these exercises to help incontinent women improve their muscle tone so they could hold their urine following childbirth.

The third individual exercise is slow–fast penile stimulation. The client is asked to stroke himself until he reaches a high level of sexual excitement then slow down rather than come to a complete stop. The last individual exercise entails the male stroking himself at a high level of arousal continuously without stopping. Kaplan (1989) has the male rate his level of stimulation from 1 to 10 (1, no arousal; 10, orgasm). She advocates that the male learn to continuously stroke himself at a level between 5 and 7 for at least two consecutive minutes before moving on to partner exercises.

When the individual exercises are completed, the nonsymptomatic partner joins the process (serving as the masturbator), and the couple repeats all the exercises. When they have completed them, the nonsymptomatic partner then mounts the man and rubs his penis near her vagina; she stops rubbing just before the point of ejaculation. (Gay couples can adapt this exercise accordingly.) In the next exercise, the partner inserts the penis but only moves enough to maintain the orgasm (quiet vagina or nondemand coitus). This can be repeated with the partners lying side by side. Finally, in the last partner exercise, the man mounts his partner (male superior position) and practices speeding up and slowing down his thrusting (as opposed to stopping it altogether), which better simulates intercourse.

In my clinical experience, couples who present with PE can simultaneously be engaged in the p–d dynamic. In this situation, the therapist must help the couple fight a three-front war: treat the underlying conflicts, the p–d dynamic, and the PE symptom as well. The following case illustrates PE in the p–d dynamic. In this situation, it was the distancer who presented with the sexual symptom.

Case 2. Brad and Lea. Brad and Lea (see Figure 6.2) were in their early thirties. They had been married for six years and had two small children. Brad appeared to be articulate, laid back, and soft spoken; he was employed as a computer programmer. Lea appeared angry and aggressive; she was employed as an attorney in a large law firm. Lea was clearly the major breadwinner in the family, and Brad didn't seem to have a problem with this, at least on the surface. Brad initiated contact with me because Lea threatened to leave him unless he learned to better meet her needs both emotionally and sexually. Apparently, Lea felt alone quite a bit. She reported that Brad rarely if ever initiated anything in the marriage and failed to engage her emotionally. She also claimed that even when she asked Brad to take care of

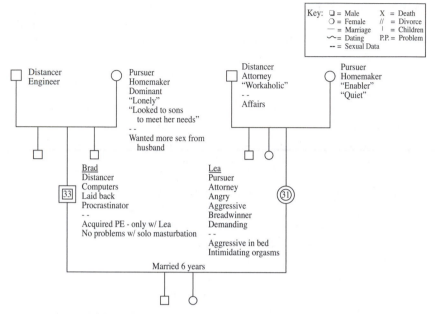

Fig. 6.2 Brad and Lea.

certain chores he either failed to do so or procrastinated. Lea was also very upset with Brad's inability to last longer during intercourse. Brad admitted that he usually lasted for a few seconds (or three or four thrusts) before ejaculating. His hypothesis was that Lea was a very passionate woman and that her behavior in bed (*e.g.*, excessive moaning and maneuvering) would trigger an early orgasm on his part. Lea thought this was an "absurd" excuse. She believed that this was simply another indication of Brad not meeting her needs. Brad believed that Lea was a very demanding woman and that very little could satisfy her. Nevertheless, he stated that he still loved his wife and did not want to lose his family. Having read about the treatment of PE on the Internet, both partners specifically requested sexual exercises in order to expedite their painful situation, but they also realized the need for marital therapy.

Brad reported that he had only one other girlfriend prior to meeting Lea and that the relationship had no sexual problems. He said that this girlfriend was inexperienced and not nearly as aggressive in bed as Lea. Brad rarely masturbated, but when he did he lasted as long as he wanted. He said that he most often fantasizes about being with Lea, but he has thoughts of other women, as well. Lea had a few lovers in the past and no chronic sexual difficulty. She was able to achieve orgasm, but according to Brad her orgasms were loud and intimidating to him.

Brad was a middle sibling of three brothers. He described his upbringing as relatively uneventful but he had little contact with his father (an engineer). His mother was the dominant force in the relationship and complained often about her husband's distance. Brad thought she was lonely and sometimes looked to her sons to meet her needs. Brad admitted that he felt somewhat sorry for his mom but that she could be a "pain in the ass." Brad said that sex was not discussed in his family of origin, but that it wasn't considered a bad thing. If anything, he got the impression that his mother would have liked more of it from her husband.

Lea was the youngest of three siblings. She reported that her father was a workaholic lawyer and that her mother was a quiet homemaker. She said that there were no problems with sex in the marriage that she knew of, but she believed that her father had at least one affair. She admitted that she used to challenge her father to try to change his behavior, but to no avail. Having had individual therapy in the past, Lea was able to refer to her mother as an "enabler." Because of the age differences between the siblings, Lea ended up spending years at home as if she were an only child. Lea denied any physical or sexual abuse in her history (as did Brad). She stated that she and Brad drank alcohol infrequently (only on a social basis).

Because Brad and Lea knew they had marital and sexual problems, I was better able to integrate working on the PE symptom and their p–d dynamic. After completing my initial evaluation (which took one session), I was able to tell them that, in my opinion, their PE symptom was related to their p–d dynamic. I immediately requested that they obtain a copy of Kaplan's (1989) PE: How To Overcome Premature Ejaculation (note that Metz and McCarthy's [2003] Coping with Premature Ejaculation is also a good source for clients), and I assigned Sensate Focus I exercises. I began with these exercises based on the facts that Brad did not have problems when he masturbated (even when he fantasized about Lea), that he had a significant amount of anxiety when he faced Lea sexually, and because Lea complained that she wanted more contact with Brad. Given their p–d dynamic, I was skeptical as to whether the couple would be successful, but I offered the assignment because, again, I thought it would prove to be a relatively benign testing ground for my hypothesis and because the couple had initially requested exercises. I tend to request that the distancer initiate exercises to encourage engagement in the relationship. It also provides a quick way to dive into the p–d dynamic because the odds are the distancer will resist; in this case, the assignment pleased Lea.

The following excerpts depict how I integrated treatment for the PE and p–d dynamic. Notice that I requested details from the couple, particularly with relation to the PE exercises. I also had to deal effectively with the resistances that the dynamic presented in order to keep the exercises moving in the right direction. Specifically, I did not push Brad too hard, but I did give him responsibility for his behavior. I also gently challenged Lea on her need for control and her own intimacy issues. Also, I gave both partners reinforcement when they stepped out of their p–d roles and moved closer to one another.

Session 2

Dr. B: How did the Sensate Focus I exercises go?

Lea: We didn't do them. Brad seemed to forget about them.

Brad: I just got kind of busy.

Lea: You're always too busy for the marriage. What's the use in coming here?

Brad: You could've reminded me about them.

Lea: It was your job to initiate … remember?

Dr. B: Lea, I think it's great that you didn't remind Brad about the exercises — it was his job.

Brad: What happens if I forget again?

Dr. B: It's your marriage — you can do what you want with it. Nobody can control you. You can help to make it great or you can help to ruin it.

Session 3

Lea: I think the Sensate exercises went well.

Dr. B: Who initiated them?

Lea: Brad did the first time and I did the second and third times.

Dr. B: Sounds productive to me. What were each of you thinking during the exercises?

Lea: Well, at first Brad was a little rough — like he was giving a massage.

Dr. B: Did you communicate this to him?

Lea: Yeah, and then he began to lighten up.

Dr. B: Brad, what about you?

Brad: I was a little nervous at first. I kept thinking I was going to do something wrong and piss Lea off.

Dr. B: Did she seem pissed off during the exercise?

Brad: Well, she did seem mad at me when I was massaging her.

Dr. B: How did that make you feel?

Brad: I was already nervous, but when she seemed angry I felt like getting out of there.

Dr. B: Did you tell her that?

Brad: No. I just changed my technique.

Dr. B: That's great. Instead of distancing you stayed with the exercise. I would, however, like you to work on telling her in the moment how you feel. Do you think that if Lea changed her approach it would help you to better meet her needs?

Brad: Yeah. I don't mind Lea telling me if I'm doing something wrong, but oftentimes she sounds like Mrs. Smith, my mean, former second-grade teacher.

Dr. B: Lea, do you have any comments?

Lea: Brad doesn't listen very well and this really irritates me. You told him it wasn't a massage, but he did it his way. He said he understood, but when it came time to doing the exercise, he did it the way he wanted to. He does this kind of thing all the time and it makes me mad.

Dr. B: The dynamic is between you and Brad, so I suspect what is agreed upon in the session will not necessarily be what happens at home for some time to come. For example, I recommended that Brad initiate the exercises but it seems you are gradually taking over this duty despite the fact that you have complained about Brad's lack of initiative. In other words, both of you will have to expect some resistance toward changing the process. Try the same exercises one more week and if all goes well we can move on.

Session 6

Dr. B: How did the stop–start exercises go?

Brad: We only had a chance to do them once, but I initiated them.

Dr. B: Good, were there any problems during the exercise?

Brad: No, I wasn't able to last very long, but I guess that will take time.

Dr. B: How long were you able to last?

Brad: About three or four thrusts?

Lea: I was stroking him very slowly.

Dr. B: So, you're expectedly still pretty sensitive, but it sounds as if the two of you did fine. Lea, did you request that Brad bring you to orgasm prior to the exercises?

Lea: No, but that was okay because I wasn't in the mood for a long drawn-out session that night.

Dr. B: May I ask why you only did the exercises once?

Lea: You'll have to ask Brad. I wanted to set aside a time to do them every night.

Brad: I didn't want to do them every night. It seemed like too much pressure.

Dr. B: Did you tell Lea that you were feeling pressured?

Brad: No, I just shut down.

Lea: Well, how am I supposed to know what you are thinking? I'm not a mind reader.

Dr. B: That's a good point, Lea, but I do have a question. If the assignment was to do the exercises three to four times per week, why did you pursue Brad to do them every night?

Lea: I'm tired of having to work so hard to get something that should come naturally in a marriage. I wanted to push things along.

Dr. B: I can understand your anxiety, but what was the outcome?

Lea: He runs from me.

Dr. B: Right. I therefore have to wonder why you would push Brad to the point that it would enable him retreat from the very thing you said that you wanted him to do in the first place — take initiative. If anything, it would guarantee that the exercises would fail.

Male Orgasmic Disorder

In contrast to PE, men who suffer from male orgasmic disorder (once referred to as retarded ejaculation) possess an involuntary inhibition of the ejaculatory reflex. That is, they cannot ejaculate when they want to. The DSM-IV (APA, 1994) defines the disorder as a "persistent or recurrent delay in, or absence of, orgasm following a normal sexual excitement phase" (p. 507). The subtypes are lifelong *versus* acquired, generalized *versus* situational, due to psychological factors, and due to combined factors (psychological and medical).

In the most common form of the disorder, the male cannot reach orgasm during intercourse, although he may be able to via manual or oral stimulation by a partner. There are some men, however, who can achieve orgasm during intercourse but only after a prolonged period of stimulation. Still others may be able to achieve orgasm only via solo masturbation. As with all of the sexual disorders, the clinician should use the client's specific circumstances to dictate where and how treatment should begin.

Kaplan (1974) considered this disorder to be somewhat rare. In support of this assertion, Masters and Johnson (1970) referred to the disorder as "ejaculatory incompetence" and reported that out of 510 couples treated only 17 suffered from this problem. Sex researchers Laumann *et al.* (1994) found that 8.3% of men reported an inability to achieve orgasm. Simons and Carey (2001) also reported that the prevalence rates of male orgasmic disorder were relatively low. In their review of the research literature on this dysfunction, the authors found that community estimates ranged from 0 to 8%.

Causes

According to Kaplan (1974), some of the physiological causes of male orgasmic disorder are lower spinal cord injuries or abdominal and pelvic surgery. Excessive alcohol and drug consumption can also be factors. As is always the case, the psychological causes vary depending on the orientation of the clinician. Kaplan reported that some psychoanalysts, for example, view the disorder as a form of impotence (*i.e.*, the male cannot complete the sexual act because on an unconscious level he feels guilty and fears castration at the hands of his father for wanting his mother). Systems or relationship therapists may look to control or power struggles (*e.g.*, the male may withhold his orgasm as an expression of hostility toward the partner). In his paper entitled, "Retarded Ejaculation: A Much Misunderstood Syndrome," Apfelbaum (2000) wrote that the disorder is a result of the male never being sufficiently aroused to reach orgasm during intercourse. He even correlated it with low sexual desire in men.

Kaplan (1974), however, described the immediate cause of the disorder as obsessive self-observation and an inability to "let go." The exercises she recommended (similar to that of Masters and Johnson [1970]) involved using masturbation to maximize stimulation while mentally distracting the male from interfering thoughts. Like *in vivo* desensitization, the goal is for the male to progressively move toward intravaginal ejaculation.

Treatment

As with all of the exercises for sexual disorders, where the clinician begins treatment depends on the client; however, the male who cannot ejaculate by himself is initially assigned solo masturbatory exercises (usually three to five times per week). Specifically, he is directed to lie on his back, relax, and think sexual thoughts while attempting to stroke himself to orgasm. The use of a water-based lubricant is recommended to increase stimulation, and in some cases the male may need to read erotic material prior to the exercises or view an erotic movie before or during the exercises. Once the male has achieved orgasm he can repeat the exercise with his partner stroking him manually or via oral sex. When he reaches a heightened state of arousal, the partner mounts him and continues to stroke him until the male is ready to orgasm. Just prior to orgasm the partner ceases stroking, lets go of the penis, and allows the male to thrust to orgasm. Kaplan (1975) referred to this latter technique as the "male bridge maneuver."

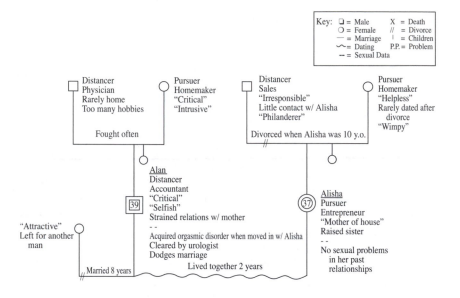

P.P. Alan suffered from acquired male orgasmic disorder.

Fig. 6.3 Alan and Alisha.

No matter the context, when one partner wants or needs something from the other, the potential for a p–d relationship to develop arises. The withheld ejaculate and the emotional satisfaction that comes with knowing that one has made his lover achieve orgasm set the table for the p–d dynamic to emerge. Whether an individual is voluntarily or involuntarily withholding, the result may be the same: a p–d struggle that may prosper for years and cause irreparable damage to the relationship.

The following case depicts a couple suffering from the p–d dynamic and male orgasmic disorder. The boyfriend is dodging his long-time, live-in girlfriend's attempts to get him to marry her, and the dynamic is metaphorically played out via the boyfriend's inability to ejaculate during intercourse. As is often the case, the couple presented the sexual problem as the main reason for attending treatment.

Case 3. Alan and Alisha. Alan and Alisha were a couple in their late thirties (see Figure 6.3). Alan was an accountant, and Alisha ran her own business. They had dated for a total of four years, and had lived together for the last two. The couple presented with Alan's inability to ejaculate during intercourse, which he had been experiencing ever since they moved in together. Alan had never had this experience in prior relationships, and he had the ability to orgasm via solo masturbation as well as when Alisha manually or orally stimulated him. It was only during intercourse and for the last two years that he had suffered from this problem. Alan was evaluated by a urologist who told him that his problem was psychological and that he should consult a sex therapist. Alan admitted that he had absolutely no control over his sexual situation, and that he was baffled by it. Alisha admitted that she was hurt by Alan's inability to achieve orgasm during intercourse. She was an attractive woman who felt that she had done everything she could have to stimulate Alan, but to no avail.

While some p–d dynamics were evident during the first few sessions, they only seemed to pertain to the sexual problem, but Alan did not present as a hard sell — he seemed to be just as disturbed by his symptom as was Alisha and was perfectly willing to seek the appropriate treatment. The p–d dynamic really became evident when it was revealed that Alisha was heavily pursuing Alan to marry her. While Alan said that he was probably going to eventually marry Alisha, he stated that he was afraid of making the commitment at this point in time. Interestingly, neither partner made the link between the p–d dynamic regarding the issue of marriage and the orgasmic disorder.

Alan was the oldest of two siblings (he had a younger sister). He reported that his parents fought quite a bit, mostly over his father's many hobbies and civic involvements. Apparently, his mother felt that her husband was not around the family much. Alan reported that he had a good relationship with his father (a physician), but that his relationship with his mother (homemaker) was strained. He said that he loved her and always would, but that she was "critical and intrusive." He gave many examples of showing his mother something he had just accomplished only to have her question whether it could have been done better.

Alan reported that the topic of sex was not taboo in his family of origin but that it wasn't necessarily discussed openly. He lost his virginity in college to his ex-wife and reported that their sex life was exciting. He said that he found his ex-wife to be very attractive and was devastated when she eventually left him (after eight years of marriage) for another man. He said that his ex-wife accused him of being "critical and selfish" — characteristics he admitted that he probably inherited from his mother. He said that he tried to convince his former wife to return to him but she refused.

Alan did not do any serious dating for a couple of years following his separation and divorce. He said that he was scared of being vulnerable to a woman and questioned his ability to sustain a healthy relationship. He did, on occasion, have sex with women he met at clubs, but he made sure not to become emotionally involved with them. Things changed when Alan was introduced to Alisha by a relative. They felt an almost instant attraction, and both admitted that they had sex on the first night they met. From that point forward, the couple was inseparable and their sex life was "great." Alan reported that they often had "marathon sex" (*i.e.*, sexual sessions that lasted for a long time) and that Alisha was willing to try anything. After two years of dating, however, Alisha began pressing Alan to marry her. When he compromised and agreed to move in with her he began experiencing inhibited orgasm.

Alisha was the older of two sisters. Her parents had divorced when she was a young girl (ten years old), and she and her sister lived with her mother. Alisha saw her mother as "wimpy" and somewhat helpless. She claimed that she, not her mother, was the "mother of the house" and that she had a great deal to do with raising her sister. She also claimed that she started her own business as soon as she could so she could support herself and her family independent of her father. Alisha described her father as a "philanderer." She also saw him as somewhat "irresponsible" in that her mother had to pursue him for child support over the years. Alisha saw her father infrequently; he was a traveling salesman who eventually moved to a distant state. It is interesting to note that Alisha did not seem to have negative feelings for her father and at the time of treatment she was in frequent contact with him. He continued to disappoint her in many ways, but she seemed to accept his flaws for the sake of maintaining contact with him. She was still close to her mother.

Alisha reported that her early sex life was uneventful. She denied any abuse, and she "was spared a stepfather" because her mother never remarried and rarely dated after her divorce. Alisha focused most of her time on her business (children's clothes), so her sex life suffered in the process. She did have boyfriends but no relationship that ever lasted too long. She reported that she never experienced any sexual difficulty in these relationships. Alisha prided herself on being attractive and was also confused by Alan's relatively new symptom. She admitted that she was hurt and depressed by Alan's symptom until she discovered (in therapy) that it had little to do with his level of attraction or lack of love.

The following excerpt describes how I discovered the link between the inhibited orgasm problem and the p–d dynamic. Up until this point the exercises had not been effective. This session represented the turning point in the treatment, and the couple was subsequently able to complete the exercises for male orgasmic disorder, thus alleviating the symptom.

Dr. B: What were you thinking about when you were having sex with Alisha the other night?

Alan: I was worried about being able to finish the act.

Dr. B: So, you were concerned that you wouldn't be able to reach orgasm?

Alan: Yeah, and it happened again. I just couldn't let go.

Dr. B: It has been very difficult for you to distract and stimulate yourself so that you can reach orgasm?

Alan: Yeah, I don't know what's going on, and Alisha's getting more and more annoyed with me.

Dr. B: Are you annoyed with her?

Alan: For what?

Dr. B: I don't know … you tell me.

Alan: I don't think so.

Dr. B: Are you feeling pressure?

Alan: I can understand her position.

Dr. B: Is that a yes?

Alan: Yeah, but I feel more pressure to marry than to ejaculate.

Dr. B: Maybe they're connected.

Alan: What do you mean?

Dr. B: Maybe you're holding back your ejaculate the way you are holding back marriage. I'm not suggesting that you marry. I'm simply pointing out a possible link between Alisha's pursuit and your withholding.

Alan: If you're right, it would be unconscious on my part. I mean, I am very nervous about marriage, but I'm not sure if or how it might have something to do with my sexual problem.

Dr. B: That's okay; I wouldn't expect you to at this point, but you do feel the pursuit, don't you?

Alan: Oh, yeah.

Dr. B: Why are you so nervous about marriage?

Alan: I don't think I've ever gotten over my ex cheating on me. I was devastated. I tried so hard to get her back. What's even more humiliating is that she ran off with a guy who makes about a third of the money I make.

Dr. B: You did admit that you mistreated her emotionally.

Alan: Yeah. I was a jerk.

Dr. B: Well, maybe you've learned a lesson.

Alan: I hope so.

Dr. B: You don't sound so confident. Are you afraid you will mistreat Alisha and she will strike back?

Alan: I don't know. I'm just afraid she will leave me, and I don't want to go through that again. I needed medication and I almost ruined my career.

Dr. B: If you could control the relationship, how would you want it?

Alan: I would like to marry Alisha, but given my fear I would just like to keep her as a lover until I gain more confidence.

Dr. B: Well, maybe that's what your penis is helping you to do. Maybe it's helping you form a compromise with your conflict. That is, you're able to get an erection and have intercourse, but not let go and culminate your relationship. To finish the act might represent closing out the informal part of the relationship and beginning the real serious stuff. You know ... the stuff that has the potential to hurt you.

Alan: Are you saying that I can't let go because I'm afraid of changing my relationship with Alisha?

Dr. B: I suspect so. It is as if your penis is helping you to distance from Alisha.

CHAPTER 7

Female Sexual Disorders and the Pursuer–Distancer Dynamic

Female Orgasmic Disorder

The DSM-IV (APA, 1994) defines female orgasmic disorder as a "persistent or recurrent delay in, or absence of, orgasm following a normal sexual excitement phase" (p. 505). The major subtypes are lifelong *versus* acquired types, generalized *versus* situational types, and due to psychological factors or combined factors (*i.e.*, psychological and medical problems). While most orgasmic disorders in females are lifelong, some women present with having achieved orgasm in the past but not with their current partners; others are only able to achieve orgasm via solo masturbation. I have encountered a few women who have reported a problem because they were only able to climax via clitoral stimulation. Most contemporary sex therapists believe this view to be the result of Freud's (1905/1953) clitoral/transfer theory in which he contended that a woman who could not achieve coital orgasm was immature and neurotic. While I will treat this issue if the client desires, I do not necessarily view this as a sexual problem.

According to Reinisch (1990), approximately 10% of all women have never had an orgasm by any means, and between 50 and 75% of all women cannot achieve an orgasm by just thrusting. Laumann *et al.* (1994) reported that 24.1% of all women in the United States suffered from female orgasmic disorder. The authors found the disorder to be the second most commonly reported sexual disorder among women (second to low sexual desire). Simons and Carey (2001) reported general community estimates of the disorder range from 4 to 24%.

Causes

Kaplan (1974) found that some of the physiological causes of female orgasmic disorder include neurological disorders affecting the spinal cord; advanced diabetes, which can result in severe neuropathy of the sensory nerves of the clitoris; liver disease; and endocrine disorders. Various medications can also have a deleterious effect, such as selective serotonin reuptake inhibitors (SSRIs) (Plaut, Graziottin, & Heaton, 2004). Apparently, poor muscle tone can inhibit female orgasm. Given this, Kegel (1952) exercises may be used to help bring on or enhance orgasm in women (see "Treatment" section, below). The psychological causes of this disorder vary. Kaplan (1974) reported that some psychoanalysts look to Oedipal conflicts to explain the problem. For example, a little girl's guilt over wanting her father and fear of reprisal from her powerful mother may manifest in the inhibition of pleasure during adult sex. She may also exhibit symptoms because of unresolved penis envy or the inability to cope with having been deprived a penis.

Other causes mentioned by Kaplan (1974) include traumas, such as incest or rape, and cognitive distortions (*e.g.*, "If I have an orgasm it will injure me"). Ellison (2003) attributed the problem to a focus on performance rather than pleasure and inadequate arousal or erotic stimulation. In a recent study, Kelly *et al.* (2004) found poor communication between partners to be correlated with the disorder. Specifically, the authors found that partners experienced a great deal of discomfort discussing sexual activity involving direct stimulation of the clitoris. Plaut *et al.* (2004) mentioned relationship problems and "too brief or absent foreplay" as factors (p. 58).

Kaplan (1974) reported that the immediate cause of female orgasmic disorder is an involuntary inhibition of the orgastic reflex. Simply put, some women fear "letting go." While maintaining control over their sexual feelings reduces anxiety, this control soon becomes reflexive and, paradoxically, out of their control.

Treatment

The objective in treating female orgasmic disorder is to maximize stimulation and minimize inhibition. If a woman has never achieved an orgasm in her lifetime, I will immediately assign readings to help her feel more comfortable with her body. Barbach's (2000) *For Yourself*, Heiman and LoPiccolo's (1988) *Becoming Orgasmic*, and Dodson's (1996) *Sex for One* serve this purpose. I then begin by assigning individual masturbation exercises. The woman is instructed first to relax and focus on her feelings while digitally stimulating her clitoris. If she is not becoming aroused it may be suggested that she fantasize about something that excites her. She may wish to read erotic material prior to the exercise or view an erotic movie before or during the exercise. If the woman is still experiencing difficulty after a week or two, it may be recommended that she utilize a vibrator as an aid to stimulate herself. The vibrator should, however, be a last resort, given the danger that the woman can become dependent on it. It might also help some women to integrate the simulation of an orgasm into their exercises. For example, a woman can be instructed to moan loudly or thrust her hips when she feels she is getting close to achieving an orgasm.

After a woman can masturbate herself to orgasm, a desensitization process via a series of home exercises is undertaken by the couple to treat the disorder. First, I may ask the woman to begin masturbating while her partner is in the room. When this is accomplished, the partner is then to stimulate the woman's clitoris with his finger. The woman can guide the partner's hand in order to help reduce anxiety. During these exercises, the woman is required to relax, go with the feelings, and fantasize about something erotic. In the next series of sessions, the couple is instructed to engage in foreplay and, when the woman is aroused, the partner should penetrate her and thrust slowly while the woman masturbates herself (lesbian couples can adapt accordingly). In the last set of exercises, the partner penetrates the woman and masturbates her simultaneously until she reaches orgasm. If the woman requests a coital orgasm, the partner is instructed to stop masturbating during intercourse just prior to orgasm and to allow the woman to increase her thrusting to climax. This technique serves as a bridge between clitoral stimulation and coitus.

It should be reiterated here that the therapist can be creative in the assignment of sex therapy exercises. Moreover, the therapist should begin where the client is, rather than blindly following a series of exercises put forth in instructional manuals or books. For example, if a woman is easily able to achieve orgasm via individual digital stimulation, I may start her immediately on couple exercises if I think she is able to tolerate them.

In my experience, female orgasmic disorder can provide a context for the p–d dynamic. While this can apply to lesbian relationships, it seems to be particularly applicable to heterosexual relationships. Many men, for example, seem to take it as a personal affront to their manhood if they cannot bring a woman to orgasm; they will therefore pursue to achieve this end. In most of the heterosexual cases I've encountered, it is the female symptom bearer who plays the role of the distancer while her counterpart plays the role of the pursuer. The following case example typifies this.

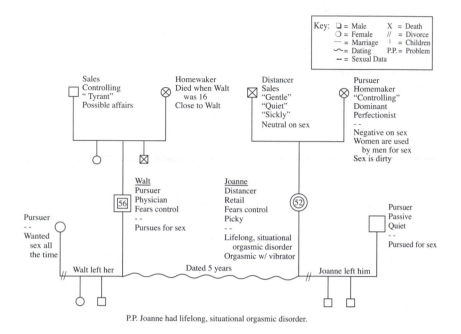

Key: □ = Male   X = Death
     ○ = Female   // = Divorce
     — = Marriage | = Children
     ～ = Dating   P.P. = Problem
     -- = Sexual Data

Sales
Controlling
"Tyrant"
Possible affairs

Homewaker
Died when Walt
was 16
Close to Walt

Distancer
Sales
"Gentle"
"Quiet"
"Sickly"
Neutral on sex

Pursuer
Homemaker
"Controlling"
Dominant
Perfectionist
--
Negative on sex
Women are used
    by men for sex
Sex is dirty

Walt
Pursuer
Physician
Fears control
--
Pursues for sex
[56]

Joanne
Distancer
Retail
Fears control
Picky
--
Lifelong, situational
    orgasmic disorder
Orgasmic w/ vibrator
(52)

Pursuer
Passive
Quiet
--
Pursued for sex

Pursuer
--
Wanted
sex all
the time

Walt left her

Dated 5 years

Joanne left him

P.P. Joanne had lifelong, situational orgasmic disorder.

Fig. 7.1 Walt and Joanne.

Case 4. Walt and Joanne. Walt and Joanne were a couple in their fifties (see Figure 7.1) who had been dating for approximately five years. Each had been married once and both had grown children. Walt was a physician, and Joanne owned her own retail clothing store but was independently wealthy thanks to a large inheritance from her deceased parents. When they presented for treatment, the partners had their own apartments. Walt initiated the treatment because he was upset that Joanne refused to move in with or to marry him. He also claimed that he would like to have sex more frequently (they were averaging sex once a month; Walt would like it at least twice a week) and for Joanne to achieve orgasm. Joanne would like Walt to stop hounding her to be closer. She likes having her own place and refers to it as her "safe haven." She does, however, want to achieve orgasm with Walt. Joanne reported that she cannot achieve orgasm via manual or oral sex with Walt or during intercourse. Furthermore, she has never reached orgasm with a man but is easily able to do so via solo masturbation with a vibrator.

Joanne, an only child, claimed that her mother was extremely controlling of her in nearly all aspects of her life. In contrast, Joanne's father was a very passive man who was sickly most of Joanne's life. According to

Joanne, he originally did not want children but acquiesced for fear of losing his wife. Joanne claimed that she loved her father because he was a "quiet, gentle man" who eventually learned to unconditionally accept her. She resented her mother's dominance and critical perfectionism.

Joanne reported that her mother always gave her negative messages about sex. She considered it potentially dirty and was concerned that Joanne would get pregnant or catch some venereal disease. She also believed that men tended to use women for sex and she constantly warned Joanne of this. Joanne claimed that her father was neutral on the subject. Joanne reported that she lost her virginity at age sixteen despite her mother's attitudes toward sex, and in fact dated several men over the years and had sexual relations with some of them. Joanne said that she would enjoy making love but when she came close to orgasm she would "shut down," or dissociate. As mentioned, she claimed that she has used a vibrator for years and could achieve orgasm as long as a man was not in the room with her.

Joanne grew up resenting control and missing a stronger, more engaged father figure in her life. Treatment determined that distancing allowed her to control her relationships. Specifically, it enabled her to protect herself from the pain associated with her disengaged father and her overbearing mother. Her conflict with Walt was evidence of this. Walt was an engaged man who appealed to Joanne because he made her feel wanted and desired; however, she needed to keep his advances at a distance for fear of being controlled by him.

Walt was a middle child of three. He described his father as a tyrant who gave him few alternatives in life and who was generally insensitive to his wife's needs. Walt's mother died a slow debilitating death from diabetes when Walt was sixteen years old. He claimed that he loved her very much and still misses her today. Walt reported that sex was not discussed in his family of origin but that he believed that his parents were sexually active up until his mother became very ill. He lost his virginity late in life (late twenties) but said that he made up for it by relentlessly pursuing women to sleep with him. His sex life with his ex-wife was significant in that it was she who pursued him for sex constantly. He said that she seemed to want to have it at least twice a day. He distanced from her, however, claiming that her pursuit seemed like control to him. Marrying a female distancer such as Joanne enabled Walt to pursue a woman to replace his mother yet not get close enough to her to risk once again experiencing loss or being controlled (like he was by Dad).

The partners' individual conflicts and their p–d dynamic were addressed in treatment, and exercises for Joanne's orgasmic disorder were integrated, as well. The following excerpts from sessions with Walt and Joanne reflect this approach. At the end of the first session, it was determined that Joanne had used a vibrator for so long that it would be fruitless to try to achieve the couple's goals without one; I believed that Walt alone could not match the level of stimulation she now needed to ultimately reach orgasm. The couple also agreed that they would be very satisfied if Joanne could reach orgasm with her vibrator while Walt was thrusting inside her. At the end of the first session, Joanne was instructed to go home, lie on her bed, and use her vibrator while relaxing and focusing exclusively on her feelings. Walt was to be sitting in a chair in her bedroom (Joanne felt more secure doing the exercises in her bedroom).

Session 2

Dr. B: How did the exercises go Joanne?

Joanne: Not too bad. At first I was aware that Walt was in the room, so I couldn't focus. I felt like an exhibitionist. So I asked him to face away from me and eventually it was as if he wasn't there. I then had an orgasm.

Dr. B: So, you felt inhibited with Walt watching? Can you pinpoint why?

Joanne: I'm not sure, but I feel pressure when he is involved. It's as if he's my teacher or boss and I have to get it right or else.

Dr. B: Or else what?

Joanne: Or else he'll be angry with me or he'll be all over me.

Dr. B: Will you be all over her, Walt?

Walt: Well, I think it's abnormal that a woman can't have an orgasm, and I think Joanne has a tendency to procrastinate.

Dr. B: Are you admitting that you do pressure her?

Walt: Yes. If I don't, I'm afraid she will have a sex life with herself and leave me out of it.

Joanne: I wouldn't do that, but I do like to be with myself. I think you bug me too much, especially when it comes to sex.

Dr. B: What could Walt do to help you progress through the exercises?

Joanne: If he agreed not to say anything during the exercises, then I think I might be able to do them while he is looking.

Walt: I agree to that.

Dr. B: Okay, then. Try the same exercise with Walt watching.

Joanne: I'd also like Walt not to harass me for sex during the week.

Walt: I haven't since we started the exercises.

Joanne: Oh, Walt! You nudge up against me almost every morning with your erection. That's your way of putting pressure on me to have sex every day. It makes me want to be with my vibrator.

Walt: [*chuckles*]

Walt kept his word, and despite intermittent resistance after a few months the couple progressed through the exercises. Joanne was able to achieve orgasm via her vibrator with Walt lying on the bed next to her; this turned out to be very uplifting to both partners. She was then able to achieve an orgasm while holding the vibrator with Walt's hand on top of hers. Next, Joanne was able to allow Walt to hold the vibrator and masturbate her; when she began to approach orgasm, she took the vibrator from his hands and finished the job. At some point, Joanne was asked to let Walt hold the vibrator while she attempted to achieve orgasm, but just prior to reaching this objective she grabbed the vibrator from his hands; she was obviously not ready for this transition. Joanne actually found it less anxiety provoking to masturbate herself with the vibrator while Walt was inside her.

The couple's sex life improved, as did their relationship, but just as the couple began to discuss the possibility of pooling their resources and moving in together Walt acted out and caused a regression in the couple's sexual activity. Their p–d dynamic flared up worse than ever. This is typically the way resistance will reveal itself in a p–d couple who presents with sexual problems. Because the sexual symptom ultimately represents a problem with intimacy, as the couple nears elimination of the symptom the defensive dynamics (in this case the p–d dynamic) or the symptom (in this case, the orgasm disorder) might flare up to prevent this closeness from occurring. The following excerpt exhibits how I confronted the couple on their sabotaging behavior and the connection of it to their problem with intimacy.

Session 24

Walt: Well, we've regressed. We didn't do the exercises this week, and Joanne threatened to break up with me.

Dr. B: Really?

Joanne: Tell him what you did, Walt.

Walt: What do you mean?

Joanne: He was pressuring me all week to have sex with him. Then he made several negative remarks about our personal life in front of another couple.

Walt: I didn't say anything about our sex life.

Joanne: No, but you criticized me because of my refusal to marry you. Do you think that approach is going to make me want to marry you? After that evening, I didn't want to do anymore exercises. I just wanted to forget about everything and tell you to find someone else to pressure.

Dr. B: Weren't the two of you discussing the possibility of moving in together?

Joanne: We were.

Dr. B: That's interesting, Walt. It seems that things were going your way and you stepped on a land mine.

Walt: I think she overreacted.

Dr. B: Well, you have to know her by now, so I suspect that on a deeper level you must have known you were taking a risk.

Walt: I didn't think she would get so bent out of shape about what I said.

Dr. B: Walt, I think you know Joanne better than I do, but even I could have predicted Joanne's reaction. There must be a side of you that truly doesn't want Joanne to get closer to you — to have sex and to live with you. I suspect you're conflicted.

Walt: I don't feel conflicted.

Dr. B: When you think of moving in with Joanne, what gets conjured up?

Walt: I want it to happen.

Dr. B: Yes, but do you have any concerns?

Walt: I am afraid she will try to control me. She has a tendency to control how I express myself, and this incident is a good example of it.

Dr. B: So, getting close might be dangerous.

Walt: Yes.

Dr. B: Well, then, perhaps stepping on a land mine every now and then buys you a little insurance against her control; however, following this type of behavior Joanne distances and you then start to pursue her again.

Joanne: If that's what he's doing it will work every time with me.

Dr. B: I agree, but that's a problem as well. I suspect you are, in fact, quick to jump on Walt and to distance. How were you feeling about the way things were going prior to this incident?

Joanne: I must admit that I'm always a little concerned about moving in with Walt and giving him any kind of power over me because he can hurt me so easily.

After processing the setback over a period of time, the couple eventually recovered and was able to complete the next exercise, which required Joanne to allow Walt to penetrate her and bring her to orgasm while holding the vibrator. The couple decided not to work on a bridge maneuver, which would have entailed Walt stopping the vibrator just prior to Joanne's orgasm and allowing Joanne to thrust to orgasm naturally. It should be noted that these exercises would not have been as successful if they had not been integrated with treatment of the p–d dynamic. Alleviation of the dynamic clearly coincided with the progress of the exercises. The couple did move in together and, in fact, married a short time thereafter.

Vaginismus (Pelvic Floor Muscle Pain)

The DSM-IV (APA, 1994) defines vaginismus (also known as pelvic floor muscle pain) as "recurrent or persistent involuntary contraction of the perineal muscles surrounding the outer third of the vagina when vaginal penetration with penis, finger, tampon, or speculum is attempted" (p. 513). The subtypes are lifelong *versus* acquired, generalized *versus* situational, and due to psychological or combined factors (*i.e.*, psychological and medical problems). Women with lifelong vaginismus have always suffered from the problem, while those with the acquired form have usually developed it as a result of a sexual trauma or medical condition. Women who experience the generalized type, or what some sex therapists refer to as primary vaginismus, cannot tolerate any form of penetration, while situational vaginismus refers to women who can tolerate certain types of penetration (*e.g.*, tampon). According to Leiblum (2000), women who reported with primary vaginismus described the pain or sensations to be "ripping, tearing, burning, or stinging" (pp. 182–183).

The point of anxiety, or when the woman begins to experience the tightening of her vaginal muscles, varies. For example, some women feel relatively relaxed during sexual foreplay but begin to tighten up when they perceive intercourse to be imminent. Others, however, may experience profound anticipatory anxiety after the first kiss. Nevertheless, given the powerful reaction to penetration, it is not uncommon for untreated vaginismus to last many years. It is in fact, a leading cause of unconsummated marriages (Kabakçi & Batur, 2003; Plaut, Graziottin, & Heaton, 2004). Some therapists find it ironic that women who suffer from vaginismus may be able to experience high sexual arousal as well as achieve orgasms via manual or oral stimulation.

In a review of a decade of research regarding the prevalence of sexual dysfunctions, Simons and Carey (2001) found that no clear, general estimate of vaginismus emerged. The authors did, however, cite studies that reported incidences that ranged from 0 to 30%, depending on the setting. Leiblum (2000) agreed that, while the incidence of vaginismus varies widely, it probably occurs with greater frequency than is reported. My clinical experience supports this notion in that I have encountered women who have hidden the disorder either by avoiding gynecological examinations or by successfully completing their examinations but not telling their gynecologists that they were having difficulty with intercourse. Most women who do seek treatment tend to do so because they are on the verge of divorce or because they wish to have children.

Causes

According to Plaut *et al.* (2004), healthy and pleasurable vaginal receptiveness usually includes the following physical components:

> ... anatomical and functional integrity of many tissue components, both in resting and aroused states. Normal trophism, both muscosal and curtaneous, adequate hormonal impregnation, lack of inflammation, particularly at the introitus, normal tonicity of the perivaginal muscles, vascular, connective and neurological integrity and normal immune response. (p. 61)

The disorder should be distinguished from dyspareunia (*i.e.*, genital pain associated with sexual intercourse); however, some researchers (Reissing, Binik, & Khalifé, 1999) have called for it to also be categorized as "either an aversion/phobia of vaginal penetration or a genital pain disorder" (p. 261). The psychological causes of vaginismus vary. According to Kaplan (1974), some psychoanalysts view it as an act of rage against men (and a wish to castrate them) associated with unresolved penis envy: "The symptom is explained as the physical expression of the woman's unconscious wish to frustrate the man's sexual desires, or, more specifically, of her wish to 'castrate' him in revenge for her own 'castration'" (p. 415). Cognitive-behaviorists (Kabakçi & Batur, 2003) recommend challenging the irrational cognitive aspects of the fearful reactions to penetration (*e.g.*, "Penetration is dirty and will cause me great physical harm") that may lead to the problem. Traumatic experiences such as rape or incest can also be culprits (Reissing, Binik, Khalifé, Cohen, & Amsel, 2003). And, from a systemic perspective, hostility toward the partner or power or control dynamics can be responsible.

Treatment

Kaplan (1974) believed that "vaginismus occurs when a negative contingency becomes associated with the act or fantasy of vaginal penetration" (p. 417). Her model of treatment called for extinction of the negative response by introducing dilators of gradually increasing size into the vagina until a dilator the size of an erect penis is able to be inserted comfortably. After the client has undergone a complete medical examination by a gynecologist, she is instructed to lubricate the smallest dilator (using a water-based lubricant such as K-Y Jelly® or Astroglide®) and insert it (with a slight twist) while exhaling and relaxing her muscles as best she can. Whenever this dilator feels comfortable, she can move on to the next one. When she has made her way through the pack of dilators, she should be ready for her partner's penis. Generally, there are four dilators per package, but it may take anywhere from a few weeks to several months for the woman to work through them. The more relaxed she is with sex in general, the more quickly the process moves and the better the prognosis. In some cases, anti-anxiety medication and relaxation tapes may help to smooth the treatment process. I may also recommend that the couple read about the disorder. The book *Sex Matters for Women* (Foley, Kope, & Segrue, 2002) is a good source to consult.

Sex therapists tend to report great success in treating vaginismus (Kaplan, 1974; Masters & Johnson, 1970). In tune with Leiblum (1995, 2000), however, it has been my experience that many women successfully negotiate the dilators but fail to achieve coitus. While this can be attributed in part to the individual's sexual history, the relational dynamics between the two partners may be a major factor. The p–d dynamic, for example, can provide a very fruitful context for vaginismus. In most cases, I have found that the male relentlessly pursues the female to have intercourse, while the female distances. The pursuit may be in the form of chronic complaining or ridiculing but can also take the form of physical harassment in which the male insists on attempting penetration despite the pain that may ensue. If the female attempts intercourse prematurely and is unable to perform, the p–d dynamic might then be reinforced. As evidence of the power and importance of the p–d dynamic in a couple's relationship, the male may insist on pursuing for intercourse even after professionals have diagnosed the problem and warned of the dangers of "forced intercourse." Of course, this plays right into the hands of the male pursuer, who, because of his unconscious conflict regarding intimacy and closeness, wishes to maintain the p–d dynamic.

The following case illustrates vaginismus within the p–d dynamic and depicts how the male can unconsciously sabotage treatment progress all the while insisting that he desperately wants intercourse. The case is typical in that the woman has procrastinated in seeking treatment for years (even having hidden her problem from her gynecologist) and has finally decided to get help because her husband has seriously threatened divorce and because both partners want to have children.

Case 5. Dan and Julie. Dan and Julie were a couple in their late thirties (see Figure 7.2) who had been married for approximately twelve years; they dated for four years prior to marriage. Dan was employed as a financial

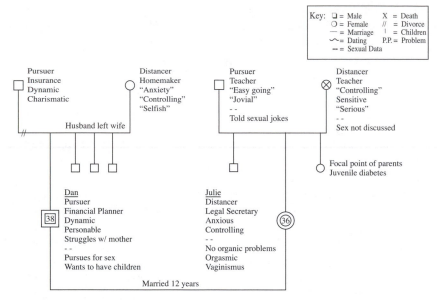

Key:
☐ = Male   X = Death
○ = Female   // = Divorce
— = Marriage | = Children
⌣ = Dating   P.P. = Problem
-- = Sexual Data

Pursuer
Insurance
Dynamic
Charismatic

Distancer
Homemaker
"Anxiety"
"Controlling"
"Selfish"

Pursuer
Teacher
"Easy going"
"Jovial"
--
Told sexual jokes

Distancer
Teacher
"Controlling"
Sensitive
"Serious"
--
Sex not discussed

Husband left wife

Focal point of parents
Juvenile diabetes

Dan
Pursuer
Financial Planner
38
Dynamic
Personable
Struggles w/ mother
--
Pursues for sex
Wants to have children

Julie
Distancer
Legal Secretary
Anxious
36
Controlling
--
No organic problems
Orgasmic
Vaginismus

Married 12 years

P.P. Julie suffered from lifelong vaginismus.

Fig. 7.2 Dan and Julie.

planner, and Julie was a legal secretary. The couple had no children. Dan claimed that he had been trying to get Julie to seek treatment for several years because she has never been able to have intercourse. Although the couple participated in other sexual acts and Julie was orgasmic via digital clitoral stimulation, she remained a virgin and the marriage was unconsummated. According to both parties, she was "too tight to penetrate." Any attempt at forced penetration was "painful." While Julie had been able to tolerate gynecological examinations over the years, she had failed to inform her gynecologist that she had a problem with intercourse. Following my evaluation of the couple, however, I spoke to her gynecologist and we both agreed on a diagnosis of vaginismus. He ordered dilators for her therapeutic process with me. At the point they entered treatment, Julie was unwilling to attempt intercourse, and Dan was threatening divorce. He said that he not only missed sex (he was not a virgin when he and Julie met) but also desperately wanted children. He was not interested in adopting a child.

Julie was the middle child of three siblings. She described her father as "jovial" and "easygoing" and her mother as more "serious and controlling." She said that her mother was particularly sensitive to criticism and was hard to talk to in general. While Julie kept a relatively low profile in her family, her biggest complaint was the attention lavished on her younger sister. Apparently, this sister has juvenile diabetes and her parents made fighting the disease a lifelong obsession. According to Julie, the parents not only became actively involved in the treatment of their child (as would be expected) but also joined and formed organizations to raise money for the research and treatment of it. Julie stated that at times her parents acted as if they did not have any other children. Julie reported that she had an active dating life, as well as a couple of long-term relationships. She claimed that she attempted intercourse on a few occasions but was impenetrable. Julie believed that her inability to consummate some of her relationships caused her to lose a boyfriend or two. She denied any sexual abuse in her history. Her mother never discussed sex, and her father told sexual jokes once in a while. She believed that her mother rarely had sex with her father.

Dan was the oldest of four brothers. He was the most competent and conservative of the group and he had long tried to keep his brothers on the right path, so to speak. He was a handsome, dynamic man to whom people seemed to be attracted. Both he and Julie agreed that Dan's father had a similar personality. Dan's parents divorced when he was in college, and although he had a relationship with both he claimed that he had always been much closer to his father. He contended that his mother was very "controlling" and for the most part would only do something if she wanted to, no matter what the task. He reported long-standing struggles with his mother to attend family events, to visit, and to do other things "that one would expect a mother to do." Dan was unclear as to whether his mother was "selfish, anxiety-ridden, or both." He was, however, certain that her reluctant behavior caused his father to eventually leave her for another woman. Dan said that his father saw his wife as holding him back in life. Dan reported a normal sexual history. He had dated several women and had had successful and pleasurable sex with a couple of past girlfriends. He reported that he had no sexual disorders and denied ever experiencing any sexual abuse. He claimed to be totally perplexed by his wife's problem but did not personalize it.

My evaluation revealed that Dan married Julie, in part, to engage in a struggle to pursue what he wanted — a good sex life and children. He had a history of fruitless pursuits, not only with his wife but also with his mother and at his long-term place of employment. He had also witnessed his father pursue his wife over the years until he finally gave up and found someone else. Julie validated this hypothesis and said that, despite Dan's talent, he seems to have "bad luck." She said that at times she felt sorry for him.

While Julie admitted that Dan's pursuit caused her to distance sexually and otherwise, she did receive attention as a result of it — something that she sorely missed as a child. In doing the exercises, she insisted on having Dan lubricate and insert the dilators. She didn't have a particular problem doing it herself; she simply preferred that he be closely involved from the beginning. This could have been a way to continue to get his undivided attention during the treatment process.

The following vignette demonstrates Dan's conflict with closeness. Although the exercises were going well, he increased his pursuit by losing his temper with Julie on several occasions. This behavior, in turn, enabled her to regress in the treatment process. Julie had been in complete control of the exercise process; it was she who determined when the couple would move on to the next dilator and at what pace. She was reluctant to take any medication for the disorder (although she did use a relaxation tape), and every time she did an exercise she prepped herself by starting with the smaller dilators before working herself up to the largest one she could tolerate at the time. This technique in of itself did not necessarily slow the process down, but it did indicate the level of her anxiety and her need for control. She spent several weeks on every dilator but progressed steadily when Dan was supportive. Dan was not an introspective fellow so the psychodynamics were not of much use to him; however, he was ultimately able to work with his wife to conquer the problem primarily using the behavioral dilator method.

> **Dr. B:** How are you two doing with the exercises? The last time we met you were on the third dilator.
>
> **Julie:** Well, I've got good news and bad news. The good news is that I've finally been able to finish up with the third dilator. The bad news is Dan refused to help me with the fourth dilator.
>
> **Dr. B:** Tell me more.
>
> **Julie:** Dan freaked out on me again and decided not to help me with the fourth dilator, so I didn't do the exercises this past week. I'm confused. I don't understand why he is flipping out on me when it is clear I'm trying. I realize it's a slow process, but I've been doing well. This makes me feel like giving up.
>
> **Dr. B:** What's up, Dan?
>
> **Dan:** I just think this is taking forever. I'm turning 40 years old soon and I want to have children. I'm sick of this.
>
> **Julie:** I understand your frustration; I'm frustrated too, but we're closer than we've ever been to having sex. Why are you on my case now?
>
> **Dan:** I'm just very upset.

Julie: This is too weird. You seem angrier with me than you did before I started treatment.

Dan: I guess I started thinking of all the lost time. I've been trying to get you to do something about this for years and now that you are the anger is coming out. I've even been thinking about divorce.

Dr. B: Julie is raising an interesting point. It seems to me that you are about to get what it is you have been saying you want, and yet you are becoming more upset. I know your history. Did you ever get what you wanted from your mother?

Dan: No, but what does that have to do with me and Julie?

Dr. B: I'm beginning to suspect that you are a man who for some reason has difficulty getting what he wants in life.

Julie: That's interesting. Tell the doctor about your work problems.

Dr. B: What about them?

Dan: They're not related.

Julie: Dan has been trying to get a certain promotion for years and they keep giving it to less qualified people.

Dan: That's true, but it's not been my fault.

Dr. B: No, but have you looked for a different job? And have you ever confronted your mother on her stubbornness? You seem to keep trying to change something to no avail. Perhaps you don't give up and move on because the object is to stay in the process of pursuing without getting what you want.

Dan: Are you trying to tell me to leave Julie?

Dr. B: No. I'm simply pointing out that you certainly have grounds for giving up on your mother, leaving Julie, and looking for a different job, but I believe that because you come from a family of origin that is riddled with the p–d dynamic it prevails over your ability to get what you want. Instead, you remain in conflict. For example, now that you are on the verge of intercourse with your wife, you are thinking about bailing out. If the dynamic is eliminated, you will be in grave danger of being close to your wife and getting what it is that you have always wanted — a sense of power, competence, and knowing that someone cares enough about you to give you what you want. This may be too much for you to tolerate at this point. Sabotaging the exercises may be a way of buying time.

Julie: It fits, Dan, and it makes sense that my first response is to consider quitting. If I have to, I'll finish up the dilators without you.

Dan was slow to connect the sexual p–d dynamic with his pursuit and failure in other contexts and to his problem with intimacy; however, after this session he rejoined Julie in the quest to conquer the vaginismus (which the couple did within 18 months) with far less animosity. Eventually, the couple was able to have intercourse on the average of twice per week. I suspect Dan was motivated by what he may have perceived to be a personal challenge by his wife to fix their problem. When the distancer takes a positive proactive stance in the treatment process, it bodes well for the overall prognosis of the case.

CHAPTER 8

Hypoactive Sexual Desire Disorder and the Pursuer–Distancer Dynamic

Kaplan (1977) and Lief (1977) pioneered the research on low sexual desire (once referred to as inhibited sexual desire, or ISD). After experiencing an inordinate number of couples presenting with little or no interest in sexual activity, they began to view this problem as a distinct disorder. It is now commonly referred to in the professional literature as hypoactive sexual desire disorder (HSDD). The DSM-IV (APA, 1994) specifically defines HSDD as a "deficiency or absence of sexual fantasies and desire for sexual activity" (p. 496), and breaks it down into the usual subtypes (*i.e.*, lifelong *versus* acquired and generalized *versus* situational). The disorder may also be due primarily to psychological factors or a combination of medical and psychological factors. While this is the most accepted definition of the disorder to date, perhaps the most graphic description of the problem was provided by Kaplan (1987), who referred to individuals with little or no sexual desire as being "in a psychogenic state of 'sexual anorexia'" (p. 11).

Pridal and LoPiccolo (2000) referred to HSDD as the "sexual dysfunction of the 1990s" (p. 58); however, the disorder is still considered the number one sexual problem experienced by couples (McCarthy & McCarthy, 2003). HSDD is by far the most prevalent sexual problem presented by women, and it is more common in women than men (Laumann, Gagnon, Michael, & Michaels, 1994). Simons and Carey (2001) found that community estimates of the disorder for females ranged from 5 to 46%, and for males from 0 to 26%.

Causes

Hormonal deficiencies, hypothyroidism, pituitary tumors, and renal dialysis can all cause low sexual desire (Plaut, Graziottin, & Heaton, 2004; Segraves & Balon, 2003). Recently, much research has been conducted on the correlation between hormonal imbalances and low sexual desire in women (Davis, 2000). Various medications can also be responsible for low sexual desire, such as antidepressants (*e.g.*, SSRIs), anti-androgens, MAOIs, and various stimulants (Plaut *et al.*, 2004; Segraves & Balon, 2003).

Some psychoanalysts attribute the problem to Oedipal difficulties. For example, with regard to the Madonna–prostitute complex, Freud (1912/1957) wrote of the man who searches for and marries someone who represents the pure, Madonna image he has of his mother — someone to whom he can transfer his affection. Because it is unacceptable to think of his mother in a sexual way, however, the man reserves his sensual attraction for one whom he perceives is impure. (Freud referred to this latter woman as the prostitute, even though no money is exchanged.) I have treated many men who have reported no desire on their honeymoon after a normal premarital sexual relationship. It is as if the partner is thrust into the Madonna role immediately after the wedding.

Cognitive behaviorists recommend changing the way sexual partners think, feel, and behave by utilizing exercises such as viewing erotic literature and becoming more sexually creative. For example, Barry and Emily McCarthy (2003) offer a number of exercises and techniques to treat this problem in their book *Rekindling Desire*. Kaplan (1995) noted that anxiety, depression, stress, a strict religious upbringing, and past or present sexual trauma or abuse can also be causal factors of low sexual desire. Psychodynamic systems therapists, most notably Schnarch (2000), have argued that poor levels of differentiation from one's family of origin can result in a decrease in passion and desire in a relationship. In addition, Weeks and Gambescia (2002) have found that relationship strife brought on by poor communication and power or control struggles may also be responsible for the disorder.

Treatment

Most therapists have admitted to having little success in treating HSDD. Polonsky (1997) wrote that when low sexual desire was the couple's chief complaint he knew treatment would not be easy. He believed that the issues were generally deeply entrenched and not usually responsive to quick solutions. If deemed appropriate, testosterone replacement in both men and women is used to treat the disorder although the long-term safety of this type of treatment in females in particular has not been established (Segraves

& Balon, 2003). Generally speaking, however, the practicing clinician needs to be equally skilled in psychodynamic, systemic, and behavioral techniques. If insight therapy fails, the psychodynamic therapist is limited, as would be the behavioral therapist if behavioral interventions fail. A couples therapist who is not skilled in sex therapy may not even diagnose the problem correctly; alternatively, a sex therapist who does not have couples therapy skills may be severely limited, particularly if the problem is symptomatic of a systemic or relationship dynamic.

Although Kaplan (1995) contended that the disorder could have a positive prognosis, in tune with Polonsky (1997), she admitted that treatment could be difficult and lengthy depending on the underlying issues involved. She wrote, "Patients with sexual desire disorders tend to have more serious underlying emotional and marital problems" (p. 5). She also believed that these individuals suffered from more severe intrapsychic sexual conflicts and relationship difficulty than those who possessed other sexual disorders and had a higher incidence of personality disorders.

Kaplan's (1995) model for the treatment of low sexual desire is based on the integration of brief, psychodynamic psychotherapy in tandem with explicit sexual exercises to enhance the individual's libido. Kaplan also advocated for the use of medication and hormonal treatment when appropriate to help alleviate the problem. For example, in menopausal women a lack of androgens can cause the loss of sexual desire. In this case, estrogen–androgen therapy, including testosterone, may be merited.

Hypoactive sexual desire disorder appears to be more closely linked to the p–d dynamic than any other sexual disorder. The vagueness of the disorder alone seems to evoke pursuing behavior from the nonsymptomatic partner. Many partners, including the symptom bearers, do not believe they have HSDD or that it actually exists. This skepticism makes it easier for the nonsymptomatic partner to personalize the disorder (*e.g.*, automatically thinking that the HSDD partner is purposely avoiding him or her). In almost all of the cases I have treated, the symptomatic partner is in control of the couple's sex life but not in control of the HSDD. As mentioned, HSDD is often correlated with serious underlying problems (Kaplan, 1995); therefore, it usually takes longer to treat than other sexual dysfunctions. This also serves to exacerbate the frustration on the part of the nonsymptomatic partner, in particular, and in turn helps increase that partner's pursuing behavior.

Most sex therapists who work with couples are accustomed to seeing one partner (more often female) present with low sexual desire, along with his or her "sexually deprived" mate (Pridal & LoPiccolo, 2000). In some cases, both partners will report HSDD, but it is an unusual occasion when mates fail to take up respective p–d roles when HSDD is the symptom (Betchen, 2001a). The symptomatic partner is the natural distancer in the sense that he or she tends to avoid the sexually pursuing partner as much as possible. It is also rare that an individual with HSDD will pursue a partner in an effort to try to raise his or her own level of desire. They tend to want to be left alone, even though they may be extremely upset that they have the disorder. I have even found that some partners sexually experiment with others rather than their partners to see if they are capable of having sexual relations.

I have seen numerous couples in which the pursuing partner is upset simply because the distancer fails to be sexually proactive or initiate the sexual process; however, this is not necessarily an indication that the distancer has low sexual desire. The female distancer, for example, may be passively trying (consciously or unconsciously) to provoke pursuit because sexual passivity is supported in her cultural background, as has been the case with many women raised in patriarchal societies. In these cases, when sex is initiated the partner can perform quite well.

Beyond the subtypes of the disorder mentioned, I believe that two case scenarios of HSDD are prominent. The first is the individual who rarely if ever initiates sex because of a low desire to have it. This individual only gives in or participates in order to save the relationship. The more severe type of HSDD involves an individual who has no desire for sexual relations and refuses to engage in sexual activity no matter what the circumstances. This individual will not respond to a sexual partner's assertiveness because he or she simply does not have the desire to do so. The following two cases depict both scenarios.

Case 6. Paul and Sandy. Paul and Sandy had been dating for approximately six years (see Figure 8.1). Sandy, an attorney, was in her late thirties and Paul, a dentist, was in his early forties. Both partners were attractive and very bright individuals. Paul was married and divorced several years prior to meeting Sandy. Paul was upset because Sandy did not appear to be interested in having sex with him. The couple was averaging sexual intercourse once every two months. Sandy never initiated the sexual process and admitted that she probably would not have sex at all if she did not worry that it might provoke Paul to cheat on her or leave her. Even so, Paul had to pursue Sandy to have sex with him until she gave in. On the particular occasions that Sandy would agree to be with Paul, she claimed that she did not feel him inside her and couldn't wait until the sex was over with. Paul confirmed that when the couple did have sex Sandy appeared disinterested, even bored.

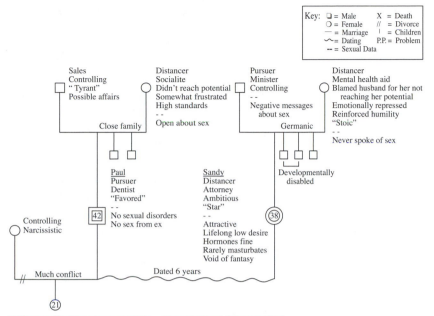

Fig. 8.1 Paul and Sandy.

Paul was not threatening to leave Sandy. In fact, he stated that he was very attracted to her and was extremely upset that she was not responding in kind. Sandy claimed that on an intellectual level she knew Paul was right about the situation but that she simply didn't have any sexual feelings. She also reported that she rarely masturbated, claimed to be void of fantasy, and felt no particular attraction or need for anybody else. Interestingly, however, she claimed that she could be brought to orgasm if Paul stimulated her clitoris with his hand for a long enough period of time. Sandy had seen a gynecologist and was cleared of any organic problems. Her hormone levels were fine. She had taken antidepressants for a period of time, but they did little to help her with her libido. Finally, although the couple averaged sex two to three times a week in the very beginning of their relationship, this high point of sexual contact lasted only one or two months. Soon thereafter the sexual symptom and p–d dynamics emerged.

Sandy had three younger brothers. She grew up in a small, rather pleasant rural town that few of her friends ever left. Sandy claimed that she could not wait to move onto bigger and better things. She was particularly fond of the cultural offerings of a big city and initially attended college and law school in New York. She later took a job with a law firm in New York, where she resided with Paul. Sandy described her home life as very conservative. Her father was a minister and her mother was a mental-health worker. She described both parents as somewhat "stoic" individuals who discouraged her from touting herself and her abilities. Although she was considered very attractive and popular in high school, Sandy said that she was trained to be humble. The family was not religious in a rigid sense, but family members rarely shared and processed their feelings. Sandy reported that perhaps the most memorable message she received as a child came from her mother, who felt that Sandy needed to be "sat upon," or held back. Sandy was clearly the "star" of her family. She had the looks, talent, and popularity, and although her father favored her and made her feel special her mother was concerned that she would get too out of control and do harm to her reputation. Sandy also believed that it was possible that her mother was somewhat jealous of the attention her husband paid to Sandy and the fact that "she wasn't able to reach her own potential" — Sandy saw her as a very bright but frustrated individual who at times blamed her "controlling" husband for her lack of personal and professional success. Another factor that contributed to Sandy's family stardom was the fact that two of her brothers were developmentally disabled and relied on their parents to help them function. To their credit, the parents did not parentify Sandy under these conditions.

Sandy claimed to have her choice of boyfriends in high school and college. She said that she usually attracted very good-looking men. Even though she had several rather long-term relationships, she tried to put off having intercourse as long a possible and lost her virginity in her junior year of college to her boyfriend of three years. She stated that she wanted to have sex with a couple of previous boyfriends but that she would have felt too guilty ("Good girls don't do it this young") and she feared getting pregnant. She did claim to have had more sexual desire in the past than now, but she admitted in retrospect that her desire level was never as high as it should have been — or at least as high as the desire levels of most of her friends. By the time she met Paul, Sandy had had sex with a couple of suitors, but for the most part they had to pursue her, and she slept with them simply to keep the relationships going or to satisfy a rare physical need. There was no evidence of any physical or sexual abuse nor any use or abuse of alcohol or drugs in her family of origin.

Paul was the oldest and "favorite son" of three brothers. He described his father as an affable, ambitious man who placed a high value on academic and cultural pursuits. He was a physician who fancied himself a "Renaissance man." Paul described his mother as a very bright, assertive individual who participated in many of her city's social activities. While Paul maintained a very close relationship with his family, he did admit that his siblings were under a certain amount of pressure to perform, whereas he felt he was given a free pass because of his favored position in the family. He claimed that his siblings were annoyed by this injustice but never really confronted the issue in a serious manner. Paul's parents were in denial regarding this matter.

Paul reported that his sex life as a young man was normal. He had many sexual partners and some long-term relationships. He claimed that he never experienced any sexual disorders, but that he did lose interest in his ex-wife near the end of their relationship. Paul reported that the marriage was wrought with conflict and that his ex-wife was controlling, manipulative, and narcissistic. He said that, like Sandy, she too stopped having sex with him, causing him to pursue her for several years until he finally gave up and filed for divorced.

The following excerpt is from an individual session with Sandy. It was in this session that I unveiled the hypothesis that I believed that she was in conflict regarding a need to feel "special" and that this conflict was behind her HSDD and, in turn, her distancing behavior. I came to this conclusion primarily based on the double message she received as a young woman: "You're a star, but you shouldn't act like one." Sandy consistently demonstrated this conflict during the treatment process in may different contexts by simultaneously expressing a certain air of superiority about herself and a surprising sense of insecurity as well. Most telling was the way she could criticize others at work yet unrealistically degrade her own abilities. She appeared to me to be a "reluctant star," one who drove through life putting the brakes on her formidable talents.

Sandy's case is a good example of a client with HSDD because of her distancing behavior, the level of sophistication of her case, and because she demonstrated vast improvement in other nonsexual areas of her life (areas which she did not initially report as problematic, such as her career) despite the fact that her level of sexual desire remained relatively low. Those who work regularly with this disorder are familiar with the fact that HSDD is often the last symptom to be alleviated (Betchen, 2001a).

> **Sandy:** Paul's been pressuring me to have more sex with him. I can understand his position, but I just don't have the desire.
>
> **Dr. B:** When's the last time you had sex with him?
>
> **Sandy:** Two weeks ago, but I really wasn't into it. He can tell I'm not completely there when I do give in, and it bothers him.

Dr. B: Are you ever concerned that Paul will have an affair or leave you because of this problem?

Sandy: Yes, but I try not to think about it.

Dr. B: Well, then, there must be a very important reason to turn yourself off to him.

Sandy: I guess, but we still don't know what that is.

Dr. B: What if you are unconsciously setting yourself up?

Sandy: For what?

Dr. B: For failure.

Sandy: It wouldn't be the first time, but in this case do you mean that I'm setting myself up for Paul to cheat on me or leave me?

Dr. B: Well, we seem to agree that you were given double messages about success in your family of origin and that this has manifested in an internal conflict.

Sandy: Yes. In fact, I recently called my mother to tell her I got a promotion at work and she didn't respond. I'm so used to this by now it was almost funny.

Dr. B: Okay, so it might be possible that this conflict around success is being expressed through your lack of sexual desire for Paul. For example, consider that one part of you does what it takes sexually to get him, and then does just barely enough to keep him. I would think that this relative lack of effort can make you special.

Sandy: Do you mean that it makes me special to have gotten such a great guy without doing that much in return?

Dr. B: Yes, but the other side of the conflict is evident by the fact that by doing so little you leave yourself vulnerable to failure.

Sandy: Because Paul could leave me. Well, it does bother me when he looks at other women.

Dr. B: You see, your conflict creates a certain amount of tension. You are never wholly "special." While Paul pursues you, you are annoyed and respond with a certain amount of distancing behavior, but you still feel somewhat special or just special enough to tolerate the arrangement. However, if he looks at other women or gives up on you completely, you will lose that specialness altogether. I doubt this will be acceptable to you.

Sandy: That's an understatement. So, then, I have to put out sexually in order to avoid failure.

Dr. B: Well, I prefer to think of it as your resolving your conflict regarding success and specialness. Your distancing by way of your lack of desire is the vehicle that seems to carry a potentially risky compromise to your conflict.

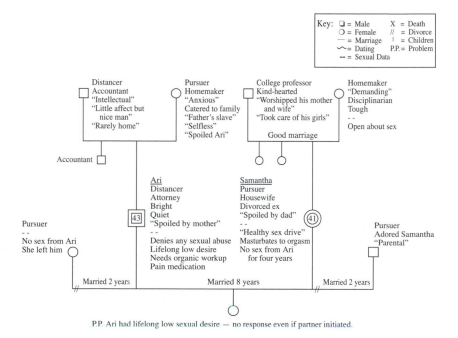

Fig. 8.2 Ari and Samantha.

Case 7. Ari and Samantha. Ari and Samantha were a couple in their early forties (see Figure 8.2). Ari was a successful attorney, and Samantha was a housewife. The couple had been married for eight years and had one young child (a daughter). This was the second marriage for both partners. Samantha's first marriage lasted approximately two years. She stated that she ended it because her husband was too "parental" and because she just wasn't in love with him. Ari's first wife left him after two years of marriage because he showed little interest in having sex with her. Samantha had to drag Ari into couples therapy under the threat of divorce, even though he lost his first wife because he lacked sexual interest in her. Samantha complained that she and Ari hadn't had any sexual contact for close to four years and that Ari showed very little nonsexual affection toward her, as well. While both partners were reasonably pleasant to one another during the sessions, it was clear that Samantha was the pursuer and Ari the distancer.

Ari was a bright but relatively quiet man. He was the younger of two brothers. His older brother and father were accountants. Ari described his father as a "nice, intellectual man" who was distant and rarely home primarily because of work and professional commitments (he was the head of his own accounting firm). Ari claimed that education was stressed in his family, and the only time he ever saw his father upset was if his sons did poorly in school (although this rarely occurred). Ari contended that his mother was an anxious, subservient woman who would do anything for her husband and sons. In fact, Ari pointed out that he had some difficulty with his mother's catering behavior. He stated that he sometimes felt sorry for her because she was so "selfless." Samantha confirmed this picture of her mother-in-law and firmly believed that Ari put little into his marriages because he was "spoiled" by his mother.

Ari reported that his parents' marriage was a good one and that he believed that they slept in the same bed and had regular sex. He claimed that because his mother did whatever his father wanted, however, it was hard to tell whether she actually enjoyed herself or was simply complying with her husband's wishes. Ari claimed that he had a relatively uneventful sexual childhood. He dated infrequently in high school, choosing to focus on athletics instead, and lost his virginity at age 18 to his college girlfriend, whom he described as "wild." This woman eventually cheated on him and he broke up with her. He had one other girlfriend in law school but admitted that he lost interest in her. As mentioned, Ari was previously married, but this woman eventually left him because he lost sexual interest in her, too. He admitted that he never really had a very strong desire for sex. Although Ari said that he used to masturbate to orgasm, he would do so rather infrequently. Interestingly, Ari reported that when he did attempt to have sex his erection was strong. He claimed that he would "get lost in the physical feelings of the act, or fantasize."

Ari had not had his hormone levels checked prior to our initial session, so I strongly recommended that he obtain a complete medical examination in order to rule out any organic problems. He also presented with a flat affect so I thought that he could be suffering from depression, even though he denied this. Finally, he was on some pain medication for a bad knee but claimed that his desire problem preceded the taking of this medication; he rarely drank alcohol.

Samantha was the youngest of three sisters. She described her parent's marriage as a happy one. Her father, a college professor, was a kind-hearted man who was very caring and loving. Samantha claimed that he was a very maternal man who "took care of all the girls in the family." Samantha said that he worshipped his mother and especially catered to his wife's every whim. Samantha described her mother as an assertive, demanding woman who ran the family home and served as the disciplinarian to the children. She was, in a sense, a traditional housewife. Samantha reported that her sexual past was uneventful. She was involved in a couple of long-term relationships prior to her first marriage but experienced no significant sexual problems. She claimed to always have a "healthy sex drive" and was disappointed when she and Ari only had sex twice on their honeymoon. She has always been able to masturbate to orgasm. As mentioned, Samantha was married once before for a brief period of time. She stated that her first husband was an adoring and caring man who had desire for her but she didn't feel the same way about him; she said that he was "too fatherly." Samantha believed that her parents had sex regularly, but the topic was not openly discussed in the household.

The following excerpt is from a conjoint session in which I exposed each partner's conflicts and pointed out how they related to Ari's low sexual desire and the couple's p–d dynamic. In the previously cited case, although she was unable to initiate sexual activity, Sandy valiantly forced herself to have sex with her husband when she felt she had to. This case differed in that Ari could not bring himself to do what he needed to in order to rescue his marriage. No matter how hard Samantha pursued, he never gave in.

> **Samantha:** He doesn't know how to be married. I think his mother spoiled him. He doesn't think he needs to do anything for a woman except bring home a paycheck. He doesn't have to spend time with me or have sex with me.
>
> **Dr. B:** What do you think, Ari?
>
> **Ari:** Maybe she's right.
>
> **Dr. B:** Are you patronizing me?
>
> **Ari:** No, I'm serious. I really don't know what's going on with me, but I do think that I do more than bring home a good paycheck. I think I'm a pretty good father.
>
> **Samantha:** That you are, but you're a terrible husband. You were never taught how to be a good husband. You didn't have to do anything at home because your mother waited on you hand and foot.
>
> **Dr. B:** What about that hypothesis?
>
> **Ari:** My mother did dote on the entire family. She was my father's slave. [*chuckles*]
>
> **Dr. B:** You found that humorous?
>
> **Ari:** Well, she seemed happy doing it.
>
> **Dr. B:** So you were okay with it?
>
> **Ari:** Well, it was easy.
>
> **Dr. B:** I'm not so sure it's easy now.
>
> **Samantha:** Why not? He gets everything he wants.

Dr. B: Except peace in the house. In fact, I would think on some level it would be easier if Ari accommodated you rather than have you after him all the time.

Ari: That's probably true because she never gives up — she's relentless.

Samantha: I don't want to give up. I want to make my marriage better. Do you want me to give up?

Ari: Not on the marriage but definitely on attacking me.

Samantha: If I give that up I'll have to live the rest of my life without sex. I don't want to do that.

Ari: You won't have to live the rest of your life without sex.

Samantha: No, then for how long?

Ari: I don't know.

Dr. B: Ari, you want Samantha to stop pursuing you but you can't promise her anything in return. That deal sounds a little familiar.

Ari: What do you mean?

Dr. B: Well, that's the deal that you, your dad, and your siblings had with your mom when you were a kid. She did the work and all of you allowed her to do it.

Ari: That's the way it was. She didn't seem to complain.

Samantha: So why did you marry me? Why didn't you marry someone more like your mother? Even your first wife wasn't like your mother. She also pursued you for intimacy. Why marry women like us? What are you … masochistic?

Ari: Definitely. [*chuckles*]

Dr. B: Samantha, that's a great question. Do you have an answer for her, Ari?

Ari: I don't know.

Dr. B: Was there ever a time when you really felt bad about the way your mother allowed herself to be treated?

Ari: Rarely, but later in life when she developed arthritis she couldn't do as much and I would get annoyed with my dad for taking advantage of her. Sometimes he would ask for something to eat and my mother would struggle to get to the refrigerator when he was perfectly healthy enough to get it for himself. Of course, it was confusing because she probably would have stopped him from getting it anyway. She was like that.

Dr. B: Is Samantha like your mother in any way?

Ari: Samantha works hard. She shuttles the kids around and keeps a nice home, but she can be childlike, demanding, and pretty spoiled herself.

Samantha: I'll admit that. My dad spoiled me also, but my mother was very tough on me.

Dr. B: Ari, do you ever feel sorry for Samantha?

Ari: Sometimes when it comes to the sex issue. I know that she's right, but I also get mad at her for bugging me about it all the time.

Dr. B: Well, this takes me back to Samantha's question as to why you married someone like her.

Ari: I don't know.

Samantha: He thought he could turn me into a slave, too.

Ari: I don't want a slave.

Dr. B: Why not? It worked well in your family of origin.

Ari: It goes beyond Samantha's unhappiness. I don't want to perceive myself as a guy who needs his wife to be a slave.

Dr. B: Perhaps a part of you does and a part of you doesn't.

Ari: What do you mean?

Dr. B: Well, you might be in conflict. Part of you may feel comfortable being doted on without having to put much back into a relationship, while the other part of you feels uncomfortable with it. It might explain why you married Samantha.

Ari: I don't get it.

Dr. B: I'm suggesting that you may have married Samantha in part because you wanted a woman to care for. By her own admittance she does demonstrate some childlike tendencies and neediness even beyond sex; yet, you seem to put little into the relationship — as if you wish to be treated the way your were as a child. Your HSDD is possibly symptomatic of your inability to decide what role to play in the marriage, which in turn leads to a pursuer–distancer dynamic, with Samantha as the pursuer and you as the distancer. Does this make any sense to you?

Samantha: It makes sense to me, but why would I marry Ari?

Ari: You were also spoiled.

Samantha: Yes, but if I were spoiled I wouldn't have left my first husband who worshipped me. And I certainly wouldn't have married you.

Dr. B: What consciously attracted you to Ari?

Samantha: He was cute and very smart. He was also a successful lawyer so I knew he would be a good provider. I also thought he was strong and protective. He was very gentle and gentlemanly.

Dr. B: And the sex?

Samantha: In the beginning the quality was okay, but as I mentioned before the frequency was never there. I thought that would change after the marriage, and I thought he had so many other great qualities that it would make up for the lack of frequency anyway. I never thought the sex would totally disappear.

Dr. B: So, is it possible that there is a part of you that really wants to be catered to the way your father catered to you, and you saw the potential for this caretaking in Ari?

Samantha: Maybe, but I left my first husband, who doted on me hand and foot.

Dr. B: That's interesting. What do you think?

Samantha: I just know that I became bored with him, but he was a very sweet man.

Dr. B: It's as if you rejected the man who met your needs to marry a man who you claim fails to meet your needs. Perhaps you have a conflict around getting your needs met. Like Ari, part of you wants to be taken care of and part of you doesn't, for some reason.

Samantha: What could that reason be?

Dr. B: I don't know yet, but I think we will need to explore what underlies both of your conflicts and resolve them in order to alleviate your symptoms.

Talmadge and Talmadge (1986) wrote, "Sex therapy techniques have a poor record of success in treating low sexual desire largely because of insufficient attention to the emotional relationship of the persons involved and to psychodynamics" (p. 5). The model presented herein suggests that HSDD can cause the p–d dynamic or even be a result of it; therefore, it is vital that relational dynamics and their underlying conflicts be considered in order to relieve the couple of their symptoms. The previous two case examples have demonstrated these important links.

Finally, some authors believe that men naturally have higher sex drives than women; therefore, while women may be programmed to be emotional pursuers or pursuers of attachment (Fisher, 2000), "men are genetically programmed to act the sexual pursuers" (Kaplan, 1995, p. 34). This may explain why men in general suffer less from HSDD than do women. Moreover, it may also explain why some men pursue for sex and then distance emotionally after they have gotten it, and why some women initially distance from sex, preferring to pursue for emotional attachment, or distance sexually after they have achieved emotional attachment.

Caution, however, should be exercised when attempting to generalize across gender lines on this matter. In my clinical experience, pursuers tend to demonstrate higher sex drives no matter what their gender (Samantha supports this hypothesis). And, if HSDD is presented by a couple, it is almost always the distancer who is the symptom bearer. This begs the following questions: Do sexually pursuing women have higher levels of testosterone than others? Because I would find it troubling to request that a sexually pursuing woman with a relatively high sex drive have her hormones checked, I cannot offer any first-hand knowledge on this issue. If they do have higher levels, however, it might explain why they act more like males when it comes to pursuing for sex. Do male sexual distancers have lower levels than other males? I have found that, while some individuals (of both genders) with HSDD have abnormally low testosterone, others do not, indicating a probable emotional or psychological cause for the symptom.

CHAPTER 9

Same-Sex Couples and the Pursuer–Distancer Dynamic

Approximately 600,000 American households are inhabited by same-sex couples (also referred to, in this chapter, as gay couples or gay male and lesbian couples) (U.S. Census Bureau, 2000). While many experts in this area (Carl, 1990; Chernin & Johnson, 2003; Nichols, 2000; Tessina, 2003) have agreed that these couples have relational problems similar to those of heterosexual couples, they also acknowledge that differences exist between the two populations (just as they do between gay male and lesbian couples) and that these differences need to be taken into account in order for same-sex couples treatment to be effective. The primary purpose of this chapter is to touch on a few of the differences that I have found to be most germane to the p–d dynamic and to offer some treatment suggestions. The differences presented by these couples may in some cases be behind the p–d dynamic or at the very least exacerbate or complicate the interaction. The first difference that distinguishes same-sex couples from others in our society is the stigma they experience.

Discrimination and Homophobia

It is a fact that gays are discriminated against in our society. Gay couples in particular tend to evoke disapproval because seeing them in partnership highlights their differences — differences that many heterosexuals disapprove of. When a heterosexual couple holds hands in public, it is often viewed with fondness; if a gay couple does so, it is considered by many heterosexuals to be aversive. Although the Gay Liberation Movement, which began in the 1970s, has helped to lessen the discrimination against gays, many people still openly disapprove of them and their unions. Many heterosexuals still view gays as perverted individuals who could change if they truly wanted to. Michael *et al.* (1994) reported in *Sex in America* that, between 1972 and 1991, over 70% of Americans believed that homosexuality was always morally wrong.

Societal disapproval and familial/parental opinions of the gay individual can often exacerbate the situation. Parents and siblings of gays may express, anger, embarrassment, and shame — attitudes and feelings that can cause the gay family member anxiety, depression, and low self-esteem. The "coming out" of a gay family member can also result in a familial schism or an emotional family cutoff. Sometimes, however, the discrimination is less overt. For example, family members (as well as friends) may unconsciously choose to deny the gay member's true sexual orientation, thus causing an unhealthy delay in the coming-out process.

Laird and Green (1996) defined homophobia as the "irrational fear, prejudice, and willingness to discriminate against lesbians and gay men" (p. 4). The many prejudices sustained by gays can lead to internalized homophobia (*i.e.*, homophobia within gays) and, in turn, problems in their intimate relationships (D'Ercole & Drescher, 2004), specifically a deleterious p–d dynamic. Interestingly enough, I have only seen this exhibited in gay individuals who were engaged in the coming-out process, not in those who have been out for some time. It seems that most gay men and lesbians need time to come to terms with their own sexual orientation before they can discard the homophobia they, too, grew up believing. Consider the following case.

Marc and Edward were two thirty-year-old gay men who had been in a tenuous relationship for approximately eight months. Prior to meeting Edward, Marc had left his wife and two young children after a long and tumultuous struggle with his sexual orientation. Apparently, Marc had been molested by a man as a young boy and needed to take some time (with the help of individual therapy) to figure out, as he put it, "which came first: the abuse or the homosexuality." He also struggled with whether he was bisexual, but his lack of passion during sex with his ex-wife, his consistent need to fantasize about men when he was with her sexually, and his frequent attractions to men (not women) at his place of employment made him finally admit to himself that he was, in fact, gay. Marc told me in a conjoint session with Edward that he thought he might be gay or bisexual when he was about twelve years old, but he had pushed these feelings aside because he so badly did not want to be gay. In fact, he informed me that for most of his life he actually "hated" gays. Marc stated that, although he believed that some of his wife's friends were suspicious of his true sexual orientation, his wife was in "complete denial" about the issue. Marc also expressed a lot of shame about the early sexual abuse. He was "worried sick" that if he left his wife he would be abandoning his children and his responsibilities. He worried what family, friends, and his "macho" colleagues would think of him (Marc worked in the construction business). He especially did not want to prove his wife's friends right about him.

Edward, on the other hand, had been out for many years and had had a series of lovers and long-term relationships. He was very attracted to Marc and complained that Marc would spend limited time with him and have "partial sex" (*i.e.,* petting but no intercourse). To Edward, Marc was a tease, and he pursued heavily to convince Marc that he needed to "let go" and "be proud of being a gay male." He also wanted Marc to move in with him sometime in the near future.

Marc admitted that he liked Edward a lot but that his sex drive was almost nonexistent. He said that he could barely kiss Edward, and only participated in any kind of sexually related activities because he did not want Edward to leave him. He said that he had no desire to have intercourse with Edward and that he avoided discussions about sex and living together as best he could. He said that he could not sexually consummate his relationship with Edward and that he definitely was not ready to "hang out with him too much or live with him." Marc therefore distanced physically and emotionally from Edward but tried to stay close enough to keep Edward pursuing. At one point, when Edward threatened to end the relationship, Marc began having panic attacks for which he was referred for medication.

The treatment with this couple was relatively brief (approximately four months). It centered on Edward reducing the pressure and empathizing with Marc's situation. Edward was unaware of Marc's history of molestation but finding out helped him to be gentle and more patient with Marc. This change, in turn, helped Marc to feel less anxious and more secure with Edward. It was also helpful for Edward to come to grips with his apparent rejection sensitivity, which was rooted in his family of origin and was at least partially responsible for his anxious pursuit of Marc. This was accomplished in individual and conjoint sessions.

In a mix of individual and conjoint weekly sessions, Marc and I processed how the abuse and his internalized homophobia were impacting his level of sexual desire and his overall distancing behavior until he eventually understood the connection and began spending more time with Edward as well as having sex with him. Marc also continued to see his children regularly and, to his ex-wife's credit, both she and Marc remained on very good terms. At the point of termination, Marc and Edward were in the process of buying a condominium together and Marc was also able to stop his medication. Although I thought that Marc could have used more help with his coming-out process and his apparent internalized homophobic attitude, he insisted that he was ready to terminate treatment. Near the end of the process, Marc stated that he never would have gone to a gay therapist (even his former individual therapist was a heterosexual). He said that a nonjudgmental, heterosexual therapist was the right prescription for him because, in part, he was made to feel accepted.

In order to successfully treat the p–d dynamic in the same-sex couple, the therapist must simultaneously consider the external discrimination that exists against this population as well as any internalized homophobia in the couple. The first step in this process is for the therapist to join with the couple. While the gay therapist will most likely have an easier time accomplishing this, possessing the same sexual orientation does not guarantee a positive outcome. It is, however, particularly important for the heterosexual therapist to demonstrate an acceptance and respect for the gay couple (see "Therapist Bias," below). This serves to preserve the therapeutic process by helping to make the gay couple feel more comfortable and supported by a member of an otherwise hostile society. Some heterosexual therapists unfamiliar with same-sex couples may use the therapy hour to learn about the gay culture, which is frowned upon, although heterosexual therapists can request clarification when needed. This will show the gay couple that the therapist is interested enough in them and respectful enough of their differences to work hard to their therapeutic benefit.

Gay partners may be overly sensitive to cues from the therapist that may signify acceptance or homophobia; therefore, it is important for therapists to be aware of their own biases (see "Therapist Bias," below) and to exhibit caring, empathy, and warmth in the therapeutic process. In discussing lesbian couples, Goldstein and Horowitz (2003) stated, "It is important for therapists to display genuineness, realness, and spontaneity in the therapeutic relationship, rather than adhere to the traditional stance of neutrality, abstinence, and anonymity" (p. 32). The authors believe that "these qualities encourage a bond of mutual identification that permits the therapeutic work to move forward" (pp. 32–33). Creating such a bond is particularly important for the heterosexual or opposite-sexed therapist when working with gay couples. The therapist might also do well to point out strengths that may be enhanced by the couple's gayness, such as self-definition and sensitivity. Overindulging the couple or failing to maintain appropriate limits within the therapeutic process is counterproductive, but validating the discrimination that a gay couple must endure is advised.

Roles and Relationship Fluidity

Falco (1991) contended that at times lesbianism may not be a part of the therapeutic issues but it "is never irrelevant" (p. 10). She claimed that it is the therapist's job to "ascertain to what level lesbianism is part of the therapy issues" (p. 10). Gay male and lesbian couples engaged in the p–d dynamic may present a more complex picture in treatment (particularly to the heterosexual therapist) than do heterosexual couples. The high level of relational equality demonstrated by same-sex couples, particularly lesbian couples (Laird & Green, 1996), may make it somewhat more difficult to discern any fixed p–d role patterns in these populations.

In some cases, I have found that the lesbian partner who has characteristics more closely associated with the distancer may quite frequently play the role of the pursuer in the relationship, and the partner who possesses pursuer traits may quite frequently play the distancer. This may not pertain as much to those lesbian partners who assume femme and butch roles and are more rigid in their p–d dynamic, as in the more common female pursuer and male distancer roles; however, the taking of a femme or a butch role is not nearly as prevalent in the gay community as some believe (Chernin & Johnson, 2003). Laird and Green (1996) stated that rigid butch and femme roles are not the norm in gay couples and that gay couples generally do not divide roles up along the "lines of traditional gender dichotomies" (p. 4).

Nevertheless, even though it has been acknowledged that there is a little pursuer in every distancer and a little distancer in every pursuer, I have generally found that the roles portrayed by lesbian couples seem to be more fluid than they are in gay male and heterosexual couples. If it were simply a matter of gender, one would think that the female heterosexual distancer, for example, would behave similarly, but this is not necessarily the case. The female heterosexual distancer oftentimes more closely resembles a male heterosexual distancer than does a lesbian distancer; this suggests that gender difference is not as much at play here as a difference more attributable to the same-sex constellation. Consider the following case example.

Desiree and Jen were a lesbian couple in their early forties. Desiree was a quiet, intellectual woman who for the most part kept to herself. Her hobbies were somewhat solitary (*e.g.*, reading and writing) and her job frequently took her on long business trips. By her own admission, she was distant or passively resistant to entering the relationship with Jen, who pursued her relentlessly. "She almost wore me down she pursued so heavily, so I finally gave in," said Desiree. Indeed, Jen presented as the energetic, vivacious, verbal partner. She had a number of outside friendships and served as the relationship's social director — always coming up with new ideas for Desiree and her to put into action. Jen clearly exhibited traits and tendencies of a pursuer. Despite the appearance of these roles, however, it was Desiree who demanded that the couple seek treatment because she felt that Jen wasn't as committed to the relationship. It was Desiree who was pressing for the couple to buy a house together and solidify the union, while Jen was very resistant to this notion.

In working with the lesbian p–d dynamic, in particular, the therapist will have to be as fluid as the roles presented. For example, while I challenged Desiree on her pursuing behavior, I also dealt with her distancing traits, the origin of these, and how they may in fact have contributed to Jen's current distancing behavior. Simultaneously, I challenged Jen's current distancing behavior because it was indeed prominent, but I also discussed her pursuing traits, as well. To view Jen exclusively as the pursuer and Desiree as the distancer would have been a stereotypical oversimplification of their behavioral roles.

Relationship Commitment

It seems that the predominant belief in our society is that gay men and lesbians do not desire long-term relationships and are unable to sustain them; yet, in reality, many gays are in long-term relationships (Chernin & Johnson, 2003). The literature has supported the notion that lesbians in particular tend to favor coupling; it is how they define themselves. Although lesbians experience the typical ambivalences when ending a relationship, their commitment to the concept of relationship may often cause them to stay in a bad union in order to avoid separation or being alone (Nichols, 1988).

According to Falco (1991), many lesbians have trouble terminating relationships because "women experience the act of breaking up a relationship as a violation of the female ethic to care for others and as a violation of the social injunction to nurture and work at a relationship" (pp. 120–121). She also believed that lesbians might want to prove wrong the predominantly heterosexual notion that their relationships are short lived. Nevertheless, the inability to terminate a relationship even when physical or emotional abuse is present may in some cases leave the lesbian couple vulnerable to chronic victim/persecutor p–d dynamics. Often the victimized partner continues to pursue the persecuting partner to cease their distancing behavior, usually to no avail.

Because of their interest in coupling, along with their greater difficulty separating sex from love (like many other women), lesbians are less prone to having flings. They are, however, prone to falling in love relatively quickly and are thus subject to affairs that seriously threaten their primary relationships (Nichols, 2000). In my experience, when a lesbian mate has fallen enough for somebody to have begun an affair, a p–d dynamic can evolve and last anywhere from several weeks to several months. In this situation, one partner plays the role of the pursuing investigator who is trying to determine whether or not the suspicious, distancing partner is having an affair.

If the affair is exposed or the cheating partner has confessed, a p–d dynamic can then develop around the victimized partner pursuing the cheating partner to end the affair. Many times I have witnessed this painful struggle, and it is interesting to note that, unlike most heterosexual adulterers, the lesbian cheater feels almost as much pain as the victimized party. Many claim that they cannot help themselves; they simply feel taken over by their newfound love.

Kelly and Robin were in their late forties and had been living together for eight years. Several months before beginning couples therapy, Kelly began having an affair with a woman she met at work and threatened to leave Robin. Kelly stated that she was "in love" with this other woman and that it came upon her very quickly. Robin desperately wanted to save the relationship and claimed that she would do what she could to salvage it if only Kelly would give her a chance.

Robin had been suspicious of Kelly's distancing behavior for some time and was keeping an eye on her as best she could (once she even followed her). Nevertheless, she claimed that she was dumbfounded when Kelly finally confessed about her affair. Aside from feeling "rejected," Robin said that she also felt "shamed" by the potential for a breakup because it would be indicative of the inability of lesbians to maintain a lifetime of monogamy.

Both Robin and Kelly had had numerous relationships in the past, including heterosexual unions. Prior to meeting one another they were each in long-term lesbian relationships (four and seven years, respectively) which they reported as dysfunctional and at times emotionally abusive. They both felt that the relationships had gone on far too long, yet both had great difficulty ending them, even after they met one another and fell in love. Robin even admitted that her previous lover was an alcoholic with serious emotional problems.

Although Kelly seemed sincerely concerned about Robin's emotional state, she openly claimed to be madly in love with a woman named Jan. Apparently, Jan had just ended a reasonably lengthy relationship and wanted Kelly to move in with her as soon as she could reconcile her situation with Robin. While it was obvious to all parties that Kelly was not interested in working on her relationship with Robin, neither she nor Robin could end it and move on with their lives. Kelly wanted Robin to break up with her so that she didn't have to take responsibility for ending the union; Robin refused, stating that Kelly being the culprit should own up to her responsibility and end it. In tune with the literature, ending the relationship (even with Kelly having someone to go to) was taboo, and both women were desperately trying to avoid having to do it. Characteristically, the relationship went on this way for nearly a year. Robin pursued Kelly to commit to her or, if need be, to terminate the union; Kelly did everything she could to distance from Robin. Kelly even moved to another apartment and more openly began seeing Jan, but still neither she nor Robin could terminate their relationship.

If the lesbian couple is engaged in the p–d dynamic with a third party as its vehicle (as Kelly and Robin were), and it does not appear as though the offending, distancing partner will ever move back toward the primary relationship, then the therapist needs to help the couple to terminate their relationship as expeditiously and painlessly as possible (but be prepared for the couple to come back together again in the future). To allow this dynamic to go on indefinitely is perpetuating a tortuous cycle. In order for a successful separation to occur, however, the therapist must show empathy for both parties and allow for a period of grieving. (Fortunately, because of the difficulty many lesbian couples have in terminating relationships quickly, they often have enough time to process the ending of a relationship.) Each partner's fantasies about new relationships should also be processed, and any internalized homophobia related to the ending of the relationship addressed. The latter will more likely come from the victimized partner; the initiating partner may need help coping with her guilt over ending the relationship because it was her action which was ultimately responsible for the termination of the union.

The concept of falling in love precipitously also needs to be addressed in therapy, and the bridging-out process (*i.e.*, leaving one partner and moving directly to another with no break in-between) must be examined in order to determine why the relationship deteriorated and to help prevent a recurrence of relationship difficulties in the future. The bulk of this work should be with the initiator of the breakup in a combination of individual and conjoint sessions.

As mentioned, gay male couples also have enduring relationships. In their study of 156 male couples, McWhirter and Mattison (1984) found that approximately a third had lived together for longer than ten years, and that some male couples had been together for forty to fifty years. Many gay men have demonstrated this type commitment to one another despite the fact that when growing up they had few, if any, relationship role models (Chernin & Johnson, 2003).

Sometimes in order to achieve a level of long-term commitment, however, gay male couples resort to means that would be upsetting or fatal to heterosexual and lesbian couples. McWhirter & Mattison (1984) found that sexual exclusivity, for example, was not nearly as important to gay male couples as were their expectations of fidelity (perhaps the male's ability to compartmentalize sex from love and commitment is a major factor here); therefore, it is not entirely unusual if a male couple has allowed outside sexual partners into the relationship in order to sustain it. The following case example involves two gay male lovers who were engaged in a p–d dynamic within the context of one partner's extracurricular sexual activities. Rather than take any moral or rigid stance on the issue, I recognized their need to be creative in order to keep their relationship alive and fresh.

Tyler and Justin were in their middle twenties. Tyler initiated couples therapy because he was highly concerned about Justin's dalliances with other men. Justin admitted to his behavior but said that he made it clear to Tyler early on that he did not consider himself monogamous, and if the relationship was to be so he would become bored. Tyler acknowledged that Justin did forewarn him about his need for greater sexual outlets; however, Tyler claimed that even though he allowed for such behavior (as long as Justin kept him informed of his behavior and practiced safe sex) Justin had consistently increased it over the past two years. Apparently, in better times, Justin was able to maintain a strong emotional and sexual life with Tyler. More recently, however, Justin's behavior had reduced the couple's time together. And, while this behavior was once used by the couple as a sexual turn on, Tyler began to find it increasingly uncomfortable.

Tyler did present as the pursuer and Justin the distancer. The more Tyler pursued Justin to decrease his outside interests and increase the time spent with him, the more time Justin seemed to dedicate to these other interests. In treating this couple, I was careful to take into account Tyler's sanctioning of some of Justin's outside sexual activities. Tyler made it clear that he felt that this arrangement was not so unusual for a gay male couple and that without the sexual flings the relationship might even become boring to him. He wanted me to help both him and Justin to negotiate a compromise in this area so that as a couple they could resolve their p–d dynamic and return to a mutually acceptable level of closeness; both partners agreed it was the only way to salvage their commitment to one another, and they were willing to work toward a compromise.

I have treated gay male couples who were adamant about maintaining monogamous relationships, as well as those who have had arrangements like that of Tyler and Justin. In the majority of the cases I have seen, however, regardless of the arrangements, the primary relationship took ultimate precedence over any outside activities. When these activities became problematic or seriously threatened the survival of the primary relationship, the couples made serious attempts to work through the problem, just as Tyler and Justin chose to do, or else they terminated the activities altogether in favor of the primary relationship.

Fusion, Sexual Desire, and the So-Called "Lesbian Bed Death" Concept

It has been established that hypoactive sexual desire disorder (HSDD) is a major context for the p–d dynamic; therefore, I believe it is necessary to discuss the concept of HSDD as it has been linked to lesbians in long-term relationships. My main point is to help free couples therapists (particularly heterosexual clinicians) from any misconceptions they may have regarding sexual frequency and desire in lesbian couples.

The concept of "lesbian bed death" was defined by Chernin and Johnson (2003) as the "rapid decline of sexual activity among lesbian couples" (p. 141). It has been contended that lesbian couples are the least sexually active couples and that lack of sexual desire is their most common complaint (Nichols, 1988). Blumstein and Schwartz (1983) found that by the second or third year of their relationship lesbian couples engaged in less genital sexual contact than heterosexual and gay male couples. More specifically, the authors found that, after two years of being in a relationship, 37% of the lesbian couples reported making love at least once a week compared to 73% of the heterosexual couples.

Various authors have hypothesized about why lesbian couples experience difficulty with sexual desire or frequency. Tripp (1975) argued that males were genetically and hormonally prewired to seek sex; without a male to pursue sex in the relationship, lesbians were free to show their true feminine nature as seekers of romance first and foremost. Other experts (Krestan & Bepko, 1980; Nichols, 1982) attributed sexual infrequency and inhibited sexual desire in lesbian couples to a state of *fusion* or *merger* (*i.e.,* a lack of differentiation or autonomy between partners in a relationship). Krestan and Bepko (1980), in their classic paper, "The Problem of Fusion in the Lesbian Relationship," believed that lesbian couples, because they consisted of two women who were socialized (as all women are) to be relational, would achieve a greater degree of closeness. The authors contended that this high level of closeness in combination with the negative effects of homophobia would result in fusion and sexual infrequency. In tune with these authors, Falco (1991) believed that societal factors play a part in the sexual frequency between lesbian partners. She contended that when two women are paired together, they may experience difficulty maintaining a satisfying sex life because they share the same "societal injunctions against sexual self-assertion, against sexual self-knowledge, and against the primacy fear of their own sexual desires" (p. 142). Moses and Hawkins (1986) found that some conflicted lesbian partners were reluctant to engage sexually because it would verify something that they feared on a much deeper level — that they were, in fact, lesbian.

In the 1970s and 1980s, the professional literature indeed seemed to focus on some combination of societal/gender expectations and internalized homophobia to explain low sexual desire in lesbian couples. More recently, however, scholars have seriously challenged the concepts of fusion (Mencher, 1990) and lesbian bed death (Iasenza, 2000). Writing for the renowned Stone Center at Wellesley College, Mencher re-examined lesbian relationships from the perspective that closeness and connection are normal, even vital, for female growth. The author warned against evaluating levels of female intimacy based on the male-derived model of autonomy and separation. She wrote that "the patterns of intimacy of lesbian couples are different from those of heterosexual and gay male relationships, and many of these distinctive features have been pathologized by labeling them as fusion" (p. 3). Iasenza called attention to the danger of defining lesbian intimacy and sexual desire using the traditional male model of sexual frequency applicable to heterosexual couples. She stated: "Asking lesbian couples about frequency is problematic because sexuality between women is not defined by discreet genital acts in the way that sex often is when a penis is involved" (p. 61). In agreement with Iasenza, Laird (1999) wrote:

> … sexual satisfaction in this society is highly linked to heteronormative images of penetration and orgasm. Lesbians may include many diverse kinds of sexual and affectionate expression in their intimate relationships — hugging, stroking, kissing, fondling — actions that are not defined as the "real" thing in social discourse and hence may be undervalued by lesbians themselves. (p. 72)

The therapist who treats the lesbian or gay male couple engaged in the p–d dynamic would do well to consider not only intrapsychic and systemic factors that contribute to the dynamic but also the highly influential social and political forces at work. It is particularly important that the therapist consider (or believe) that homosexuality is a normal variant of human sexuality and that gay sex is a normal variant of human sexual behavior.

Therapist Bias

Therapist bias regarding sexual preference as well as the therapist's degree of comfort with his or her own sexual orientation can evoke significant countertransference reactions when working with any couples; however, they can be particularly important variables in the treatment of gay male and lesbian couples. Siegel (1997) wrote, "The same therapist who could listen to stories about a gay or lesbian sexual relationship may respond very differently to a gay or lesbian couple's demonstration of affection or sexuality within the session" (p. 9). Direct exposure to a same-sex couple's interaction may reveal unresolved issues, beliefs, or values that are consciously denied on the part of the therapist.

Indeed, the gay therapist who is relatively free of internalized homophobia and who has experienced at least one relatively long-term gay relationship would, in most cases, be a better therapeutic match for a gay couple. The experience, empathy, and intimate knowledge brought by the gay therapist to treatment would prove invaluable to the gay couple. Goldstein and Horowitz (2003) wrote:

> Most practitioners are likely to see themselves as reasonably empathic people, but, regrettably, it is often difficult for therapists to understand and accept others' life experiences when they differ greatly from their own. Although gay clinicians are not free from blind spots that place constraints on their empathy, they have been extensively exposed to the mainstream culture. In contrast, many nongay therapists, who have been socialized and trained in a heterosexual society and lack familiarity with gay and lesbian life, face special challenges in clinical work with this population. (p. 32)

On the other hand, Chernin and Johnson (2003) warned that having a gay therapist does not guarantee that the therapist is free of homophobia. It also does not mean that the individual is equipped with the appropriate treatment knowledge idiosyncratic to gay couples or possesses the ability to join and empathize with gays. The authors claimed that an objective, caring therapist of either gender or sexual orientation can provide affirmative, ethical therapy to gay male and lesbian couples.

While I am in tune with the concept of client–therapist similarity, I do believe that the client–therapist difference can, in some cases, prove to be a special asset to the gay couple (as it was in Marc and Edward's case). Gay male and lesbian couples can come to view a genuine, empathetic, heterosexual therapist as accepting of them, which might encourage the couple to own and be proud of who they are.

It is a misconception that lesbians and gay men seek out only gay therapists (Laird and Green, 1996). Gay male and lesbian couples do see heterosexual therapists for treatment. While I do not contend that all heterosexual therapists who work with gay couples need to be experts about gay life or even certified sex therapists, they should at least be somewhat familiar with the professional literature regarding the treatment of this population, should be aware of the community and group activities available to them, and should attend a Sexual Attitudes Reassessment (SAR) seminar. The SAR is a two- to three-day workshop that exposes one to sexual differences via lecture, video, and small group process. It provides sexual desensitization to those wishing to become more comfortable and knowledgeable about human sexuality on a broader spectrum. These seminars are usually held at universities, medical schools, or freestanding couples/sex therapy institutes.

CHAPTER 10

Difficult Cases and Case Failure

As mentioned earlier, couples therapists must avoid certain pitfalls or risk premature termination of the treatment process; for example, entering into a power struggle with the pursuer or chasing the distancer can spell the demise of the therapy. However, avoiding these problems or skillfully handling any transference or countertransference that may arise does not guarantee that the therapy will be successful. Some couples simply cannot change their patterns, no matter how much effort is exerted, and others simply refuse to change.

The focus of this chapter is on those couples who, for whatever reasons, have presented me with the most difficult and challenging pursuer–distancer dynamics. Some of these couples were ultimately successful in alleviating their p–d symptoms, others were not, and some are still in treatment, continuing to struggle toward a more positive end. These couples presented p–d symptoms across a variety of different contexts, both sexual and non-sexual. Some couples were chosen not only for their degree of difficulty but for their uniqueness, as well. I can say without hesitation that all couples therapists will eventually confront a difficult, symptom-producing p–d dynamic and that this type of couple will either fail to improve their relationship or end up divorced. Although this is the reality of couples therapy, it is particularly the reality when working with the p–d dynamic. Rather than be discouraged, it is my hope that couples therapists will learn from these cases.

Triangulated Children

If you recall from the literature review, Guerin *et al.* (1996) discussed the p–d interaction as a triangular dynamic anchored in each partner's past rather than simply a dyadic interaction. Not surprisingly, this notion follows Bowen (1978), who contended that a couple will triangulate in an effort to avoid the anxiety that comes when two partners are in danger of intimacy. The next case clearly supports these authors. The couple's p–d dynamic was at first intricately tied to the triangulation of their oldest child; it then shifted to their second child as the oldest was about to leave home.

Lou and Janie were in their middle forties and had been married for twenty-five years. They had two teenage children — a son, Steve, and a daughter, Leah. Janie demanded that Lou attend marital therapy with her but Lou was extremely resistant to the idea. The couple had already seen two marital therapists, and each time Lou had found a reason to become angry with the therapist and drop out of treatment. Because the previous marital therapists were female, Janie thought that Lou might work better with a male therapist. Janie threatened divorce unless Lou acquiesced to treatment, so he did.

One might assume that Janie would turn out to be the pursuer in this marriage, but in fact Lou was a male pursuer; he even went so far as to specifically refer to Janie as a "distancer." The reason he said he was fed up with marital therapy was because he was tired of pursuing Janie to spend more time with him and to have more frequent and higher quality sex. He said that Janie needed to do some of the work and that he felt she was not putting much effort into making their marriage better. Janie complained that Lou was not functioning up to his capability and that he had quit a secure job to pursue a career in the art world. Although she admitted that she initially sanctioned this move, she was livid that Lou had done little to make this career work and that she had to carry the financial load for the family. She also claimed that Lou was demanding and argumentative and that this behavior served to reduce her attraction for him.

As treatment went on it was evident that Lou could be difficult and at times unreasonable. He had a bad temper and seemed to look at life only through his own lens. He also held family members accountable for their behaviors but was always able to justify his own actions. To Lou's credit, however, he was clearly concerned about the welfare of his children, was good at setting limits with them, and was able to admit that he did not want them to follow in his footsteps. As a result, he confronted them when their school grades deteriorated and held them accountable for any poor behavior.

At some point in the treatment, Lou began to discuss his children in more detail and mentioned that he believed that Janie sabotaged any punishment or limit that he imposed on the children. He said that Janie was liberal to the point of harmful. One example he gave was that she allowed their daughter to stay home from school one day a week for several weeks in order to rest and gather herself. Apparently, the daughter also held a job and Janie was concerned that she would wear herself out. Lou felt strongly that school should come before work and that if necessary his daughter should quit her job. When Lou adamantly refused to accept Janie's decision, his daughter sided with her mother, thus completing the triangle. As this dynamic continued, the mother–daughter coalition solidified, and the father–daughter relationship deteriorated. Although Janie said she could not support Lou's aversive punishments and outbursts, it became clear that Janie was, albeit unconsciously, using her daughter against Lou, and Lou was exacerbating the situation via his temper and explosive and intimidating parental style.

Lou and Janie's dance was evidence of the link between the p–d dynamic and triangulation which was further validated by the fact that, whenever the partners attempted to increase their closeness, a problem would invariably develop with the daughter that would conveniently take the focus off the marriage and back onto the daughter. After the couple was able to detriangulate their daughter (which took approximately two years of treatment to accomplish), the son became the new point of the triangle and was even more difficult than the daughter given that he was somewhat oppositional as well as physically imposing. Further evidence of the link between the p–d dynamic and the triangulation emerged when the son was finally detriangulated with the help of a family therapist. At this point, the couple's p–d dynamic escalated beyond what it had been upon intake. Lou was angrier than ever. He was so relentless in his pursuing attacks on Janie that it was difficult for her to speak. Janie's response was to sink even more into herself, mumbling at Lou in defiance. Indeed, the marriage seemed to be in serious trouble.

When I helped the couple to connect their intimacy issues with the p–d dynamic and subsequently to the triangulation of the children, their relationship experienced some improvement, but Janie still had difficulty accepting that she could be passive–aggressively powerful and Lou refused to accept that his reactions to his wife and children contributed to the p–d dynamic. The couple continues in treatment today but it remains a highly toxic process. Lou was correct in saying that Janie was a distancer, but he didn't see anything wrong with his neediness and his angry, relentless pursuit of her. He said a husband should have a right to closeness. Janie admitted that she wanted more distance than Lou but felt that she could be closer if he was less demanding and more empathetic.

The case of Lou and Janie is perhaps a particularly difficult one for a number of reasons. First, the joining process was difficult. Lou was particularly angry and argumentative; he was clearly one of the most relentless pursuers I have encountered. He was also extremely bright and thus more capable of building cases against other family members, defending himself against change, and challenging me. With regard to the latter, it was difficult at times to stay calm and not personalize any of his challenges. Lou was also suspicious of therapy because of his prior negative experiences. Janie's unconscious passive–aggressiveness was also problematic. Her prior parentification in her family of origin contributed to a need for control and a need to defend her children from perceived injustices. Also, most marital therapists do not have to get as involved in the family dynamics as this case warranted; however, teens Steve and Leah were doing their best to maintain the dysfunctional family system and thus were in desperate need of detriangulation. At times, their acting out behavior bordered on dangerous.

Death and Distancing

When I was a young boy, my father captured a pheasant and put it in a wire cage. The bird was so distraught over the situation that it repeatedly slammed itself against the sides of the cage until one day it simply fell over and died. At the risk of being anthropomorphic, I must admit that I always believed the bird chose its fate — that it would rather have died than be trapped. My work with the following couple brought this story to mind.

Sean and Margaret were two physicians in their early forties. They had been married for eight years and had two young children. While this was Margaret's first marriage, it was Sean's third. He had four children from his previous marriages, and, despite the strain, he always seemed to meet his financial obligations to these individuals. The couple initially presented for treatment because Sean was openly having an affair and was thinking of leaving Margaret and moving in with his new girlfriend (a woman nearly half his age). Margaret was extremely distraught over this situation and wanted to save her marriage. She was perfectly willing to forgive Sean for his indiscretion if he would end his affair and commit to her. Not surprisingly, it was Margaret's idea to attend martial therapy; however, it was my impression that Sean's affair had progressed to the point where his departure from the marriage was imminent. Unfortunately, I was right, and within four sessions Sean confronted Margaret with the bad news. He subsequently moved out of the marital home and secured an apartment.

Under most circumstances, I would offer each partner a referral for individual therapy, but because they both were not quite sure about the ultimate outcome of the marriage, I agreed (at their request) to see them individually for a while to see if the marriage could still be salvaged. Despite being the initiator of the separation, Sean made it clear that he was in no hurry to obtain a divorce.

In my individual work with Sean it was evident he was a distancer in his marriage to Margaret. He not only carried on an affair and initiated a separation but throughout his marriage he was rarely home. He worked long hours and spent a great deal of time with friends and colleagues after work. Margaret said that on weekends he spent much of his time alone working on his hobbies.

Sean also demonstrated distancing tendencies in past relationships. Each of his ex-wives initially pursued him to spend more time with her, and when he initiated separations from them they fought hard to keep him. After getting to know Sean's pattern, I likened him to a missionary. His dynamic was to unconsciously choose women who were in need of a "good father." (All of Sean's wives were younger than he and had distancing fathers.) Coming to their rescue, Sean advised them, helped them gain self-confidence, and, when he felt that they were better able to stand on their own two feet, moved on to needier partners. It all seemed to give Sean a great sense of control and importance. He was always the sage in his relationships.

Sean distanced from the treatment, as well. He would only commit to biweekly sessions and seemed at times to treat me like one of his wives — other things took priority over our work together. Nonetheless, Sean was likable so I stuck with him, but I did not spare him the consequences of his distancing behavior. I repeatedly pointed out how his distancing manifested itself in and out of my office. I challenged him on his pattern and hypothesized that he had a conflict with commitment because of a parentified past. I also questioned why he consistently failed to enjoy the fruits of his labors (i.e., women with new-found self-esteem and confidence).

During the treatment, Sean's young girlfriend (who was unemployed) soon began to pursue him to end his marriage to Margaret and to start a life with her. As expected, she wanted a house and children of her own. While Sean understood her position, he now had to include Margaret and their two children in his already burdensome financial situation, without benefit of Margaret's somewhat substantial income. Nevertheless, he bought a new home and began to fall behind in his payments to his ex-wives, who in turn increased their pursuit of support. One ex-wife even threatened to take him to court.

Although Sean was trying to take all of this pressure in stride, I could tell he was under enormous stress and that his psychological "escape hatches" were beginning to close. Soon, Sean began to understand his pattern and to question whether he wanted to rescue any more women or put anyone else through his dysfunctional process. He also began to see his limitations for the first time, but, because of the strength of his internal conflict, he could not end his relationship and go back to Margaret.

Meanwhile, Margaret was making progress in her individual treatment. She began to realize that her need for a man like Sean was connected to her controlling, yet distancing, father and she soon became strong enough to file for divorce. Ironically, Sean became enraged when Margaret initiated the divorce process. He did not like her newfound power being used against him; moreover, he no longer had an excuse to avoid marrying his new girlfriend. His stress increased tenfold from this point forward.

When Sean failed to show up for a session one day, Margaret called to tell me that he had suffered a massive stroke and died. I do believe that Sean wanted out of his dilemma and that his conflict had created so much stress for him that it may have triggered a biologically predisposed organic problem. Regardless of the origin of his fatal illness, however, Sean performed his final distancing maneuver, although I am sure he would have consciously preferred a different escape route. Similar to my father's pheasant, Sean gained his freedom but at a tremendous cost.

When One Partner Has Attention-Deficit/Hyperactivity Disorder

Attention-deficit/hyperactivity disorder (AD/HD) is a multidimensional disorder that is linked to neurological, physiological, psychological, and behavioral problems that may lead to a multitude of symptoms such as hyperactivity, impulsivity, distractibility, emotional lability, hypersensitivity (physical and emotional), forgetfulness, and maturational lag (Betchen, 2003). Although experts such as Amen (2001) have discovered as many as six types of the disorder, the DSM-IV (APA, 1994) identifies three major ones: the hyperactive–impulsive type (AD/HD–HI), the inattentive type (AD/HD–I), and the combined type (AD/HD–C). The hyperactive type is marked by a general lack of self-control. People with this type have a constant need for activity, are very impatient, and bore easily. Inattentive types have difficulty paying attention, particularly to detail. They also have a tendency to drift and appear as if they are in a fog. The combined types have characteristics of both.

There was a time in the not-to-distant past when AD/HD was thought to dissipate in adolescence (Munoz-Millan & Casteel, 1989); however, recent research has indicated that up to 4% of the adult population suffers from it (AD/HD Information Library, 2002). One of the consequences of this confusion is that the correlation between adult interpersonal difficulties and AD/HD has been relatively overlooked (Ratey, Hallowell, & Miller, 1995). The reality of the disorder is that symptoms associated with it affect not only an individual's day-to-day functioning but also efforts to establish and maintain intimate connections (Hallowell, 1999; Nadeau, 1996). According to Nadeau (1993), adults suffering from AD/HD are so often wrapped up in their thoughts that they are usually unable to establish the closeness and communication that can lead to sexual intimacy.

According to Weiss (1997), marital therapy that fails to recognize AD/HD will result in inappropriate treatment of the couple; therefore, it is vital for couples therapists to be aware of the many symptoms suggesting this disorder. With regard to the p–d dynamic, couples therapists need to be cognizant of the fact that many of the behavioral traits of the inattentive type, for example, resemble those of the distancer, and *vice versa*. I do not, however, believe that partners with AD/HD precisely fit the p–d model presented herein because much or all of their non-intimate behavior is caused by their organic difficulty, not necessarily because of a core issue with intimacy. Nevertheless, the result is too often the same, and the partners of inattentive types in particular sound very much like the partners of distancers (*i.e.*, pursuers). That is, they complain that they feel neglected and as if they are living alone. As a result, they, too, clamor for more contact, which eventually sets up the p–d relationship in the AD/HD couple.

While the model proposed in this book has not been specifically designed to treat couples with AD/HD, the psychodynamic components of it can be useful (Halverstadt, 1998) as long as other interventions that are more behaviorally driven are included. For example, Nadeau (1996) recommended a multimodal approach to help AD/HD-affected couples achieve intimacy that includes not only family-of-origin work but also medical and educational components, homework assignments, cognitive restructuring, communication and social skills training, and, in some cases, auxiliary treatment such as coaching by an AD/HD specialist. I believe strongly that medication is a necessity in the treatment process because of the organic nature of the problem. Psychostimulants such as methylphenidate HCl (Concerta®; Johnson & Johnson, 2002) or an extended-release formula of amphetamine mixed salts (Adderall XR®; Shire Laboratories, 2002) are two of the most common longer lasting drugs used for the treatment of AD/HD.

Even with medical treatment, however, I have found that treating a couple affected by this disorder can prove to be a very difficult task. When the individual who acts as the pursuer keeps the distancer in treatment, the prognosis is often more positive, but when both partners have AD/HD treatment is usually short lived and unsuccessful. The following case reveals some of the specific difficulties I experienced with a couple in which one partner suffered from the inattentive type of AD/HD.

Rex and Mara had been married for twenty-one years and had three children. Rex was in his early fifties and Mara was in her middle forties. Rex was pursing Mara to stay married to him. He was very emotional about wanting to keep the marriage together but Mara was unsure about doing so. During the sessions she would space out or seem preoccupied. She often had to be asked to refocus on the topic at hand. When it came to deciding to stay married to Rex, she simply couldn't provide an answer. Meanwhile, she refused to have sex with him. At his insistence, they slept in separate beds in the house, and she had decided against accompanying the family on vacations. Rex was tearing his hair out pursuing Mara at every turn but to no avail. Mara even obtained her own individual therapist but still could not make up her mind about her marriage.

Because of her inability to maintain her focus, her ability to be easily distracted, her apparent disorientation in sessions, her lack of goals, and her difficulty with decision-making, I referred Mara to a specialist to be tested for AD/HD. I strongly suspected that she suffered from the inattentive type. I knew that this form of AD/HD was most common in females and because of its passive nature was the most difficult of the three types to diagnose (Solden, 1995).

As predicted, Mara was diagnosed with the inattentive type of AD/HD and prescribed medication. The couple was advised to continue their marital treatment. I also contacted Mara's individual therapist, who confirmed that Mara was stuck as to whether to stay with or leave her husband. The therapist said it would probably be up to Rex to decide what to do with the marriage.

I believed that the key to the treatment of this couple was to alleviate the couple's parent–child dynamic and to get each partner, particularly Mara, to take partial responsibility for it in the first place. More specifically, Rex needed to deal with his overfunctioning and to learn to take care of himself — artifacts from his family of origin. Mara needed to organize herself and learn to make decisions and set goals. She also needed to take responsibility for parentifying Rex so that she could alleviate some of the anger she had for him. (Hallowell and Ratey [1994, pp. 217–218] reported that individuals with AD/HD are "proverbial 'fence sitters'" because of the difficulty they have building and retaining a "historical self" on which to base future decisions; this renders them more dependent on others.)

Unfortunately, the preceding treatment plan was more easily conceived than carried out. Mara could not let go of the disdain she had for Rex's parental style, even though it was pointed out to her numerous times that she probably selected Rex, in part, to structure her life. Rex was not a critical parent, but he was intrusive and controlling, and the family-of-origin work failed to alleviate his caretaking. It is not unusual for an individual with AD/HD to marry a structured individual with obsessive–compulsive traits to help with limit setting and structure, but this combination frequently turns into a problematic parent–child dynamic, as it did in this case (Betchen, 2003).

It took a few weeks of frustrating treatment, but because Rex could not secure any kind of commitment from Mara he decided to end couples therapy and seek a divorce. Mara's resistance to taking her medication on a consistent basis (which did make a difference in her attitude and behavior) and her inconsistent attendance in treatment (either forgetting to show up for a session or finding an excuse not to attend) helped to speed Rex's decision along. Unfortunately, several months later friends of Rex and Mara whom I also had been treating volunteered the fact that Rex never followed through with the decision to leave Mara. The couple was still floundering in their situation and, no doubt, their p–d dynamic as well.

In Pursuit of Marriage

We live in a couples-oriented society. In 2003 alone, approximately 2,443,000 marriages were recorded (U.S. Census Bureau, 2003). After dissolution of their marriages, people still tend to remarry at an astounding rate. For example, one study found that 81% of the women under age 25 remarried within 10 years after divorce, and 68% of the women over 25 years of age remarried within 10 years after divorce (U.S. Department of Health and Human Services, 2002). Even those individuals not interested in marriage or those who cannot marry for legal reasons (*i.e.*, same-sex couples) seek out more permanent-type partnerships. As previously noted, Fields and Casper (2001) found that nearly 8 million men and women were cohabitating in the year 2000, representing 3.8 million unmarried-partner households. These statistics do not even account for those individuals who maintain separate residences but still consider themselves in monogamous relationships.

While couplehood is an admirable objective, the pressure to find a permanent partner can be emotionally overwhelming. This is particularly true for childless women who feel the tick of their biological clocks. I cannot even count the number of single individuals who have expressed sadness to me following their attendance at someone else's wedding. Many individuals have told me that they are embarrassed to attend events alone. Some worry about becoming ill or dying alone. The size and closeness of one's family of origin are factors in determining how well the latter issue is handled. The following case is that of a talented, yet somewhat desperate woman who pursued the man she loved to live with and eventually marry her. Unfortunately for both partners, they were not able to resolve their differences and collaborative p–d dynamic.

Warren and Alice were a couple in their early fifties. They had been dating for four years prior to coming in for couples work. Alice was a professional woman with a high-powered job, a hefty income, and a beautiful home. Alice was proud of her accomplishments as a single woman but made it clear that she wished to marry more than anything in the world. Marriage was something she had never achieved and she felt that Warren was the man she wanted to spend the rest of her life with.

Warren was also a professional man but was currently unemployed. He had been married and divorced once and had two grown children. Unlike Alice, Warren's financial situation was tenuous. He was recently laid off from his job and was having problems paying his mortgage. Warren's solution was to rent out his home and obtain a small apartment until he secured satisfactory employment. Alice vehemently disagreed with Warren's plan. She wanted Warren to move in with her with an eye toward marriage. She had plenty of room in her spacious home and considered this to be a good deal for Warren, given that it would clearly elevate his lifestyle. Moreover, Alice stated, by moving in with her Warren would be conveying the message that he was indeed serious about the relationship.

Warren, however, rejected Alice's proposal and this response set off a p–d dynamic that would sometimes border on violent. While Warren initially stated that Alice was a "controlling pain in the ass," he later said, "My house is all I've got. If I give it up and move in with her I'll be swallowed up … I'll become her boy." Alice was pressing; in fact, she needed anti-anxiety medication to help her cope with Warren's distancing. She made it clear that Warren was demonstrating that he did not love her.

I also thought that Alice's offer was a good one. I thought that she was a woman of great quality and that she truly loved Warren. I did not feel that she simply wanted him because no one else was available. I did, however, feel that her pursuit was damaging to the relationship and clearly was not going to work with Warren. She seemed to have a conflict around intimacy and victimization that she was playing out via her pursuit. I also felt that, although Warren blamed Alice's aggressive personality for why he would not commit to her, I believed that he had a history of sabotage and that he was using distance to ruin a potentially good life for himself.

Although I worked on the preceding issues and how they were connected to each partner's family of origin for over a year, the p–d dynamic only seemed to escalate, particularly as Warren moved closer to renting an apartment. Assigned readings on the p–d dynamic enlightened the couple but had no great impact. Finally, when Warren had his home rented and an apartment picked out, he terminated the relationship with Alice. Stunned, she retreated to individual therapy with someone she had seen in the past.

While I certainly felt bad for Alice, it was clear that Warren was not ready for a committed relationship with her. In this type of situation, it is better for the pursuing partner to give up and look elsewhere. Forcing an individual into a relationship usually only ends in disaster. If someone doesn't want you, then you should learn not to want them, even if it means you have to remain single. It is better to be single than to be in a miserable, abusive relationship. These were my final words to Alice.

The Ultimate Distancer

As noted, some therapists believe that when the pursuer backs off the distancer usually closes in, thus the treatment concept of backing off the pursuer to bring in the distancer. While I do believe that the distancer will close if the pursuer curbs his or her pursuit, the extent to which this will occur depends on where the distancer is on the p–d continuum. For example, distancers who are close to or at the extreme end of the distancing side of the continuum may move in only slightly. Doing so may take the form of sitting at the breakfast table a little longer as if to indicate that the distancer is willing to spend extra time with his or her mate. Someone closer to the pursuing end of the continuum will come in closer.

Some individuals, however, fail to offer little or any movement even when the pursuers refrain from or limit their pursuit. These distancers simply continue to distance, bearing out their corresponding pursuers' worst nightmares — that if they stop pursuing they will lose total connection or be abandoned. The following case depicts this type of distancer. This individual most resembles the most extreme version of the distancer.

Jay and Gwen were a couple in their middle forties who had been married for five years. Gwen was clearly the pursuer in this marriage. She was extremely angry and frustrated with Jay and dragged Jay into marital therapy because she claimed that he was not engaged in the marriage. She specifically said that Jay held few if any conversations with her, never complimented her, and never initiated sex. Gwen was threatening divorce unless Jay learned to show more interest in the marriage. Typical of a distancer, Jay claimed that he was relatively happy with the marriage, with the exception of Gwen's constant nagging, of course.

It took several months of treatment, but Gwen began to curb her pursuing behavior and work on her own internal conflicts. She eventually was able to get in touch with how her need for a "caring, responsible father" caused her to marry and pursue someone like Jay. Indeed, Gwen's father was a very difficult man to get close to and was rarely home with his wife and children. On the other hand, Jay could not seem to move in an inch. In fact, as Gwen pulled back he increased his distancing by choosing to engage himself in more solo activities.

I could do very little to help Jay save his marriage, and in fact I probably worked too hard to help him. In perhaps the most significant session of our work together, Gwen tearfully said that she believed that she had no alternative but to end her marriage. She said that the thought of it was extremely painful to her, but that Jay couldn't give her even the slightest sign that he cared for her. Rather than address Gwen during this crucial moment, Jay looked at me and said that he didn't want a divorce, but couldn't say why. He just mumbled that he had no control over the situation. The only thing Jay needed to let Gwen know at that moment was that he cared about her, but he couldn't. It was as if his car was about to crash but he couldn't lift his leg to step on the brake to save himself. Jay was indeed paralyzed, but Gwen wasn't; she soon thereafter filed for divorce.

Both pursuer and distancer need to be prepared for the fact that either of them might not be able to change, and as a consequence the end of the relationship may be inevitable. Too many couples avoid treatment for fear they will discover the ultimate truth about the viability of their relationships. It is, however, the risk that all couples must endure in order to have a chance at intimacy.

No Sexual Attraction, No Sexual Desire

I have already described at some length the difficulties associated with treating low sexual desire. Therapists can spend years trying to help a couple rekindle their love lives, oftentimes to no avail; therefore, no discussion on case difficulty and failure would be complete without at least one example of a struggle with a sexual desire problem. I feel confident in asserting that nearly all therapists who work in the relationship field have coped with such a struggle with little or no success.

I was at a professional meeting several years ago when a group of sex therapists began discussing whether or not an individual who was able to be attracted to others both in the past and present could become attracted and desirous of his or her partner if that attraction had never existed to begin with. The overwhelming response was "no." The theme of the meeting centered on low sexual desire and how to treat it. The therapists were expressing the frustration and helplessness they often experienced when they tried to improve the quality or frequency of sex between partners when at least one of them holds little or no attraction for the other and never has. Treating an acquired low desire is certainly difficult enough, but successfully treating individuals who have never even felt an inkling of sexual attraction for their partners is, I dare say, next to impossible.

Whether the problem lies with pheromones (*i.e.*, chemical substances made by the body to stimulate other members of the same species), neurotransmitters in the brain (Fisher, 2000), or emotional conflict, when it comes to creating attraction, I remain pessimistic about the progress. If at least a hint of attraction has existed, the therapist can perhaps help the disinterested partner to build upon it. If one partner has never felt any semblance of attraction, perhaps it is possible that the therapist could help that partner discover an interest level that he or she was never aware of and thus unable to feel because of an internal blockage or conflict. I have, however, never achieved success in this manner.

In terms of the p–d dynamic, the interaction presented herein is similar to that of couples who present with acquired low sexual desire in which an attraction once existed — the partner who desires sex pursues and the one who has low or no desire distances. In the case that follows, however, it is the sexually attracted, desirous partner who pursues and the indifferent partner who has never had an attraction that distances. As with low sexual desire in couples, it is rare when both mates are unattracted to each other (Betchen, 2001a).

Lenore and Scott were a couple in their early forties who were married for nine years. Scott reported that Lenore was not very attracted to him and that she was not interested in sex. Lenore agreed and said that she was, in fact, never attracted to Scott but she decided to marry him because he was a relentless pursuer. As Lenore put it, "He would not go away." Scott verified his wife's comments. He admitted that he constantly called her and begged for dates. Lenore reported that at times she would not answer the phone or would abruptly hang up on Scott in order to dissuade him from contacting her. Nevertheless, Scott kept coming back until he apparently wore Lenore down. Midway through the couples work, Scott remarked in Shakespearean jest, "Be careful what you wish for."

Actually, Scott was a handsome, charming man with a good sense of humor. Although Lenore admitted that he was by general standards good looking, she was not attracted to his look, found his sense of humor distasteful, and was not interested in having sexual relations with him. An examination of the couple's history revealed that even during their dating process Lenore showed a lack of sexual interest in Scott. At times, Lenore had forced herself to have sex, but it was obvious to both partners that she simply had no interest in this pursuit. Nevertheless, just as he did prior to the marriage, Scott consistently pursued Lenore to have sex with him to show that she loved and accepted him as a life partner. He was totally enamored of her and saw it as a challenge to get her to love and desire him. The more he pursued, however, the more adverse, prickly, and distant Lenore was to him.

The couple was in therapy for several years and enjoyed many improvements in their communication patterns, problem-solving ability, and general lifestyle; however, Lenore was never able to reach an acceptable level of attraction and desire for Scott. Her deep-seated family-of-origin issues and correlating conflicts with intimacy were too difficult to overcome. She did, however, decide to stay with Scott, probably out of her own insecurity and fear of abandonment. Scott, not one to give up on anything easily, accepted his fate, but he did manage to relax more and greatly curb his pursuing behavior. Scott's pursuing behavior and his inability to end his relationship in order to seek out someone more accepting of him could be traced back to his mother, who was difficult to please and by whom Scott never felt accepted. Although Scott was able to put some of this insight to use (*e.g.*, increasing his self-esteem and curbing his pursuit), his fantasy to one day get his mother to love and accept him proved to be too strong of a transference for him to give up on Lenore.

CHAPTER 11
Other Contexts and the Pursuer–Distancer Dynamic

As noted previously, many different contexts can serve as vehicles for the pursuer–distancer process. The context of sexuality, for example, has been discussed at great length earlier in this book; however, the couples therapist will most likely have to contend with several other contexts that are particularly fertile for the p–d dynamic. In this chapter, I will attempt to discuss some of the more common contexts and raise specific issues within these contexts that will inevitably confront the therapist. This chapter is not meant to provide an exhaustive discourse on the contexts presented, as that is well beyond its scope; rather, its purpose is to enlighten the therapist with regard to how these particular contexts can and often do interact with the p–d dynamic in couples. It is recommended that couples therapists have some familiarity with each specific context in order to better service the couples.

Intimate Partner Violence

Intimate partner violence (*i.e.*, violence committed against persons by their current or former spouses, boyfriends, or girlfriends) exists to varying degrees in all ethnic and racial groups regardless of socioeconomic status, but Gelles (2000) contended that because it is "typically hidden in the home, there has been, until quite recently, a general lack of awareness of the extent and seriousness of the problem" (p. 784). It does seem to be common knowledge, however, that women are at greater risk of being victimized by their intimate partners than are men. For example, in 2001, the rate of intimate partner violence against women averaged 5.0 per 1000; the rate for men averaged 0.9 per 1000. More specifically, in 2001 women were victims in approximately 588,490 violent crimes committed by intimate partners, and men were victimized 103,220 times by their partners (Rennison, 2003).

Intimate partner violence particularly merits serious attention because it tends to be compulsive in nature and escalates over time, thus proving to be potentially deadly. Approximately 35% of female murder victims die at the hands of a partner each year (Lissette & Kraus, 2000). In 2000, 1247 women and 440 men were murdered by their intimate partners (Rennison, 2003).

Gelles (1995) pointed out that regardless of the rate of violence or who initiated it, women were seven to ten times more likely to be injured in these acts than are men. It is also contended by some experts that women tend to strike out for the most part as a defensive measure against their abusive intimate partners (Loseke & Kurz, 2005).

Intimate partner violence is most often associated with shame and embarrassment; therefore, as Gelles (2000) stated, it is often kept secret from those outside the immediate family. Even within the family system the abuse is oftentimes protected by a denial of the seriousness of the transgressions and is allowed to thrive free of intervention. On those occasions when it is reported, the victimized partner may characteristically fail to follow through with prosecution. Reasons for this may be related to not wanting to deal with the complexities of the criminal justice system, the unconscious need to preserve the abusive dynamic, or a fear of further retaliation from the perpetrator.

During my work on a spouse abuse grant in the late 1970s, I heard several police officers express concern about responding to domestic disputes because of risks associated with intervening in such potentially explosive situations and the reluctance of many victims to cooperate with the authorities even though they may have been the ones who made the distress calls. Although it was clear to me at the time that most police departments lacked the appropriate training required to handle these types of calls, today (even though the same barriers to appropriate intervention exist) most police departments are far more aware of the problem and seek professional consultants to train their officers in handling intimate partner violence disputes.

Daniel (2000) reported that a major reason why intimate partner violence exists and is difficult to alleviate is because it is learned in the family of origin; that is, most perpetrators and victims tend to come from homes in which they one way or another experienced abuse or violence. As adults, these individuals unconsciously choose one another and replicate the abusive cycle. Although the types and levels of domestic abuse and violence vary, this chapter focuses on the physical violence between adult partners and how it can serve as a context for the p–d dynamic. In my clinical experience, it is often the batterer (generally the male) who plays the role of the distancer and the victim (generally the female) who plays the role of the pursuer. The following case depicts the p–d dynamic within the context of intimate partner violence.

Ben and Allie were married for approximately four years when they presented for couples treatment. Ben was forty, and Allie was in her late twenties. Although Allie initiated therapy, Ben admitted that he and Allie needed help. Allie tearfully described Ben's terrible temper and how he had pushed and slapped her on occasion. Ben said that Allie "asked for it." He specifically said that she was obsessive and therefore could not let go of something that bothered her. As a result, Ben claimed that she nagged him until he couldn't take any more — and then he would strike. In essence, Ben portrayed his behavior as defensive; it was the only way he felt he could stop Allie from badgering or provoking him. Initially, Ben did not admit that he had a bad temper. In fact, he said that he had tried to leave the room or house in order to avoid fighting with Allie, but she would follow him from room to room or block him from leaving the family home.

Ben was an only child who was severely parentified; his parents were very reliant on him to help with the family business to the extent that he was not able to participate in school or social activities. One particularly telling example Ben offered of his parentification was when he joined the basketball team in high school and his parents showed up at a practice to insist that he quit the team and return to work. To make matters worse for Ben, he reported that the family business could be very stressful in part because of its seasonal nature. The income needed to support the family the entire year needed to be made in a short few months. It was during these months that Ben suffered the most, eventually developing chronic migraine headaches. Ben's father was a hard-working individual but not an affectionate man. According to Ben, he was a philanderer and a "bully" in a passive, manipulative manner. Ben's mother was "always ill" and used this as well as her dominant personality to bully both Ben and her husband. No physical abuse occurred in Ben's family of origin, but both parents (in their own style) were constantly after him to do things for them and the family business.

Ben admitted that he fantasized about escaping from home, but that he felt too dependent and obligated to do so. Ben also reported that his first wife was a demanding "whiner." He admitted that he was abusive to her, particularly when he perceived her as being whiny or demanding. He eventually left this woman after two years of marriage because he was not comfortable with her style and felt he would never be able to please her. Although Ben believed that he did the right thing by escaping his ex-wife, to this day he said that he still feels some guilt about leaving.

Allie was the youngest sibling of three sisters. Her father was known to be physically abusive with his wife and daughters, particularly on the occasions when he would drink too much. Allie reported that "all the girls" in the family, particularly she, constantly pursued her father to stop drinking and distancing and to stay home. Apparently, he would disappear for long stretches at a time and was irresponsible in terms of supporting the family financially. Although Allie was the youngest sibling, it was she who challenged her father most often and as a result ended up taking the brunt of his abuse. Allie described her mother as a passive, manipulative woman who seemed to relish the roles of "martyr" and "victim."

Ben and Allie were a good example of how the p–d dynamic could lead to or exacerbate a violent dyadic situation. Ben presented in conflict: Because of his parentification, he needed to take care of someone to feel useful, yet he hated the burden this need brought with it. While he was conscious of the fact that he was marrying a beautiful, much younger woman, he was less aware of the level of need she presented and how it would awaken the hostility in him. When Allie showed even the slightest annoyance or disappointment in him, Ben would overreact (as if he were dealing with his parents and ex-wife) and distance from her as best he could.

Allie, however, was also in conflict: She longed for a good man to take care of her, but was unable to allow one to treat her well. While she was conscious of the fact that Ben was an older, more mature man who seemed particularly caring, she was unaware of the resentment inside him and the anger and disappointment she held toward men. As a result, she judged Ben harshly, and angrily pursued him (as she did her father) to meet an unattainable standard for a spouse.

Ben and Allie's p–d dynamic is relatively common; however, severe parentification in conjunction with a history of abuse renders this couple more prone to a violent p–d dynamic. In fact, typical of intimate partner violence and the aforementioned p–d interactional sequence, after Ben would hit Allie she would retreat to her room or a friend's home (distancing) to sulk, until Ben sought her out (pursuing), swearing never to hit her again. Interestingly, Allie felt the same way after her father struck her, and Ben felt guilt-ridden and ashamed whenever he tried to rebel against his parentified duties in his family of origin. Eventually, however, the cycle would start over again with both partners reverting back to their natural p–d roles.

Just as the couples therapist must work quickly to calm the p–d dynamic so deeper work can take place, it is absolutely imperative that violence in a relationship be dealt with first and foremost. The couple may need to be referred to a program for abuse before couples therapy can take place or resume, or each partner might benefit from attending groups for perpetrators and victims, respectively, in conjunction with the couples work. Ben and Allie were sent to a program for partner violence after an attempt made in couples therapy to alleviate the violence failed. Even the coping mechanisms (*e.g.*, Ben was to begin counting in an effort to calm himself when he began to anger; meditation), limit-setting recommendations (*e.g.*, Allie calling the police), and planned escape routes (*e.g.*, Allie was to have a bag packed and as soon as Ben began to get physical she was to grab her bag and evacuate the house) failed to prevent this couple from engaging in violent behavior. As recommended by Mack (1989), even a "no-violence contract" was discussed, but to no avail.

Following the violence program, however, the couple returned to conjoint therapy to work on their underlying issues and the p–d dynamic in general. Over the next couple of years, both partners worked to solve their respective internal conflicts which ultimately led to their addressing the p–d dynamic and their intimate partner violence. Ben processed his conflicted feelings about being parentified in his family of origin and how his parentification correlated with his reaction to Allie's demands, resulting in his becoming a perpetrator of spousal violence and abuse. He also came to realize how his distancing only exacerbated the couple's problems. Allie processed her anger and disappointment with regard to her parents (particularly her father) and realized that her pursuit only tapped into Ben's severe parentification, which in turn prevented her from getting her needs met by a man. This behavior also modeled her mother's victimization — something she consciously abhorred.

When Berns *et al.* (1999) examined the demand/withdraw interaction in the context of marital violence, they separated the male batterers in their study into type I and type II batterers. Type I batterers were found to be belligerent and defensive, with a tendency to strike quickly. They were more likely to have had a history of violent behavior in and outside the home and to use or threaten to use a knife or gun on their wives. They were also more likely to meet the criteria for antisocial or addictive personalities. Type II batterers exhibited their anger in a slower, more gradual fashion, increasing their threatening behaviors as the interaction continued. Only a very small percentage of these men had histories of violent behavior outside the marriage. In terms of the demand/withdraw interaction, Berns *et al.* were somewhat surprised to find, uncharacteristically, that each spouse in the violent marriages they studied exhibited both demand and withdraw tendencies; that is, the batterer was found to be both demanding and withdrawing, and the victim was found to be both demanding and withdrawing.

Although I believe that Ben could be classified as a type II batterer, the case of Ben and Allie does not necessarily support the authors' findings with regard to the demand/withdraw dynamic. (The authors did caution that their sample size was both small and unequal.) I can, however, attest to the fact that males can exhibit pursuing or demanding behavior in the context of a violent relationship, just as many of the type I husbands did. In an effort to attain and maintain total dominance and control, these men may pursue an irrational level of dedication and general subservience from their female partners. Even when these victimized partners gather up the courage to leave these men, the men may relentlessly pursue them deep into the legal system often using whatever financial and legal resources they can to maintain control. I have witnessed this type of pursuit from men even after their partners have ended the relationship and moved off the premises (if the couple was residing together), as well as, in extreme cases, after both partners have remarried others. Some of these pursuing men may also be prone to commit femicide (*i.e.*, murder of a woman) and participate in stalking behavior.

In their national study, "Stalking in America: Findings from the National Violence Against Women Survey," Tjaden and Thoennes (1998) found that over 1,006,970 women were stalked annually. Of all the stalkers, 87% were men, and 54% of the females were stalked by an intimate partner. The authors also found that the average stalking case lasts 1.8 years. McFarlane *et al.* (1999) reported that 76% of the femicide victims and 85% of the attempted femicide victims she and her colleagues examined and interviewed had been stalked by their intimate partners in the year just before their murder. The Internet has become yet another vehicle for extreme pursuit or stalking behavior. Cyberstalking, or the use of the Internet, e-mail, or other electronic communication devices to stalk another person, is rapidly becoming a major problem in our society. In tune with the statistics previously mentioned, the majority of cyberstalkers are men, and the majority of cyberstalking victims are women (U.S. Department of Justice, 2001).

The following case depicts a pursuing male stalker and his distancing, victimized wife. The husband in this case did not physically batter his spouse, but he did exhibit some of the emotionally abusive, controlling, and irrational characteristics of the type I batterer discussed by Berns *et al.* (1999).

Renee and Barry were a very attractive couple who had been married for approximately six years when they entered marital treatment. Renee was a soft-spoken woman in her middle thirties, and Barry presented as a dynamic and charismatic man in his early forties. The couple had three young daughters. Barry was the dominant personality in the relationship. He controlled everything. He controlled all the finances in the house, and much of the couple's assets were in his name alone. He made all business decisions and decided where the couple would live. While Renee was initially attracted to Barry's dominance (she eventually discovered that this attraction was unconsciously rooted in a distaste she had for her passive father), she began to eventually feel suffocated and controlled in what she perceived as an unfair manner. She initiated treatment in an effort to get Barry to curb some of his controlling methods and to compromise more with her in the marriage. Barry, on the other hand, demonstrated an indifference to his wife's concerns (in much the same way as his father reacted to his "martyr" mother). He believed that she was not sophisticated enough to make big decisions, and because he had a track record of success he felt that he should run their lives.

After about two months of treatment, it was obvious to Renee that Barry had no intention of compromising with her on any issue so she decided to seek a divorce. It was at this point that Barry's controlling, dominant behavior intensified to a level that clearly shocked Renee. Specifically, Barry became an obsessive pursuer. He began to follow Renee, attempted to tape her telephone conversations, harassed her friends to convince her to cease divorce proceedings, and badgered her every time he saw her. Again, he did not resort to physical violence or threats of physical harm like the type I or type II batterers described by Berns *et al.* (1999), but he made it clear that he was not going to let go of Renee.

Although the couple terminated marital therapy after Renee's decision to leave the marriage, she would call me from time to time to inform me of the situation. Apparently, the divorce process dragged on for four years, with Barry fighting every inch of the way, even though it cost him a substantial sum of money. Even after Renee moved out of the family home and obtained an apartment, Barry bought a house nearby her and kept track of her dating. Renee claimed that Barry's behavior had cost her a boyfriend and that her financial resources were dangerously low because of the constant suits Barry had brought against her. Renee was angry with the judicial system because she felt it was not protecting her from Barry's stalking and constant harassments. She also noted that male judges were indifferent to this type of behavior against women. Although Barry almost lost a live-in girlfriend because of his obsession with Renee, Renee informed me that he finally left her alone soon after he married this girlfriend.

Employment (Work)

In an industrial society, work and financial success are prized commodities. Working hard in order to achieve financial independence is the goal of most people. Although this capitalistic philosophy has allowed our society (and societies like ours) to prosper to a greater extent than others, the natural inclination to beat the competition and achieve wealth has, for many, evolved into a "win at any cost" attitude that has skewed the values of society away from nurturing relationships. Political and corporate leaders like to preach marriage and family values; however, we are also told that in order to get ahead we need to give 110% to our work. I recently saw one television commercial that recommended giving 200%. The message is conflicting at best, with both men and women struggling mightily to balance their lives. The result: Stress levels are up, and more and more people are taking medication for relief. Intimacy is down, and the divorce rate continues to hover just below 50% (U.S. Bureau of the Census, 2003). When the economy is suffering, these problems are exacerbated.

I do not pretend to have a solution to the ills of society, but I do see firsthand how career and work can prove deleterious to a relationship, particularly a marriage. Given the positive reinforcement that work is accorded in our society, it is easy for an individual to hide behind it in order to create space in a relationship. This is what makes work a convenient vehicle for the p–d dynamic. One partner distances via work or career under the guise that he or she is performing a noble deed for the relationship and family; the other partner pursues to be made a priority. Work is clearly one of the contexts most often presented by couples engaged in the p–d dynamic.

Dean and Mary were a couple in their late thirties who had been married for ten years. Mary was a housewife, and Dean was employed as a supervisor at a major computer company. They had one infant son. Mary dragged Dean in for marital therapy. She was an angry, animated, passionate individual, and Dean presented as a quiet, restrained, polite man.

Mary complained that, although Dean had always worked long hours, he had unnecessarily increased the time he spent at work to the point where he was barely home. Moreover, she claimed that they had plenty of money and that much of this extra time dedicated to his career was unnecessary, particularly given that the couple had just had their first child. Mary also reported that Dean was obligated to spend time in the Army Reserves, as well, but she did not have as much trouble with this as long as he could better balance his job and home responsibilities. Dean's defense was that he felt the need to earn more money now that the couple had a child. He did admit, however, that Mary seemed to "want too much of him." He also resented Mary's attacking style, which he said turned him off and at times made him want to spend more time at work. He described his job as somewhat solitary and calming except when he had to confront one of his employees, which he admitted he wasn't very good at.

Mary was a middle child in a big Irish Catholic family of six children. She described her father as a philanderer who drank too heavily and was rarely home. She described her mother as a nice woman, who was completely overwhelmed with domestic responsibilities. When asked what her role in the family was, Mary stated that she was her mother's main helper and would often fight with her father to put more of an effort into the family. Mary felt sorry for her mother, but on some level she was annoyed with her inability to stand up for herself.

Dean was an only child. He described his father as passive and disengaged and his mother as overbearing and very intrusive. Dean claimed that his mother was so controlling that he "couldn't escape her." Apparently, she was reluctant to let him out of her sight, but every chance Dean had he would get away from home and stay away for as long as he could. Dean said that he understood why his father enjoyed his time away from home and that he longed to do the same. Upon finishing high school, Dean entered the military and never returned to live home again. Although Dean had little empathy for his mother's position and seemed to hold her totally responsible for his family dynamics, he did at one point comment that his father left him to the mercy of his mother.

During the course of treatment, Mary's anger and hostility became more and more evident. At times, it seemed that she had very little control over her outbursts. To her credit, however (unlike many pursuers), Mary was conscious of her lack of control and didn't like this about herself. At one point during the therapy she said, "I hate nagging Dean; I never wanted to be like this." Dean, on the other hand, was in denial. He blamed the marital problems solely on Mary's temper and aggressive style; he didn't believe he contributed to the couple's problems in any way. This attitude served to increase Mary's rage, which in turn led Dean to increase his work hours. At one point during the treatment Dean began to work longer evening hours as well as volunteer for overtime. Mary began to suspect an affair, but it was clear to me that Dean was simply locked into the same p–d dynamic that his parents experienced and that he experienced with his mother. Mary pursued Dean with the same rage and zeal with which she had pursued her father.

Following approximately 16 months of treatment, Mary had learned to control herself (*i.e.*, approach Dean differently). In order to do so, she needed to see the p–d dynamic in her family of origin more clearly and to connect it to her current relationship with Dean. It was imperative that she resolve her conflict. Although she wanted a man to approve of her and to love her (as her father was unable to), she also distrusted men and undervalued her appeal to them (as she felt her father did). She also needed to give her mother more responsibility for her plight.

Dean took longer to come around (as distancers usually do); however, he eventually took responsibility for his conflict. Not having had a relationship with his father, he needed his mother, but he also wanted to escape her intrusiveness. When Dean began to accept his conflict, he was better able to balance his view of his family of origin. Specifically, he began to give his father some responsibility for being a distancer and to grieve over this loss. Doing so enabled him to feel some empathy toward his pursuing mother and wife.

It was particularly important to Dean that he avoid triangulating his son into the same type of dynamic he had experienced in his family of origin — this served as a great impetus for his change. Another vital component of Dean's transformation was that, instead of running from his wife, he learned to confront her and tolerate her responses no matter how offputting they may have been. I appealed to Dean's military background by asking him to stand and fight (not in a physical way, of course). Mary supported my point by admitting that she would rather have it out with Dean and know where he stood than deal with the excruciating pain of thinking he didn't love her and that he wanted to get as far away from her as possible. Ultimately, Dean curbed his work hours, and the couple began discussing the issue of having another child — something that was important to Dean, as he was an only child. Mary was considering the notion even though, prior to marital therapy, she was resistant to the idea of having another child with an absent husband.

It is interesting to note that when the distancer does use work as an escape hatch in a relationship, it is very common for the pursuer to think that he or she is having an affair (as Mary suspected of Dean). It is certainly possible to distance via an affair (as will be discussed in the following section), but the therapist needs to approach this subject with caution and skepticism and must maintain a systems perspective. At all times, the therapist must realize that the p–d process in and of itself is a powerful enough dynamic to exist in one context at a time. In the case of Dean and Mary, the p–d dynamic existed in the world of work, not in the world of an extramarital affair.

As discussed earlier, more and more women are entering the work world and are taking positions of great responsibility. In the not-too-distant past, men were the distancers via their careers and women were the pursuers in this context. Although equality on the whole is a welcomed change, the proliferation of dual-career couples has made it easier for the p–d dynamic to thrive in this context. Couples therapists need to be aware of this, for it is unlikely that we will ever return to our patriarchal past. Male couples therapists in particular must approach this issue free of prejudice. They must be careful to remember that it is the p–d dynamic that is usually the major problem, not the context in which it is played.

Infidelity (Affairs)

Pittman (1989) defined infidelity as a breach of contract within a relationship. Although I have certainly seen enough couples treat it as such, I tend to favor Levine's (2003) assertion that therapists should not pathologize infidelity based on their own value systems. In this sense, I agree with Levine that the couple should be the "meaning maker" of the affair. Nevertheless, I have specifically treated couples who have consciously or unconsciously used infidelity (defined by the two partners of the following case example specifically as extramarital or extracohabitational sex) to avoid intimacy. In support of this, Brown (1999) identified "intimacy avoiders" as one of five different types of affairs. These are partners who are frightened of intimacy and therefore must keep barriers between them at all times. In this case, the affair serves as the couple's barrier. When a p–d dynamic develops as a buffer against intimacy, the affair simply serves as the context for the p–d dynamic.

While an unexposed affair can trigger or be the result of a p–d dynamic, the victimized partner usually presents as unaware of the transgression. (Many marital therapists believe that most partners are, at least on a preconscious level, aware that an affair is taking place, but they rarely bring this awareness to a conscious level because of the pain it would cause them.) Thus, the pursuing and distancing that the couples therapist sees may be that of the pursuer demanding that more time be spent with him or her and the distancer spending an inordinate amount of time with his or her lover.

In my clinical experience, however, the p–d dynamic is better fueled by those couples for whom the affair has somehow been exposed. When both partners know of the affair and the unfaithful one refuses to end the extramarital or extracohabitational relationship, a p–d dynamic may be sparked, with the pursuer seeking an end to the relationship and the partner refusing to do so and possibly escalating the dynamic by spending even more time with the lover. I have treated a number of these cases, and despite the fact that they sometimes resemble a sadomasochistic control struggle they can last for months before a resolution is reached. The following case depicts a couple whose problems with intimacy manifested into a severe control struggle, which in turn led to an affair and a severe p–d dynamic.

Ray and Glenda had been married for fifteen years. Ray was in his late thirties, and Glenda was in her early forties. The couple had two preteen-age sons. Ray owned his own consulting firm, and Glenda was a court stenographer. Glenda insisted that Ray attend couples counseling with her because he was having an affair with a secretary he had met while on a consultation call to a large law firm. Glenda was enraged with Ray's behavior and insisted that he end his affair immediately. She said that she had tried cajoling Ray to give up the woman and had even threatened divorce, but to no avail. She admitted that the affair was always on her mind and that she angrily pursued Ray every day to put an end to his indiscretion.

Ray openly refused to give up his lover and was put off by Glenda's angry pursuit and especially her inability to accept any responsibility for his marital unhappiness. He did state, however, that he still loved Glenda and wished to stay married to her. He said that he had no intention of seeking a divorce to be with his lover (although his lover was unaware of this) but he needed to keep her in order to persuade Glenda to consider modifying her controlling, stubborn personality. He said that until he saw proof that Glenda was willing to "back off of him" and to look at herself, he couldn't take the chance of ending his extramarital affair. In essence, his lover was the only power card he felt that he had in trying to get Glenda to consider changing her behavior. He said he was afraid to go back to the way the marriage used to be (prior to his affair), with Glenda constantly pushing him around and controlling every aspect of his life.

Glenda was the younger of two siblings. She described her father as caring, quiet, and passive and her mother as very controlling. She said she was "daddy's little girl," but she had regular control struggles with her mother. Glenda was briefly married to a man whom she described as "selfish." The marriage lasted approximately six months before she divorced him. Ray was the youngest of three brothers. He described his father as very domineering and a "rugged individualist"; he described his mother as a "powerless" woman who was subservient to her husband.

Glenda was in conflict. She feared being dominated as she and her father were in her family of origin, so she became the dominant one, but she also wanted to be treated the way "dear old Dad" treated her. The more she expected of Ray and the more controlling she was, however, the less likely Ray was to treat her well. Ray was also in conflict. He didn't want a wimp for a wife (like his mother was); he wanted an older, strong woman but he also didn't want to be controlled. Glenda was both strong and controlling. Ray's extended affair was an attempt to get what he wanted — a strong woman who would not control him.

During the course of treatment, as Glenda gained more insight into her conflict, she began to curb her angry pursuit and appeal to Ray in a softer manner to end his affair, and Ray began to respond. In fact, the less Glenda angrily pursued and the more she demonstrated that she was interested in examining her own personality, the closer Ray came to ending his affair. Several months into the treatment, with a greater understanding of his own conflict about Glenda's power, in conjunction with her change, Ray ended his relationship with his lover. He then became less distant with Glenda and began to focus more on his marriage to her.

In this case, a control struggle between Ray and Glenda led to Ray's affair and a p–d relational dynamic that did not dissipate until the control struggle ended. When confronted with a situation such as this, however, the couples therapist should be aware that a so-called statute of limitations exists; that is, the victimized partner may only withstand this sort of treatment for a limited period of time. Everyone's threshold for this sort of behavior is different, depending on the victim's nature, emotional conflict, and past relational experiences. Many times, unless the couples therapist works quickly, the victimized partner will reach a turn-off point and give up on the relationship. Once this point is reached, it is as if a switch has been thrown and there seems to be no turning back to the primary relationship. As a preventative measure, I warn the adulterous partner about this sort of thing so they know they cannot carry on their behavior indefinitely without severe repercussions. Some adulterers care, but others are so engaged in the process that they are willing to take the risk rather than go back to the way things were prior to the affair.

In some rare instances, a victimized partner may wait until the affair has ended to terminate their relationship. I view this as a "counter-control" maneuver, where the victimized partner is more interested in narcissistic retaliation or regaining control than rescuing the relationship. Given this, it would be wise for couples therapists to evaluate the sincerity of the victimized partner and to confront him or her on this issue well before the adulterer gives up the affair.

It might come as a surprise to many, but Laumann *et al.* (1994) found that the rate of extramarital and extracohabitational sex is less than 25% in the United States. The authors of this study determined that over 90% of the men and over 75% of the women reported fidelity within their marriage over its entirety. These statistics are certainly a far cry from those once reported by Hite (1981, 1987), who found that approximately 70% of the women in her study who were married more than five years and 72% of the men married two years or more were unfaithful. It must be kept in mind, however, that respondents often are not very forthcoming about their sexual activity, particularly when it comes to admitting to an act that they are ashamed of or fear may have grave consequences if exposed.

Alcohol Dependence and Abuse

Alcohol dependence (*i.e.*, addiction to or chronic use of alcohol) and abuse (*i.e.*, impaired functioning via alcohol) have long been major problems in our society. According to the DSM-IV (APA, 1994), they are among the most prevalent mental health disorders in the United States, with 8% of the population having alcohol dependence and 5% abusing alcohol. The U.S. Department of Health and Human Services (2003) reported that, in the year 2003, 6.8% of the population 12 years or older (16.1 million people) admitted heavy drinking behavior, and 14.8 million people 12 years or older were dependent on or abused alcohol.

While dependence on any substance can serve as a buffer against intimacy (the substance is triangulated between the partners and prevents an intimate relationship from forming), addiction to alcohol is one of the most common contexts for the p–d dynamic. Similar in style to the co-dependent–dependent couple combination about which so much has been written in the addiction literature (Beattie, 1996), the pursuer pursues the addict to control or stop his or her drinking and to make the pursuer the focus of affection, while the addict distances via alcohol as if married to the substance. The more the pursuer pursues, the more the addict drinks, sometimes hiding this behavior or staying out all night in order to feed the addiction. It may seem to the enabling pursuer that the distancing alcoholic is having a sexual affair; while this is possible, it is entirely plausible that the affair is solely with the alcohol. The pursuing partner may find this difficult to believe but one of the responsibilities of the couples therapist is to better educate the pursuer about being in a relationship with an addictive personality.

While the p–d and codependent–dependent interactions share much in common, distinct differences can be observed. For example, the sheer presence of the substance adds a dangerous component that is ordinarily absent in a typical p–d process. Alcohol alters the dynamic somewhat because the inebriated partner may be emotionally and physically out of control. Bennett (1995) indicated that alcohol abuse is strongly correlated with violent situations between partners. Pursuing a drunken partner can result in the harm or even death of a pursuer, and the therapist as well as both partners should be aware of this potential danger.

Of course, not all alcoholic partners are the same, a fact that I find often confuses many couples. In addition to the many dangerous mean drunks are the unassuming quiet drunks, who chronically drink too much and fall asleep on the couch; the binge drinker, who may only drink on the weekends; and the alcohol dependents, who drink only on holidays. I have lost count of how many couples I have seen who have denied alcohol problems in their relationships based on the fact that the alcoholic partner does not seem to fit the stereotypical profile of the mean drunk or the drunken bum. Couples should be advised of the variety of high-functioning alcoholics out there. Two important similarities they all seem to share, however, are their inability to be intimate and their inability to stop drinking once they start or at least until they are inebriated.

The job of the couples therapist is not only to educate the p–d couple with regard to the role alcohol plays in their relationship but also to first and foremost help them to get some immediate control over the substance abuse. My philosophy is to recommend that the couple either complete a program for alcoholism prior to attending couples sessions or attend one simultaneously. If a couple rejects this treatment approach, I will refuse to conduct ongoing couples therapy with them. In my opinion, it is no use working with a couple who can leave the office and drink away whatever they learned or accomplished that night. I will, however, perform an evaluation of the couple and offer them a few sessions (usually up to four) in an effort to encourage them to seek substance treatment. If, after approximately four sessions, they do not seek alcohol treatment as (at least) an adjunct tool, I will terminate them.

To this point I have been referring predominately to the treatment of the alcoholic couple, not the treatment of the alcoholic partner. I have done so because I believe, in tune with systems theory, if the couples therapist focuses exclusively on the addict then the collusion of the couple will prevail and very little progress will be made. Just as the typical pursuer sabotages intimacy when the distancer makes an attempt at closeness, the pursuing codependent will do the same. For example, the codependent

partner may react impotently to the partner's drinking, deny the seriousness of the problem or its impact on the entire family, or buy alcohol for
the partner only to become upset if the partner abuses it, which is almost
guaranteed to happen.

One woman who complained incessantly about her husband's drinking
promptly lost a book I lent her on alcoholism in relationships. I believe that
this woman was unconsciously, yet passive–aggressively, sabotaging the
treatment process in order to maintain the alcoholic dyad. The term "codependent" indicates that this partner is addicted to or dependent on the
alcoholic and his or her dysfunctional behavior. The couples therapist must
take this partner's dependency on the alcoholic very seriously because it
may be as difficult, if not more so, to alleviate. It is, in fact, typical of a
codependent to actually leave or divorce an alcoholic the moment he or she
begins to improve.

If the alcoholic p–d couple agrees to attend an alcoholic program that
will address the relational system (*i.e.*, the alcoholic's addiction as well as
the codependent's behavior), then the couple can be seen in therapy. In
couples treatment, it is the therapist's job to integrate the treatment of the
alcoholic relationship and the p–d dynamic. Discussing the particulars of
how to treat an alcoholic couple is beyond the parameters of this chapter;
however, the bulk of the treatment approach will entail making sure the
couple stays in their respective substance programs, helping them to gain
insight into the origin of their alcoholic and codependent behaviors and to
connect this insight to their current behavior (particularly their p–d
dynamic), and learning to set personal limits both internally and externally.
As mentioned, educating the alcoholic p–d couple is an important treatment component as well. Toward this end, it is recommended that readings
specific to the alcoholic couple be assigned. Janet Woititz's (1986) book,
Marriage on the Rocks, is a brief, readable book on the topic that still holds
great meaning today. The following is a case example of a couple engaged
in an alcoholic p–d process and how they were treated.

Jack and Tina had been married for eleven years and had five children.
Tina was a housewife, and Jack was a manager in his family's real estate
business. When they initially reported for treatment Tina was extremely
angry. She said that Jack had a severe drinking problem, and that she has
been trying to convince him to seek treatment for many years. Now, she
said, unless he addressed his problem she was prepared to divorce him.
Apparently Jack had a short temper, particularly when he was inebriated,
and he would snap at her and the children. She reported that he drank
every day during his lunch break and continued his drinking in the evening
at home. Weekends were especially problematic because Jack got drunk

with his friends. Even though Jack lost his temper several times at work, because he was employed in his family's business his job was never at risk. He did, however, have difficulty at times getting along with other family members and employees of the company. Once, in a drunken rage, he broke a chair in the office while arguing with one of his sisters.

Jack presented as a very nice man. He was friendly and soft spoken. He did admit that he was anxious about his wife leaving him, but with some prodding he meekly admitted that he was angry with her behavior as well. Specifically, he found her to be "controlling" and "nagging." He said that he did drink (mostly beer) but did not consider himself an alcoholic. He said that his job was very stressful and that his parents demanded top performance, so he drank to reduce his stress. When questioned about his temper, he related it to the stress from work and Tina's behavior, as opposed to his drinking. It was clearly difficult for him to confront Tina, but he eventually revealed that she was "always on him" and never satisfied. Tina acknowledged that Jack worked very hard and was under constant stress. Although she agreed with Jack that his work often exacerbated his drinking problem, she seemed more upset by the fact that instead of seeking treatment he would become upset with her and, in turn, drink more.

Jack was the second oldest of six siblings. He described his family as very critical and competitive. Apparently, all the children were vying for their parents' approval and the opportunity to be promoted within the company. Jack had to cope with constant power struggles. He described his father as a hard-driving businessman who worked incredibly long hours to create his own company and support his large family. Jack said that his father was very demanding and had little time for any of the children as they were growing up, but because Jack made an extraordinary effort he was the closest to his father of all the children. Jack held less fondness for his mother. He did not disdain her, but he felt that she was manipulative and controlling. He said that he tried to stay away from her as much as possible but when she wanted something she would go to any lengths in the family to get it, often conspiring with other family members. Jack described her as someone who never gave up when she set her mind to something. Although he understood that his father did little to help his mother raise their sizable family, he still did not approve of her personality or questionable tactics. Interestingly, neither of Jack's parents nor grandparents had substance abuse problems, but the family of origin did seem to have a number of workaholics and a significant amount of stress.

Tina was the oldest of three sisters. Her parents divorced when she was a young child, and for most of her life she was parentified into the role of the family caretaker. Although she did this job with little internal conflict,

her sisters resented her for being put in charge of them. To further complicate matters, even though Tina's mother wanted Tina to take over, she
often resented and resisted Tina's well-meaning interventions. Eventually
they developed a parent–child dynamic where Tina was the parent and her
mother was the child. Tina had very little contact with her father, who may
have had a drinking problem (Tina was vague about this). Nevertheless,
she did perceive him to be highly irresponsible. She reported that both she
and her mother pursued her father to be more responsible but failed.

The first order of treatment for this couple (following the assessment)
was to help Jack stop his drinking; therefore, I recommended that Jack
attend an alcohol-related program to be evaluated and treated for alcoholism. In denial about the extent of the problem and upset by my joining
Tina in the pursuit of this treatment, Jack strongly resisted. I knew, however, that I had a lot of leverage in this case because if I terminated the
couples work Tina claimed that she was prepared to terminate the marriage. Even Jack admitted that he had never seen her so serious and determined before and that was why he agreed to marriage counseling with
her. After three sessions, Jack agreed to an evaluation but not a treatment
program.

As anticipated, Jack was diagnosed with alcoholism. In speaking with
the evaluator, I was told that he thought that Jack did not merit detoxifica-
tion and could get away with an outpatient program as long as he followed
through with it. Tina was happy with my attention to Jack's drinking but
began to nag and threaten him again when he said that he would only
agree to attend Alcoholics Anonymous (AA) meetings. I, however, calmed
Tina and agreed to this plan with the stipulation that Jack attend these
meeting on the average of three times per week along with weekly marital
sessions. It was also mandatory that Jack get a complete physical by his
family physician. If he failed to live up to this agreement, he would have to
attend a professionally led program or I would terminate the marital work
and leave him at the mercy of his wife. While I recognized that Tina's
rigidity regarding the treatment plan was correlated with the couple's p–d
dynamic, I chose not to focus on it. My preference was to set up the alcohol treatment as quickly as possible and return to the p–d treatment,
which I surmised would not end simply because Jack chose to attend treatment for his disease.

To my surprise, Jack was a model patient. He got his physical and was
cleared of any significant problems other than a stomach ulcer (probably
related to his excessive drinking) for which he was receiving medical attention. He regularly attended his AA meetings, and he decided to give up
alcohol completely. He reported that his toughest struggle was when he

would go to a bar with his brothers after work (a tradition). Often, he would decline the invitation, but when he accepted he ordered several club sodas and his brothers were supportive.

To Jack's credit, he also requested individual sessions at times when he felt that Tina was driving him too hard or he was frustrated at work. It was during these sessions that I encouraged him to freely express some of his dissatisfactions about the marriage and Tina's controlling tendencies, something he was always fearful to do. He did not think it would help his marriage (primarily because of Tina's resistance to changing herself), but he became convinced that it was a better alternative than getting drunk and failing his family.

Tina knew about and welcomed Jack's individual sessions, but when I tried to maintain balance in the marital treatment by inviting Tina for individual sessions she resisted. Most of the time she told me she was too busy to see me, and when she did come in she insisted on focusing on Jack. Tina also broke her therapeutic contract by failing to attend a Codependent's Anonymous Group (CODA); she said that she was fine and didn't need the help. Jack perceived Tina's attitude toward the treatment as arrogant and typically controlling. After gathering some confidence, he finally said to her in a conjoint session: "I guess everybody is screwed up but you. It must be great to be perfect."

As anticipated, even though Jack had clearly made progress in treatment, Tina offered very little positive reinforcement in his struggle with alcoholism and her attacks on him continued. Jack struggled to stay present during these barrages, but his frustration was apparent. It became clear that, although Tina didn't enable Jack's drinking by some of the typical conventions previously mentioned, she did so by being critical and impossible to satisfy. Indeed, her pursuit of Jack and his imperfections was relentless. Moreover, the proof continued to emerge that she was far more of a threat to the intimacy and long-term health of the marriage than Jack.

Although I began to delve into the families of origin of Jack and Tina during the assessment phase of treatment and in the individual sessions, the bulk of the psychodynamic work took place after Jack's alcoholism was under control. Jack eventually realized that in his marriage to Tina he had replicated a lifelong conflict: He desired the security of a large family and an engaged maternal figure but he also felt criticized and controlled and therefore wanted to escape. He was escaping or distancing from his demanding family of origin and his critical, demanding wife by staying drunk as much as possible. He eventually learned to stay present and confront her regardless of the consequences. Distancing from Tina by drinking only increased her desire to angrily pursue him (as if he were her father).

Tina proved difficult because she too was replicating a deep, unconscious conflict from her family of origin: Given her prior parentification, she needed to remain parental and in control, but she married a distancing alcoholic like her father who turned out to be more of a burden than anticipated. To resolve this conflict, she needed to give up some of her control (including curbing her constant criticism of Jack) and learn to trust a man to be responsible. Critical pursuit simply did not work for her or the marriage; it only increased Jack's distancing via alcohol. By the end of approximately 10 months of marital therapy, Jack still had not touched a drop of alcohol, had curbed his temper, and was expressing his feelings at home and at work more directly. While Tina never attended a CODA group, she did read two assigned books: Beattie's (1996) *Codependent No More* and Woititz's (1986) *Marriage on the Rocks*. She also did some significant work on her family of origin, particularly as it related to her being the child of an alcoholic, and eventually she curbed her critical pursuing. Overall, the couple's alcoholic p–d dynamic was greatly alleviated.

Again, because the p–d dynamic is a process, innumerable contexts exist in which it can thrive. Although my objective was to discuss the dynamic in some of its most common contexts, I in no way meant to underestimate the damage that can accrue in a relationship when the context seems more benign. For example, one context that I only touched on is that of leisure activities or hobbies. I have seen numerous couples, for example, for whom the game of golf has been triangulated as a context for the p–d interaction. In these cases, it was almost always the male partner distancing via golf and the female "golf widow" pursuing him to spend more time with her or the family. The male golfer invariably complains that his female paramour wishes to sap his life of all extracurricular activity and enjoyment. Many of these men have stated that they believe they are seen by their partners as only a "paycheck." Their female partners usually treat this defense as ridiculous and childlike. Many female golf widows view their male partner's behavior as obsessive and irresponsible; consequently, the p–d dynamic may continue indefinitely and do irreparable harm to the relationship.

Epilogue

Building upon the work of others can be quite intimidating. It is far too easy to question whether one is adding anything of significance to the previous work. In my years of studying the pursuer–distancer dynamic, I have long been impressed with the writings of those who have dedicated themselves to the understanding of this significant and seemingly timeless interaction in the lives of couples. During my exploration into the history of the dynamic, I was surprised to see it addressed in the psychoanalytic literature of the 1940s, and I was equally amazed at the large number of clinicians and scholars of marriage and family therapy who have attempted to expound upon the existing practice and theory of the dynamic.

In this book, I have tried to cover as many aspects of the dynamic as possible. I do not claim to have addressed all that needs to be examined nor do I think that I have provided all the answers to this complex interaction. My primary objectives were to give professionals who work with couples a way to identify this dynamic in their work, a perspective on the emotional origin of the dynamic, and a model that might help to alleviate the dynamic when needed. I have also tried to emphasize the dynamic in different contexts (*e.g.*, sex) and across certain populations (*e.g.*, gay males and lesbians) and to show how societal influences and cultured gender differences have affected the interaction as depicted in part, by the rapidly increasing male pursuer–female distancer dynamic.

The model presented provides a rather flexible perspective on the dynamic, preferring to view pursuing and distancing on a continuum rather than representative of individuals with fixed personalities or personality disorders. While I do think an individual is more prone to pursuing or distancing (and therefore more likely to act the part in more than

193

one context), I believe that a little pursing and distancing exists in each and that shifts can take place depending on with whom a person is matched and the context in which he or she is operating. I do not think a pure pursuer or a pure distancer exists. I think the number of pursuing and distancing traits and tendencies exhibited by an individual and the intensity at which they exist also depend on where the individual is on the continuum. Ultimately, however, the traits and tendencies to pursue or distance originate out of experiences from the family of origin; context, gender differences, and societal influences are also factors.

The approach of mixing linear conflict theory with the more circular and systemic family-of-origin work might appear somewhat contradictory. (The models closest to this line of thinking are those of object relations couples therapists such as Scharff and Scharff [1991] and relational psychoanalysts such as Mitchell [2002].) But, I have found this combination to be particularly powerful when working with the p–d dynamic and with couples in general. As we age, the areas of choice seem grayer and the stakes higher. Most of the time there just does not seem to be a "right" answer. Choosing which pair of jeans to wear to school may at one time have seemed vital, but having to choose an individual with whom to spend a lifetime and how close we allow ourselves to be during this process can stir up overwhelming anxiety. Rendering ourselves somewhat powerless to a mate is indeed one of the scariest things we can do; this is why many people desperately seek a compromise by either failing to commit to any one person at any level or by settling on connection at a distance. When all compromises fail to prove satisfactory, however, a choice must be made to become intimate or not. Without choosing to take this kind of risk, true intimacy would be impossible to achieve. Underlying conflicts with regard to intimacy place us in the jeopardy of developing defensive dynamics such as the p–d interaction; yet, I believe the only way out is to explore the family of origin in an effort to decipher these conflicts and to resolve the anxiety associated with them. This will enable us to commit to a reasonably close, long-lasting union free of chronic intrusiveness and elusiveness.

Although this book has been aimed primarily at those who work with the p–d dynamic in the therapeutic or clinical setting, it is my hope that a continued effort will be made by those in the profession to explore and expound on its impact on other settings as well. One area that may prove worthy of investigation is that of the p–d dynamic in the supervision process. While the tone and scope of this book do not allow for a greater discourse on this matter, I doubt few supervisors of marriage and family therapy have escaped this type of engagement with those whom they supervise. A recent example I've experienced involved Michelle, a supervisee who wanted to study couples but was reluctant to deal with any of their sexual problems (even if a sexual issue was the presented symptom). Consequently, Michelle did everything she could to distance from this topic with her clients, and when this seemed unavoidable she would request to refer the case. True to the isomorphic process, Michelle and I eventually became engaged in a p–d dynamic (Betchen, 1995). I, playing the role of the pursuer, encouraged Michelle to explore her underlying concerns regarding sex and how they were being played out in the treatment and supervision process. She, in turn, eluded or distanced from me as she did her clients.

Only with great effort and patience did Michelle and I salvage our supervision process. To her credit, she was willing to construct her own genogram (Braverman, 1997; Munson, 1984) and discuss how her rigid parents, the overresponsible expectations of her self, and her strict religious upbringing had turned her off to sexual matters. Many such supervision cases, however, can become mired in a chronic p–d dynamic with no end in sight, other than the strong recommendation that the supervisee seek personal therapy or termination of the supervisory process. If the supervision takes place in a private setting rather than in a teaching clinic or institution, the supervisor has even less control in overcoming the problematic dynamic because he or she has less leverage in the supervision process.

In a related matter, a second hope of mine is to see a continued effort in support of integrating couples and sex therapy in the profession. If the marriage between marriage and family therapy is deemed appropriate, then certainly the marriage between couples and sex therapy makes even more sense. The truth is that the energy it would have taken for Michelle to have avoided all sexual problems in her quest to become a sufficient couples therapist might have been insurmountable. At the very least, her objective would have limited her clinical capabilities.

A mentor of mine once told me that if a particular goal was easy to achieve, then it wouldn't be so special and anyone remotely interested could achieve it. Making a successful and fulfilling life with another human being is not easy. As mentioned, today's divorce rate is approximately 50%, and I believe that at least another 10 to 15% of the couples who stay together may be doing so out of emotional or financial dependence or because divorce is an unacceptable alternative given their moral or religious values or the laws of their families of origin. Those of us who work with couples know that a fear of intimacy is a major culprit in the problems experienced by couples. Given the pervasiveness of the p–d dynamic, it is safe to say that it is, and will remain, a major force confronting all couples and couples therapists.

References

AD/HD Information Library. (2002). *Lesson one: What is ADD ADHD?* Retrieved March 13, 2002, from www. newideas.net/.

Amen, D. (2001). *Healing ADD: The breakthrough program that allows you to see and heal the 6 types of ADD.* New York: Berkley Publishing Group.

APA. (1994). *Diagnostic and statistical manual of mental disorders* (4th ed.). Washington, D.C.: American Psychiatric Association.

Apfelbaum, B. (2000). Retarded ejaculation: A much misunderstood syndrome. In S. Leiblum & R. Rosen (Eds.), *Principles and practice of sex therapy* (3rd ed., pp. 205–241). New York: Guilford.

Arledge, R. (Producer). (1970). *Monday night football* [television broadcast]. New York: ABC.

Barbach, L. (2000). *For yourself: The fulfillment of female sexuality* (rev. ed.). New York: Signet.

Bateson, G., & Jackson, D. (1964). Some varieties of pathogenic organization. In D. M. Rioch & E. Weinstein (Eds.), *Disorders of communication* (pp. 270–290). Baltimore, MD: Williams & Wilkins.

Bateson, G., Jackson, D., Haley, J., & Weakland, J. (1956). Toward a theory of schizophrenia. *Behavioral Science, 1*, 251–264.

Beattie, M. (1996). *Codependent no more: How to stop controlling others and start caring for yourself.* New York: HarperCollins.

Bennett, L. (1995). Substance abuse and the domestic assault of women. *Social Work, 40*, 760–770.

Bepko, C., & Krestan, J. (1985). *The responsibility trap: A blueprint for treating the alcoholic family.* New York: Free Press.

Berlin, I. (1958). *Two concepts of liberty.* Oxford: Clarendon.

Berman, E. (1982). The individual interview as a treatment technique in conjoint therapy. *American Journal of Family Therapy, 10*, 27–37.

Berman, E., & Hof, L. (1987). The sexual genogram: Assessing family-of-origin factors in the treatment of sexual dysfunction. In G. Weeks & L. Hof (Eds.), *Integrating sex and marital therapy: A clinical guide* (pp. 37–56). New York: Brunner/Mazel.

Berns, S., Jacobson, N., & Gottman, J. (1999). Demand/withdraw interaction patterns between different types of batterers and their spouses. *Journal of Marital & Family Therapy, 25*, 337–347.

Betchen, S. (1991). Male masturbation as a vehicle for the pursuer/distancer relationship in marriage. *Journal of Sex & Marital Therapy, 17*, 269–278.

Betchen, S. (1995). An integrative, intersystemic approach to supervision of couple therapy. *American Journal of Family Therapy, 23*, 48–58.

Betchen, S. (1996). Parentified pursuers and childlike distancers in marital therapy. *The Family Journal, 4*, 100–108.

Betchen, S. (1997). *Sexual pursuer–distancer dynamics in couples therapy.* Paper presented at the annual meeting of the Society for Sex Therapy and Research, Chicago.

Betchen, S. (2001a). Hypoactive sexual desire in a couple with unresolved loyalty conflicts. *Journal of Sex Education and Therapy, 26,* 1–11.

Betchen, S. (2001b). Premature ejaculation as symptomatic of age difference in a husband and wife with underlying power and control conflicts. *Journal of Sex Education and Therapy, 26,* 34–44.

Betchen, S. (2002). Treating the male pursuer–female distancer dynamic in couples therapy. *Directions in Clinical and Counseling Psychology, 1,* 139–148.

Betchen, S. (2003). Suggestions for improving intimacy in couples in which one partner has attention-deficit/hyperactivity disorder. *Journal of Sex & Marital Therapy, 29,* 103–124.

Betchen, S., & Ross, J. (2000). Male pursuers and female distancers in couples therapy. *Sexual and Relationship Therapy, 15,* 15–31.

Bird, H. W., & Martin, P. (1959). Further consideration of the "cold, sick" husband. *Psychiatry, 22,* 250–254.

Blumstein, P., & Schwartz, P. (1983). *American couples.* New York: William Morrow.

Boszormenyi-Nagy, I. (1965). A theory of relationships: Experience and transactions. In I. Boszormenyi-Nagy & J. Framo (Eds.), *Intensive family therapy: Theoretical and practical aspects* (pp. 33–86). New York: Harper & Row.

Boszormenyi-Nagy, I., & Krasner, B. (1986). *Between give and take: A clinician's guide to contextual family therapy.* New York: Brunner/Mazel.

Boszormenyi-Nagy, I., & Spark, G. (1973). *Invisible loyalties.* New York: Harper & Row.

Bowen, M. (1959). Family relationships in schizophrenia. In A. Auerback (Ed.), *Schizophrenia: An integrated approach* (pp. 147–178). New York: Ronald.

Bowen, M. (1966). The use of family theory in clinical practice. *Comprehensive Psychiatry, 7,* 345–374.

Bowen, M. (1978). *Family therapy in clinical practice.* New York: Aronson.

Bowen, M. (1980). Key to the use of the genogram. In E. A. Carter & M. McGoldrick (Eds.), *The family life cycle: A framework for family therapy* (p. XXIII). New York: Gardner Press.

Braverman, S. (1997). The use of genograms in supervision. In T. Todd & C. Storm, Eds., *The complete systemic supervisors: Context, philosophy, and pragmatics* (pp. 349–362). Needham Heights, MA: Allyn & Bacon.

Brown, E. (1999). *Affairs: A guide to working through the repercussions of infidelity.* San Francisco, CA: Jossey-Bass.

Burch, B. (1986). Psychotherapy and the dynamics of merger in lesbian couples. In T. S. Stein & C. J. Cohen (Eds.), *Contemporary perspectives on psychotherapy with lesbians and gay men* (pp. 57–71). New York: Plenum.

Carl, D. (1990). *Counseling same-sex couples.* New York: Norton.

Chernin, J., & Johnson, M. (2003). *Affirmative psychotherapy and counseling for lesbians and gay men.* Thousand Oaks, CA: Sage Publications.

Chodorow, N. (1978). *The reproduction of mothering: Psychoanalysis and the sociology of gender.* Berkeley, CA: University of California Press.

Christensen, A. (1988). Dysfunctional interaction patterns in couples. In P. Noller & M. A. Fitzpatrick (Eds.), *Perspectives on marital interaction* (pp. 31–52). Philadelphia: Multilingual Matters.

Clunis, D. M., & Green, G. D. (2000). *Lesbian couples: A guide to creating healthy relationships.* New York: Seal Press.

Collins, R., & Coltrane, S. (1995). *Sociology of marriage and the family: Gender, love, and property.* Chicago: Nelson-Hall.

Daniel, R. (2000). Identifying persons susceptible to domestic violence. *Directions in Mental Health Counseling, 10,* 83–92.

Davis, S. (2000). Testosterone and sexual desire in women. *Journal of Sex & Marital Therapy, 25,* 25–32.

Deluca, P. (2002). *The solo partner: Repairing your relationship on your own* (2nd ed.). Alexander, NC: Alexander Books.

DeMaria, R., Weeks, G., & Hof, L. (1999). *Focused genograms: Intergenerational assessment of individuals, couples, and families.* Philadelphia: Brunner/Mazel.

D'Ercole, A., & Drescher, J. (Eds.). (2004). *Uncoupling convention: Psychoanalytic approaches to same-sex couples and families.* Hillsdale, NJ: The Analytic Press.

Diedrick, P. (1991). Gender differences in divorce adjustment. In S. Volgy (Ed.), *Women and divorce, men and divorce: Gender differences in separation, divorce, and remarriage* (pp. 33–45). New York: Haworth Press.

Dodson, B. (1996). *Sex for one: The joy of selfloving* (reissued ed.). New York: Crown.

Drobnič, S., & Blossfeld, H. P. (2001). Careers of couples and trends of inequality. In H. P. Blossfeld & S. Drobnič (Eds.), *Careers of couples in contemporary societies: From male breadwinner to dual-earner families* (pp. 371–386). New York: Oxford University Press.

Elium, J., & Elium, D. (2003). *Raising a daughter: Parents and the awakening of a healthy woman* (rev. ed.). Berkeley, CA: Celestial Arts.

Ellison, C. R. (2003). Facilitating orgasmic responsiveness. In S. Levine, C. Risen, & S. Althof (Eds.), *Handbook of clinical sexuality for mental health professionals* (pp. 167–185). New York: Brunner/Routledge.

Fagan, P. (2003). Psychogenic impotence in relatively young men. In S. Levine, C. Risen, & S. Althof (Eds.), *Handbook of clinical sexuality for mental health professionals* (pp. 217–235). New York: Brunner/Routledge.

Falco, K. (1991). *Psychotherapy with lesbian clients: Theory into practice.* New York: Brunner/Mazel.

Fields, J., & Casper, L. (2001). America's families and living arrangements: Population characteristics. *Current Population Reports* (P20-537, pp. 1–16). Washington, D.C.: U.S. Census Bureau.

Fisher, H. (1992). *Anatomy of love.* New York: Fawcett Books.

Fisher, H. (2000). Lust, attraction, attachment: Biology and evolution of the three primary emotion systems for mating, reproduction, and parenting. *Journal of Sex Education and Therapy, 25,* 96–104.

Fogarty, T. (1976). Marital crisis. In P. Guerin (Ed.), *Family therapy: Theory and practice* (pp. 325–334). New York: Gardner Press.

Fogarty, T. (1979). The distancer and the pursuer. *The Family, 7,* 11–16.

Foley, S., Kope, S., & Segrue, D. (2002). *Sex matters for women: A complete guide to taking care of your sexual self.* New York: Guilford.

Freud, S. (1905/1953). Three essays on the theory of sexuality. In J. Strachey (Ed. and Trans.), *The standard edition of the complete psychological works of Sigmund Freud* (Vol. 7, pp. 125–245). London: Hogarth Press and the Institute of Psychoanalysis.

Freud, S. (1910/1957). Five lectures on psycho-analysis. In J. Strachey (Ed. and Trans.), *The standard edition of the complete psychological works of Sigmund Freud* (Vol. 11, pp. 9–55). London: Hogarth Press and the Institute of Psychoanalysis.

Freud, S. (1912/1957). On the universal tendency to debasement in the sphere of love. In J. Strachey (Ed. and Trans.), *The standard edition of the complete psychological works of Sigmund Freud* (Vol. 11, pp. 177–190). London: Hogarth Press and the Institute of Psychoanalysis.

Gelles, R. J. (1995). *Understanding domestic violence factoids.* Retrieved September 20, 2004, from the Minnesota Center Against Violence and Abuse (MINCAVA) website: www.mincava.umn.edu/documents/factoid/factoid.html.

Gelles R. J. (2000). Estimating the incidence and prevalence of violence against women. *Violence Against Women, 6,* 784–804.

Gilligan, C. (1982). *In a different voice: Psychological theory and women's development.* Cambridge, MA: Harvard University Press.

Goldberg, M. (1987). *Keeping it together: The fine art of marital survival.* Philadelphia: Marriage Council of Philadelphia.

Goldstein, E., & Horowitz, L. (2003). *Lesbian identity: Contemporary psychotherapy.* Hillsdale, NJ: The Analytic Press.

Gottman, J. (1994). *What predicts divorce? The relationship between marital processes and marital outcomes.* Hillsdale, NJ: Lawrence Erlbaum Associates.

Gottman, J., & Levenson, R. (1988). The social psychophysiology of marriage. In P. Noller & M. A. Fitzpatrick (Eds.), *Perspectives on marital interaction* (pp. 182–200). Philadelphia: Multilingual Matters.

Guerin, P., & Pendagast, E. (1976). Evaluation of family system and genogram. In P. Guerin (Ed.), *Family therapy: Theory and practice* (pp. 450–464). New York: Gardner Press.

Guerin, P., Fay, L., Burden, S., & Kautto, J. (1987). *The evaluation and treatment of marital conflict: A four-stage approach.* New York: Basic Books.

Guerin, P., Fogarty, T., Fay, L., & Kautto, J. (1996). *Working with relationship triangles: The one–two–three of psychotherapy.* New York: Basic Books.

Gurian, M. (1996). *The wonder of boys: What parents, mentors and educators can do to shape boys into exceptional men.* New York: Tarcher/Putnam.

Gurian, M. (2002). *The wonder of girls: Understanding the hidden nature of our daughters.* New York: Atria Books.

Hales, D. (1999). *Just like a woman: How gender science is redefining what makes us female.* New York: Bantam.

Hallowell, E. (1999). *Connect: 12 vital ties that open your heart, lengthen your life, and deepen your soul.* New York: Pantheon.

Hallowell, E., & Ratey, J. (1994). *Answers to distraction.* New York: Bantam.

Halverstadt, J. S. (1998). *ADD and romance: Finding fulfillment in love, sex, and relationships.* Dallas, TX: Taylor.

Heiman, J., & LoPiccolo, J. (1988). *Becoming orgasmic: A sexual and personal growth program for women* (rev. ed.). New York: Simon & Schuster.

Hendrix, H. (1988). *Getting the love you want: A guide for couples.* New York: HarperPerennial.

Hite, S. (1981). *The Hite report on male sexuality.* New York: Knopf.

Hite, S. (1987). *The Hite report: Women and love.* New York: Knopf.

Iasenza, S. (2000). Lesbian sexuality post-stonewall to post-modernism: Putting the "lesbian bed death" concept to bed. *Journal of Sex Education and Therapy, 25,* 59–69.

Johnson & Johnson. (2002). *FDA approves Concerta 27 mg tablet for ADHD.* Retrieved May 21, 2002, from www.jnj.com/news_finance/477.htm.

Kabakçi, E., & Batur, S. (2003). Who benefits from cognitive behavioral therapy for vaginismus? *Journal of Sex & Marital Therapy, 29,* 277–288.

Kantor, D., & Lehr, W. (1975). *Inside the family: Toward a theory of family process.* San Francisco, CA: Jossey-Bass.

Kaplan, H. S. (1974). *The new sex therapy: Active treatment of sexual dysfunctions.* New York: Times Books.

Kaplan, H. S. (1975). *The illustrated manual of sex therapy.* New York: Times Books.

Kaplan, H. S. (1977). Hypoactive sexual desire. *Journal of Sex & Marital Therapy, 3,* 3–9.

Kaplan, H. S. (1983). *The evaluation of sexual disorders: Psychological and medical aspects.* New York: Brunner/Mazel.

Kaplan, H. S. (1987). *Sexual aversion, sexual phobias, and panic disorder.* New York: Brunner/ Mazel.

Kaplan, H. S. (1989). *PE: How to overcome premature ejaculation.* New York: Brunner/Mazel.

Kaplan, H. S. (1995). *The sexual desire disorders: Dysfunctional regulation of sexual motivation.* New York: Brunner/Mazel.

Kegel, A. (1952). Sexual functions of the pubococcygeus muscle. *Western Journal of Surgery in Obstetrics and Gynecology, 60,* 521–524.

Kelly, M., Strassberg, D., & Turner, C. (2004). Communication and associated relationship issues in female anorgasmia. *Journal of Sex & Marital Therapy, 30,* 263–276.

Kindlon, D., & Thompson, M. (2000). *Raising Cain: Protecting the emotional life of boys.* New York: Ballantine Books.

Krestan, J., & Bepko, C. (1980). The problem of fusion in the lesbian relationship. *Family Process, 19,* 277–289.

Laird, J. (Ed.). (1999). *Lesbians and lesbian families: Reflections on theory and practice.* New York: Columbia University Press.

Laird, J., & Green, R.-J. (Eds.). (1996). *Lesbians and gays in couples and families: A handbook for therapists.* San Francisco, CA: Jossey-Bass.

Laumann, E., Gagnon, J., Michael, R., & Michaels, S. (1994). *The social organization of sexuality: Sexual practices in the United States.* Chicago: University of Chicago Press.

Leiblum, S. (1995). Relinquishing virginity: The treatment of a complex case of vaginismus. In R. Rosen & S. Leiblum (Eds.), *Case studies in sex therapy* (pp. 250–263). New York: Guilford.

Leiblum, S. (2000). Vaginismus: A most perplexing problem. In S. Leiblum & R. Rosen (Eds.), *Principles and practice of sex therapy* (3rd ed., pp. 181–202). New York: Guilford.

Lerner, H. (1989). *The dance of intimacy: A woman's guide to courageous acts of change in key relationships*. New York: Harper & Row.

Levine, S. (1991). Psychological intimacy. *Journal of Sex & Marital Therapy, 17*, 259–267.

Levine, S. (2003). Infidelity. In S. Levine, C. Risen, & S. Althof (Eds.), *Handbook of clinical sexuality for mental health professionals* (pp. 57–74). New York: Brunner/Routledge.

Lief, H. (1977). What's new in sex research? Inhibited sexual desire. *Medical Aspects of Human Sexuality, 11*, 94–95.

Lissette, A., & Kraus, R. (2000). *Free yourself from an abusive relationship*. Alameda, CA: Hunter House.

Loseke, D. R., & Kurz, D. (2005). Men's violence toward women is the serious problem. In D. R. Loseke, R. J. Gelles, & M. Cavanaugh (Eds.), *Current controversies on family violence* (2nd ed., pp. 79–95). Thousand Oaks, CA: Sage.

Loulan, J. (1984). *Lesbian sex*. San Francisco, CA: Spinsters Ink.

Mack, R. (1989). Spouse abuse: A dyadic approach. In G. Weeks (Ed.), *Treating couples: The intersystem model of the Marriage Council of Philadelphia* (pp. 191–214). New York: Brunner/Mazel.

Martin, P., & Bird, H. W. (1959). A marriage pattern: The "lovesick" wife and the "cold, sick" husband. *Psychiatry, 22*, 245–249.

Masters, W., & Johnson, V. (1966). *Human sexual response*. Boston: Little, Brown & Company.

Masters, W., & Johnson, V. (1970). *Human sexual inadequacy*. Boston: Little, Brown & Company.

McCabe, M. (2001). Evaluation of a cognitive behavior therapy program for people with sexual dysfunction. *Journal of Sex & Marital Therapy, 27*, 259–271.

McCarthy, B. (1989). Cognitive-behavioral strategies and techniques in the treatment of early ejaculation. In S. Leiblum & R. Rosen (Eds.), *Principles and practice of sex therapy: Update for the 1990s* (2nd ed., pp. 141–167). New York: Guilford.

McCarthy, B. (1999). Relapse strategies and techniques for inhibited sexual desire. *Journal of Sex & Marital Therapy, 25*, 297–303.

McCarthy, B. (2001). Relapse prevention strategies and techniques with erectile dysfunction. *Journal of Sex & Marital Therapy, 27*, 1–8.

McCarthy, B., & McCarthy, E. (2003). *Rekindling desire: A step-by-step program to help low-sex and no-sex marriages*. New York: Brunner/Routledge.

McFarlane, J., Campbell, J., Wilt, S., Sachs, C., Ulrich, Y., & Xiao, X. (1999). Stalking and intimate partner femicide. *Homicide Studies, 3*, 300–316.

McGoldrick, M., & Gerson, R. (1985). *Genograms in family assessment*. New York: Norton.

McWhirter, D., & Mattison, A. (1984). *The male couple: How relationships develop*. Englewood Cliffs, NJ: Prentice-Hall.

Mencher, J. (1990). *Intimacy in lesbian relationships: A critical re-examination of fusion*. Work in Progress, No. 42. Wellesley, MA: Stone Center Working Papers Series.

Metz, M., & McCarthy, B. (2003). *Coping with premature ejaculation: How to overcome PE, please your partner and have great sex*. Oakland, CA: New Harbinger Publications.

Metz, M., & McCarthy, B. (2004). *Coping with erectile dysfunction*. Oakland, CA: New Harbinger Publications.

Metz, M., Pryor, J., Nesvacil, L., Abuzzahab, F., & Koznar, J. (1997). Premature ejaculation: A psychophysiological review. *Journal of Sex & Marital Therapy, 23*, 3–23.

Michael, R., Gagnon, J., Laumann, F., & Kolata, G. (1994). *Sex in America*. Boston: Little, Brown & Company.

Milsten, R., & Slowinski, J. (1999). *The sexual male, problems and solutions: A complete medical and psychological guide to lifelong potency*. New York: Norton.

Minuchin, S., & Fishman, H. C. (1981). *Family therapy techniques*. Cambridge, MA: Harvard University Press.

Mitchell, S. (2002). *Can love last? The fate of romance over time*. New York: Norton.

Mittelmann, B. (1944). Complementary neurotic reactions in intimate relationships. *The Psychoanalytic Quarterly, 13*, 479–491.

Moore, T., Strauss, J., Herman, S., & Donatucci C. (2003). Erectile dysfunction in early, middle, and late adulthood: Symptom patterns and psychosocial correlates. *Journal of Sex & Marital Therapy, 29*, 381–399.

Mornell, P. (1979). *Passive men, wild women*. New York: Ballantine Books.

Moses, A. E., & Hawkins, R. (1986). *Counseling lesbian women and gay men: A life-issues approach.* Columbus, OH: Merrill.

Munoz-Millan, R., & Casteel, C. (1989). Attention-deficit hyperactivity disorder: Recent literature. *Hospital and Community Psychiatry, 40,* 699–707.

Munson, C. (Ed.) (1984). *Family of origin applications in clinical supervision.* New York: Haworth Press.

Nadeau, K. (1993). Partners of ADD adults. *Chesapeake Bulletin, 5,* 1.

Nadeau, K. (1996). *Adventures in fast forward: Life, love, and work for the ADD adult.* New York: Brunner/Mazel.

Napier, A. (1978). The rejection–intrusion pattern: A central family dynamic. *Journal of Marriage and Family Counseling, 4,* 5–12.

Nichols, M. (1982). The treatment of inhibited sexual desire in lesbian couples. *Women & Therapy, 1,* 49–66.

Nichols, M. (1988). Low sexual desire in lesbian couples. In S. Leiblum & R. Rosen (Eds.), *Sexual desire disorders* (pp. 387–412). New York: Guilford.

Nichols, M. (2000). Therapy with sexual minorities. In S. Leiblum & R. Rosen (Eds.), *Principles and practice of sex therapy* (3rd ed., pp. 335–367). New York: Guilford.

Oberndorf, C. P. (1938). Psychoanalysis of married couples. *The Psychoanalytic Quarterly, 28,* 453–475.

Pittman, F. (1989). *Private lies: Infidelity and the betrayal of intimacy.* New York: Norton.

Plaut, S. M., Graziottin, A., & Heaton, J. (2004). *Fast facts: Sexual dysfunction.* Oxford: Health Press.

Polonsky, D. (1997). What do you do when they won't do it? The therapist's dilemma with low desire. *Journal of Sex Education and Therapy, 22,* 5–12.

Polonsky, D. (2000). Premature ejaculation. In S. Leiblum & R. Rosen (Eds.), *Principles and practice of sex therapy* (3rd ed., pp. 305–332). New York: Guilford.

Pridal, C., & LoPiccolo, J. (2000). Multielement treatment of desire disorders: Integration of cognitive, behavioral, and systemic therapy. In S. Leiblum & R. Rosen (Eds.), *Principles and practice of sex therapy* (3rd ed., pp. 57–81). New York: Guilford.

Ratey, J., Hallowell, E., & Miller, A. (1995). Relationship dilemmas for adults with ADD: The biology of intimacy. In K. Nadeau (Ed.), *A comprehensive guide to attention deficit disorder in adults: Research, diagnosis, treatment* (pp. 74–92). New York: Brunner/Mazel.

Reinisch, J. (1990). *The Kinsey Institute new report on sex: What you must know to be sexually literate.* New York: St. Martin's Press.

Reissing, E., Binik, Y., & Khalifé, S. (1999). Does vaginismus exist? A critical review of the literature. *Journal of Nervous and Mental Disease, 187,* 261–274.

Reissing, E., Binik, Y., Khalifé, S. Cohen, D., & Amsel, R. (2003). Etiological correlates of vaginismus: Sexual and physical abuse, sexual knowledge, sexual self-schema, and relationship adjustment. *Journal of Sex & Marital Therapy, 29,* 47–59.

Rennison, C. M. (2003, February). *Intimate partner violence, 1993–2001* (Publication No. NCJ 19783). Retrieved September 21, 2004, from the Bureau of Justice Statistics, Crime Data Brief: www.ojp.usdoj.gov/bjs.

Rimm, S. (1999). *See Jane win: The Rimm report on how 1000 girls became successful women.* New York: Crown.

Sager, C. (1976). Sex therapy in marital therapy. *American Journal of Psychiatry, 33,* 555–558.

Sager, C., & Hunt, B. (1979). *Intimate partners: Hidden patterns in love relationships.* New York: McGraw-Hill.

Sbrocco, T., Weisberg, R., Barlow, D., & Carter, M. (1997). The conceptual relationship between panic disorder and male erectile dysfunction. *Journal of Sex & Marital Therapy, 23,* 212–220.

Scharff, D., & Scharff, J. S. (1991). *Object relations couple therapy.* Northvale, NJ: Aronson.

Schnarch, D. (1991). *Constructing the sexual crucible: An integration of sexual and marital therapy.* New York: Norton.

Schnarch, D. (1997). *Passionate marriage: Sex, love, and intimacy in emotionally committed relationships.* New York: Norton.

Schnarch, D. (2000). Desire problems: A systemic perspective. In S. Leiblum & R. Rosen (Eds.), *Principles and practice of sex therapy* (3rd ed., pp. 17–56). New York: Guilford.

Segraves, R. T., & Balon, R. (2003). *Sexual pharmacology: Fast facts*. New York: Norton.

Segraves, R. T., Saran, A., Segraves, K. B., & Maguire, E. (1993). Clomipramine versus placebo in the treatment of premature ejaculation: A pilot study. *Journal of Sex & Marital Therapy, 19*, 198–200.

Semens, J. (1956). Premature ejaculation: A new approach. *Southern Medical Journal, 49*, 353–358.

Shaddock, D. (1998). *From impasse to intimacy: How understanding unconscious needs can transform relationships*. Northvale, NJ: Aronson.

Sharpe, S. (2000). *The ways we love: A developmental approach to treating couples*. New York: Guilford.

Shire Laboratories. (2002). *FDA approves Adderall XR for once-daily treatment of attention deficit/hyperactivity disorder*. Retrieved May 21, 2002, from www. shirelabs.com/news/10-12-2001_1.html.

Siegel, J. (1997). Applying countertransference theory to couples treatment. In M. Solomon & J. Siegel (Eds.), *Countertransference in couples therapy* (pp. 3–22). New York: Norton.

Simons, J., & Carey, M. (2001). Prevalence of sexual dysfunctions: Results from a decade of research. *Archives of Sexual Behavior, 30*, 177–219.

Solden, S. (1995). *Women with attention deficit disorder: Embracing disorganization at home and in the workplace*. Grass Valley, CA: Underwood Books.

Solomon, M. (1997). Countertransference and empathy in couples therapy. In M. Solomon & J. Siegel (Eds.), *Countertransference in couples therapy* (pp. 23–37) New York: Norton.

Spelling, A. (Producer). (1964). *Daniel Boone* [television series]. New York: NBC.

Strand, J., Wise, T., Fagan, P., & Schmidt, Jr., C. (2002). Erectile dysfunction and depression: Category or dimension? *Journal of Sex & Marital Therapy, 28*, 175–181.

Strassberg, D., de Gouveia Brazao, C., Rowland, D., Tan, P., & Slob, A. K. (1999). Clomipramine in the treatment of rapid (premature) ejaculation. *Journal of Sex & Marital Therapy, 25*, 89–101.

Symonds, T., Roblin, D., Hart, K., & Althof, S. (2003). How does premature ejaculation impact a man's life? *Journal of Sex & Marital Therapy, 29*, 361–370.

Talmadge, L., & Talmadge, W. (1986). Relational sexuality: An understanding of low sexual desire. *Journal of Sex & Marital Therapy, 12*, 3–21.

Tessina, T. (2003). *Gay relationships for men and women*. New York: Tarcher/Penguin.

Tiger, L. (1999). *The decline of males*. New York: Golden Books.

Tjaden, P., & Thoennes, N. (1998, April). *Stalking in America: Findings from the national violence against women survey*. Washington, D.C.: U.S. Department of Justice, National Institute of Justice Centers for Disease Control and Prevention.

Toman, W. (1976). *Family constellation: Its effects on personality and social behavior*. New York: Springer.

Tripp, C. A. (1975). *The homosexual matrix*. New York: Signet.

U. S. Census Bureau, Statistical Abstract of the United States. (2000). *Married-couple and unmarried partner households: 2000*. Retrieved March 24, 2004, from http://www.census.gov/prod/2003pubs/censr-5.pdf.

U. S. Census Bureau, Statistical Abstract of the United States. (2003). *Marriages and divorces — number and rate by state: 1990–2001*. Retrieved September 18, 2004, from http://www.census.gov/statab/www/.

U. S. Department of Health and Human Services. (2002). *Cohabitation, marriage, divorce, and remarriage in the United States* (DHHS Publication No. PHS 2002-1998). Hyattsville, MD: Author.

U. S. Department of Health and Human Services. (2003). *SAMHSA's 2003 national survey on drug use and health*. Retrieved September 18, 2004, from http://oas.samhsa.gov/NHSDA/2k3NSDUH/2k3results.htm.

U.S. Department of Health and Human Services. (2004). *Moratality data from the national vital statistics system*. Retrieved December 20, 2004, from http://www.cdc.gov/nchs/about/major/dvs/mortdata.htm.

U. S. Department of Justice. (2001, May). *Stalking and domestic violence: Report to Congress*. Washington, D.C.: Author.

Waelder, R. (1960). *Basic theory of psychoanalysis*. New York: International Universities Press.

Waldinger, M. (2003). Rapid ejaculation. In S. Levine, C. Risen, & S. Althof (Eds.), *Handbook of clinical sexuality for mental health professionals* (pp. 257–274). New York: Brunner/Routledge.

Walters, M., Carter, B., Papp, P., & Silverstein, O. (1988). *The invisible web: Gender patterns in family relationships.* New York: Guilford.

Watzlawick, P., Beavin, J., & Jackson, D. (1967). *Pragmatics of human communication: A study of interactional patterns, pathologies, and paradoxes.* New York: Norton.

Weeks, G., & Gambescia, N. (2000). *Erectile dysfunction: Integrating couple therapy, sex therapy, and medical treatment.* New York: Norton.

Weeks, G., & Gambescia, N. (2002). *Hypoactive sexual desire: Integrating sex and couple therapy.* New York: Norton.

Weeks, G., & Hof, L. (Eds.) (1987). *Integrating sex and marital therapy: A clinical guide.* New York: Brunner/Mazel.

Weiss, L. (1997). *Attention deficit disorder in adults: Practical help and understanding* (3rd ed., rev.). New York: Cooper Square Press.

Wexler, M. (1992). Marital therapy: When women avoid intimacy. *The Family Psychologist, 8,* 15–16.

Wexler, M. (1993). Male pursuers in intimate relationships. *New Jersey Psychologist, 3,* 21–23.

Wile, D. (1993). *Couples therapy: A nontraditional approach.* New York: John Wiley & Sons.

Woititz, J. (1986). *Marriage on the rocks: Learning to live with yourself and an alcoholic.* Pompano Beach, FL: Health Communications.

Zilbergeld, B. (1992). *The new male sexuality.* New York: Bantam.

Index